Hope you enjoy the book.

Lorne H.

The HARASEN LINE

A Broadcaster's Memoir

Lorne Harasen

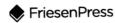 FriesenPress

Suite 300 - 990 Fort St
Victoria, BC, V8V 3K2
Canada

www.friesenpress.com

Copyright © 2016 by Lorne Harasen
First Edition — 2016

ISBN
978-1-4602-8344-8 (Hardcover)
978-1-4602-8345-5 (Paperback)
978-1-4602-8346-2 (eBook)

1. BIOGRAPHY & AUTOBIOGRAPHY, EDITORS, JOURNALISTS, PUBLISHERS

Distributed to the trade by The Ingram Book Company

For Velma.....
the journey of life with her
has been all you could ask for.

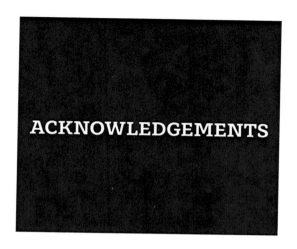

ACKNOWLEDGEMENTS

I WANT TO ACKNOWLEDGE THE SUPPORT AND ASSIS-tance I received in writing and publishing this memoir. First and foremost I want to thank Velma my partner of many years for the encouragement she provided in getting me to start the project and keep working at it as well as being a proof reader. My granddaughter, Dr. Lisa Harasen was tremendously helpful. She is a medical doctor but she can make a computer do anything she wants it to do. Elsewhere in the book I have acknowledged the great encouragement I received from my son in law Nigel Lane, and friend and book merchandiser John Kress.

I need to reserve a special word of thanks for Molly Ashlie of FriesenPress for her assistance in so many ways. She was patient with this irascible old man and she had many good suggestions. Hard to teach an old dog new tricks isn't it Molly!

Finally I want to thank my many guests over the years and my listeners for tuning in such large numbers. You all gave me an interesting and rewarding life.

The TABLE OF CONTENTS

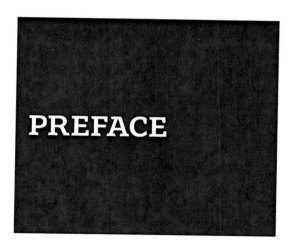

PREFACE

I WAS BORN IN YORKTON, SASKATCHEWAN, ON APRIL 17, 1938. I have no problem with people knowing my age. I had two younger brothers, who are now deceased. My father served in the army during World War II. While he was away, my mother and brother and I moved to Kamsack, a railway divisional point for Canadian National Railways (which my dad joined when he returned from the war).

Kamsack had a great high school drama program, in which I participated through the four years of high school. I won awards and I was absolutely certain that I would continue to be active in at least amateur theatre when I left school. Would you believe it? I have never since set foot on a dramatic stage. Just never got around to it. My daughter who showed no interest in drama in school went into amateur theatre after university as an actor and then as a director earning critical acclaim for casting.

Growing up, I always had a job. I delivered the *Winnipeg Tribune* (since we lived close to the Manitoba border), I worked in a soda fountain, delivered groceries, helped maintain a big yard, and shovelled snow in that same yard.

I was a Cub and Boy Scout and I was an army cadet in high school and spent two summers at Dundurn Canadian Forces Camp. I briefly contemplated a military career but my mother made that fanciful thought very brief. She was not having any of it!

I curled and was a running back and placement kicker in high school football. I started downhill skiing at age five. Over the years, I managed to ski Whistler, in British Columbia, and every province east, up to and including Quebec's Laurentians as well as Montana's Big Sky and White Fish. My wife and I were joined by our good friends Gerry and Ellie Welsh for many trips. Gerry was also my "haberdasher." No, that's not the name of a reindeer. I bought my suits and ties and shirts from Gerry.

I married my wife, Velma, some fifty-seven years ago. She was a copywriter in the radio station in Yorkton. Both of us have been active in our church and community. We have three children. Greg is our oldest. He is a semi-retired veterinarian who, a few years ago, sold what was probably the largest small-animal practice in the province. His wife, Karen, is also a vet. They spend the winter in Arizona. Lori, our only daughter, now retired, was an Agrologist with Farm Credit Canada. Her husband, Nigel Lane, is an engineer. Paul, our youngest, is a partner in a large Regina law firm and his wife, Dr. Debra Shepherd, is an obstetrician and gynecologist. I will not be needing any of her services!

We have five grandchildren, ranging in age from fourteen to twenty-nine years. Shannon, the eldest, is pursuing a master's degree so she can teach drama and voice. Her younger sister, Lisa, is finishing her second year of medical residency in family medicine. The boys are Mark, Owen, and Luke. None have indicated any interest in broadcasting but they do have good marks!

I knew what I wanted to do for a living when I was in the fifth grade. As a kid, I was a fan of radio and I was interested in the people who worked in the medium. The experience that clinched my ambition was when my fifth grade teacher, Frank Tappin, would place a loudspeaker in another classroom, leaving the microphone in our room, and we would provide news and sportscasts, a radio drama complete with sound effects, and a bit of music.

Tappin left teaching at the end of that year and took an announcer's position at CKRM Regina. He didn't stay there very long. I think his next job was in the general insurance, notary public field. He never returned to teaching or broadcasting. Many years later, I had him as a guest on my CKCK radio show.

As the end of high school approached, I began to write to and visit radio station program directors and, in some cases, sent tapes of me reading commercials or newscasts. My favorite station was CKCK Regina. I admired the on-air staff and the programming and overall sound of the station. That view was shared by a majority of the listening public in Saskatchewan because CKCK, the first radio station to go on the air in the province, was generally number one. My letter to Jim Grisenthwaite of CKCK radio resulted in an invitation to come to the station when I was next in Regina for an audition.

I accepted Grisenthwaite's invitation while on Christmas holidays in Regina with an aunt and uncle. I was given a script and led to a studio, where I was seated behind a CKCK microphone. Never before or since have I felt so nervous. Needless to say, I was totally freaked out and I was not signed up as the latest radio prodigy!

Jim Grisenthwaite's Assistant Program Director, the late Bob Macdonald, took an interest in me and acted as an advisor. He didn't have to do that, because my audition was less than stunning, but he did and I appreciated it.

I continued to send out tapes and letters. I just wasn't prepared to quit. One of my letters was to Merv Phillips, Program Director of CJGX Yorkton. I was getting desperate because high school was coming to an end and my parents were telling me that this radio business was nonsense and, like my father, I should take a job with Canadian National Railways and have a union protect me.

In my letter to Phillips, I stated that I would take even a menial job sweeping the station's floors at minimum wage. He wrote back to me saying that CJGX was no longer hiring inexperienced announcers but that my enthusiasm interested him. He asked me to drop in to see him on my next visit to Yorkton. It was only a sliver of light at the end of the tunnel, but there was some hope.

Near the end of June, 1956, my mother had a medical appointment in Yorkton and I was called upon to drive her to the city. When we got there, I said to myself that I was going to give it one more chance and I climbed the long stairs of the Smith-McKay block where the CJGX studios and offices were located.

The hallway had a large window that looked in to the radio station's main control room. I watched the activities for a few minutes when all of a sudden a man came down the hallway; I was certain it was Phillips. Indeed it was. I introduced myself and reminded him of his invitation.

I should note here that I was the last to broadcast from the long-standing Smith-McKay studios. I was working a Saturday evening shift in winter when a fire broke out in either the restaurant or photo studio below. I got out safely but I couldn't save my hat and coat. It was too smoky. I went out down a fire escape and got into a cab that just happened to be there.

Getting back to Merv Phillips... he invited me into his office, where he talked to me about broadcasting and my interest in a broadcast career. He next took me to a studio and gave me a newscast to read. I told myself that I'd better not blow this audition like the one at CKCK because this could be my last chance. I went through it flawlessly. Merv Phillips said little but asked if I would come back to the station in an hour.

When I returned, Phillips took me into Station Manager Jack Shortreed's office, where I was told that they were prepared to hire me as a junior staffer at the princely sum of $135 per month. I was to start in two weeks, on the first day of the Yorkton Exhibition. I was eighteen years old and

I thought I had died and gone to heaven! I told my mother that I was being paid $150 per month. It was a long time later that I confessed that I started at that paltry sum of $135 per month.

I think it was about two days later that I received a letter from Canadian National Railways offering me the job of Assistant Station Agent at Makaroff, Manitoba. I don't recall the salary but it had to be more than $135 per month. Makaroff is so small that a night on the town takes three minutes.

Within six months I had my first job offer. CKOM Saskatoon wanted me to read news for them. I took a bus to Saskatoon and accepted the job, only to be talked out of it by Merv Phillips. About a month or two later, CFQC, also of Saskatoon, offered me a job as early morning newscaster. I accepted. I left that job in less than a year because I was out of my depth. I didn't know a lead story from a load of hay. I was sent to cover a baseball tournament (sports was part of journalism, according to CFQC) at the Saskatoon Exhibition and I cribbed notes from the good-natured sportswriting veteran, the late Cam Mackenzie of the *Star Phoenix*. The CFQC newsroom had a staff of twelve, including the late Don Wittman who was Sports Director. Bill Cameron and Ian Bickle were the leaders. It was a professional newsroom that was winning awards from the United States. Canada had little or nothing in the way of journalistic awards.

For five days of the week, my alarm rang at 4:00 a.m. I was off on Saturday and I put in a half-day on Sunday. I finished my Sunday shift after reading the 10:00 p.m. news and went home, only to get up at 4:00 a.m. the next morning. The radio station provided a cab for the early morning announcer and the newsman. I always reminded the cab company not to honk the horn; I would be awake at that ungodly hour.

The very early start to my day was starting to get me down, along with the fact that I was completely without jour-nalistic competence. I began my career as a staff announcer. I could read the news, but reporting and editing was another matter. I was drawn to the CFQC offer because the station was also into television. I asked about that but nothing came my way. I got to read a short afternoon telecast during the last week of my employment but that was all. I heard that a television license had been granted to some Yorkton applicants and because I could learn the journalism ropes more easily, I returned to CJGX. On my last day in Saskatoon, Station Manager Vern Dallin presented me with a set of gold cufflinks, which I still wear from time to time.

My return to Yorkton included one setback; the TV licensees had wanted the radio on-air staff to also work for them. Some big thinker on the radio side declined the offer because they felt that the television station would not last because merchants could not afford the higher advertising rates. Can you believe it?

My return to Yorkton enabled me to settle into a work situation that I could handle. It also provided an opportunity to expand my personal life. I was soon introduced to Velma Stadler, who worked in the station's copy department. We married on June 6, 1959, at St. Gerard's, in Yorkton, and as I write this we are in our fifty-seventh year of marriage. Two of our three children were born in Yorkton: Greg and Lori Ann.

Life was good in Yorkton. We built a new home and settled into the community with a reasonably good standard of living. I was eventually named News Director. I would read the 12:30 noon major news and then go home for lunch. On my way out I would stop and check the Broadcast News newswire. On one occasion, I put on my hat and coat and stopped just as the teletype spelled out the bulletin from Dallas, Texas, informing the world that President Kennedy had been shot. I immediately sat down in front of the newsroom microphone to report the shocking news.

During the summer of 1965, I thought I would try my hand at radio sales. Mine was a rural territory, so I would leave town on Monday and return on Friday. I soon concluded that sales was not my cup of tea. The few weeks that I spent on the road were not a loss. I made some sales but I was not likely to become a sales leader. It was another side of private radio. It taught me to appreciate the work of the sales staff and to see the station from the advertiser's point of view. In particular, I recognized the importance of news and public affairs programming. Farm news as a part of news coverage was particularly important for the listening area of CJGX.

On one sleepless night on the road, I concluded that I wanted out of sales and to get back to news. I knew that I couldn't go back to the news job in Yorkton, because I had been replaced. I had heard that CKCK radio in Regina was looking for a person to fill a senior news position. I telephoned News Manager Grant Kennedy to inquire if such was indeed the case. He replied that it was and that he would be pleased to talk about it with me if I would come to Regina. From the tone of his remarks, it sounded to me like he was highly interested in my services.

I drove to Regina and met with Kennedy. The job was for Radio News Editor, which included city hall reporting and backup reporting at the legislature. One larger newsroom covered both radio and television. I ran the radio side and Jim Oxman handled the television bureau. There was to be a constant exchange of news material between the two newsrooms.

I told Grant Kennedy that I would take the job. He said he would send me an official written offer with salary and other details. While I was talking to Grant, Jim Struthers, General Manager, and Ron Lamborn, of the sales department, were looking for a salesperson and wondered if I might be interested. I told Grant Kennedy to kill that idea and he did.

I returned to Yorkton and informed my wife, who, typically, was supportive in every way. I tendered my resignation to George Gallagher, put the house up for sale, and got ready for the move to the capital city.

During my time at CKCK we were number one in most categories. Audience numbers hit some record-breaking levels for the medium in Saskatchewan. From a radio point of view we owned the province. I have to say that most of my years at CKCK were the happiest of my career. I worked in a beautiful new radio station with good equipment, a staff that was happy to be a part of the station, and a highly capable executive.

General Manager Jim Struthers was a brilliant, creative leader with a sense of humour that didn't quit. He came to the top job at the station from the newsroom. The pattern was usually that general managers came from the sales department. I used to refer to Jim Struthers as the Jackie Robinson of the news business. Gary Miles, who started out as a disc jockey, was very effective in sales and later succeeded Struthers. Gary was very much like Struthers except he was loud in clothing and voice and brash in a colourful way. At one time, he drove a convertible with a pet St. Bernard in the back seat. Howie Dean was Chief Engineer. He could build or repair almost anything in the technical field. Dennis Stafford was a highly competent promotional person and a good friend. Doug Alexander, who remains a friend to this day, was Program Director, on top of his job at all times.

I must express something about Harold Crittenden, who was vice president of the company that owned CKCK. Without doubt, he was one of the finest men I have ever been associated with. He came up through the ranks to his top job but he conducted himself like a good father rather than an authority. "Crit" fostered a sense of family rather than employment. His office wasn't located in the CKCK buildings but in the Regina Inn, where it didn't look like he was looking over everyone's shoulder. Crit and his wife, Myrtle, always came to the CKCK kids' Christmas parties, where they acted like grandparents. When I was leaving CKCK, Mr. Crittenden, who was then living in eastern Canada, sent me a touching telegram, which I have kept.

When I began my time at CKCK, on-air staff included morning man, Johnny Sandison, who was a very good friend, mid-morning announcer Fred Sear, afternoon country host Porky Charboneau, and a sterling news anchor, Jim MacLeod. Doing sports was John Badham, who had million-dollar tonsils and a sense of humour to match.

The morning after a City Council meeting, I was invited to join Fred Sear on the air and provide background and an explanation of some of the major or controversial council decisions. This was to be the background of something that changed my broadcast career and life forever.

I must say that I enjoyed my time covering City Hall, even though covering Mayor Henry Baker was an adventure. I had good relationships with council members and department heads. This was also the beginning of a long and close personal friendship with Hewitt Helmsing, who was a very young member of council. He and his lovely wife Gay who later was also a Councillor, and their children Clayton (our God son), and Bruce, and Heather are really family to us.

An unfortunate situation at City Hall was the fact that all council members were elected as members of slates. Politics ruled supreme, which didn't serve the city very well. At a time when decisions were needed, council was mired in bitter debate and controversy.

I was also covering the legislature, as a backup measure, and doing a weekly fifteen-minute City Hall program on CKCK TV. Fifteen minute TV shows were an oddity. I was soon named the main legislative reporter. Later, I was the first broadcaster to be elected President of the Saskatchewan Legislative Press Gallery Association. As I was leaving the City Hall beat, Council did something unprecedented by passing a resolution of commendation for me for the "excellence" of my work at City Hall and offered best wishes for the new assignment at the legislature. I sent back a letter of appreciation in which I stated that I was particularly pleased that the resolution passed unanimously rather than by a vote of six to five!

In 1967, Jim Struthers called me into his office and wondered if I might be interested in hosting an open line program. My sessions on Fred Sear's show prompted the idea. Competing station CKRM had a couple of open line shows, and our management felt that we were giving our competitors that audience by default. Being a competitive sort, I said I would be willing to give it a try.

To begin with, my show was to be known as *The Harasen Line;* it would be twenty-five minutes long. When I left the show almost ten years later, it was four-and-a-half hours long. When we began the program we discussed what posture I would adopt. Mean or nice? We finally decided that it would be difficult to maintain a phony posture. I would deal with each situation as it presented itself. Some thought I was too tough. Some believed that until I brought home a tape to play on my show after I guested on Jack Webster's show on CKNW Vancouver. Webster was a bombastic performer who was loud, fearless, and totally in charge. I could go after people, but not as loudly or forcefully as Jack.

While doing radio five days a week, I also did some reporting and I was seen regularly on television. For a time, I conducted a TV open line show, an interview program, and hosted a documentary show which resulted in three major awards.

The TV open line was a tricky effort because we couldn't use the seven-second delay device that we used on radio. Basically, a delay device on radio is a tape seven seconds long. Everything said by a caller or the host is uttered seven seconds before the listener hears it. If a caller uses profanity or says something libelous, the host has seven seconds to decide if those statements should be deleted. He presses a button, which puts the program on the air live. He can dispose of the offending caller; once that is done, he then presses the button and goes back to the delay system. A delay system on television would not be practical because what was being said on the TV picture would not be synchronized with what the viewer was hearing.

Seven seconds may sound like an unreasonably short amount of time in which to decide if something is profane or legally actionable. Take a look at the second hand on your watch as it marks out seven seconds. Unless you are sleeping at the switch, that is more than enough time to decide if something is not air-worthy. Mind you, when I first began broadcasting, you would not dare say "damn" or "hell" on the air. Today just about everything goes. CBC is just one place where the so-called ultimate expletive is loud and clear. Private broadcasting is not far behind in that department.

I was named Director of Public Affairs for CKCK radio and CKCK television and was spared from doing any reporting for the newsroom. By about the mid-1970s, I was worn out and tired of carrying the load of work and the nuisance of a high public profile and I resigned. I made a mistake in resigning in September of 1974 and not leaving until mid-November of the same year. I didn't want to leave the station high and dry at rating time. When I left CKRM, I announced my departure on my final show.

I took a job in the information division of Saskatchewan Wheat Pool, an organization for which I had a great deal of respect. During my time at the Pool I continued to do some broadcasting. My work put me in close contact with the highly competent Information Director Ian Bickle, with whom I had worked at CFQC Saskatoon in the 1950s. I also worked in close touch with President Ted Turner, the executive, and the board of directors. They all were people of integrity and substance. I have maintained my friendship with Ted Turner over the years and I'm pleased to see that the Turners are enjoying a well-earned retirement.

I guess one of my main contributions to Saskatchewan Wheat Pool was that I was able to convince delegates to open the farm policy side of the two-week annual meeting to media coverage. For the previous half century, the meeting had been closed and the organization had tried to compensate for that with news releases, which is not good practice. Needless to say, the business side of the Pool remained closed and rightly so.

In May of 1978, George Gallagher, a former colleague at Yorkton radio, had purchased CKRM Regina and came calling with an offer to join the station as an open line host, with a future appointment to the management team. CKRM was dead last in every audience category and was virtually invisible in the community. I took more than a week to decide. A significant factor in my decision to accept the offer was a substantial raise in pay (I had two children at the University of Saskatchewan at the same time).

Gallagher unloaded the station a few years later because a business project in Texas was in trouble financially and he needed the money. The Hill family of Regina purchased the station, after having purchased CKCK Television and sold the TV station for a handsome profit. The Hill purchase of CKRM brought Bruce Cowie to the radio station, which brought executive competence and stability. He appointed me Director of Administration and Community Relations; I was second in command while still doing some regular on-air work. The Hills were good employers. Paul Hill expanded the family's broadcast holdings and other enterprises later. They are Saskatchewan's wealthiest business family and they deserve to be. They could make it anywhere but they have always made Regina and the province their first consideration.

I remained with CKRM until the end of 1995. I think I did my best work there. Experience was the reason. An opportunity to work in government beckoned and I thought it might be a good way to round out my working life. When I was reading morning news at CFQC Saskatoon in the 1950s, Roy Romanow was a part-time high school sports broadcaster at CKOM, in the same city. We stayed in contact over the years. When he was Premier and a guest on my show, I would chide him during commercial breaks about when he was going to get serious and get a real job.

I am writing this book after a long period of time in which many people have urged me to do so. At the top of the list is Nigel Lane, my son-in-law, and John Kress, the best book merchandiser I have ever known, who once owned the Book and Brier in Regina. Nigel just wouldn't take no for an answer and I finally succumbed to his urging. He is a fine son-in-law who was smart enough to marry our daughter Lori, so why not write? I hope I haven't disappointed Nigel or John. I have written this book to entertain and also to inform a bit.

Some have wondered if I would use this book to even the score with those who may have double-crossed or made life miserable for me. I have decided not to. There were only three or four and some are either dead or senile. I really fixed them by not attending their funerals or visiting them in their oblivious worlds!

In my work I have been honoured by my peers, my church, community, province, and country, all for doing work I have loved. So many people go to work each day hating what they do. I must emphasize that my church is very important to me. I have tried to serve it in it's lay ministries, as school trustee and through the Knights of Columbus.

Regina has been a great place to live and raise a family. It has been good to all of us and it has provided many opportunities for members of our clan. Early in my career I worked and socialized with the same broadcast people. That was not the best idea. Our closest friends have been Dave and Barbara MacLeod, Gerry and Ellie Welsh, Paul and Angie Sprentz, and Peter and Kathy Maier. I must also mention a cousin, a Winnipeg businessman, the late Ed Werbowski, who was like a brother to me. They spoke of my work very little and that was just fine with me. None were in broadcasting.

TOPICS

THIS WAS PROBABLY THE MOST COMPLEX PART OF WHAT we did each day. I found myself really starting from scratch when I began at CKCK, because they hadn't had a program like mine before. Many years later, when I went to CKRM, they had had some call-in programs years before, but on the whole their audience wasn't even close to being a broadcast factor in Regina and beyond. CKCK had a dominant position in the province, so launching something new or different wasn't as difficult as trying to raise the corpse that CKRM was in the late 1970s. People were not aware of the station's existence; it wasn't heard as you travelled around the city and heard radios in service stations and barber shops. The station didn't even have microphone flashes, which are the attachment on microphones that identify the station in a news scrum or remote. The amazing part of all of this was the fact that CKRM (which was CJRM early on) was an old broadcaster in the province. Frequent ownership changes and incompetence on the part of management and pro-grammers ran the station into the ground.

Very early in the process at CKCK, we decided that our subject matter should be as topical as possible. Obviously, that meant being in touch with what was happening in the newsroom. It meant being in touch with what was happening in the city, province, and beyond.

Now, that wasn't enough, because there are standing questions in society that may not be immediately topical but are never far from the minds of people. Capital punishment, rules of the road, taxes, government decisions, censorship, the cost of living, and the list goes on.

One of the keys to choosing a topic or a guest was that you hit people where they live. We chose issues that make the average guy angry. These are the concerns that come up at a coffee row or the workplace. The open line show provided opportunities to vent frustration or anger. At times, there was an opportunity for listeners to tear a strip off the guy in charge, such as the mayor or cabinet minister.

I generally tried to place the people in charge at the disposal of my listeners. Those in charge included municipal leaders, provincial premiers, cabinet ministers, opposition members, dissenters of various kinds, police, educators, and union and religious leaders.

You generally tried to provide balance in a discussion. At least, "the other side" should have the opportunity to be heard. You didn't allow callers to abuse those they disagreed with, but a contrary view expressed forcefully and respectfully was always welcome. Some callers failed that basic requirement, but there were many who were a treat to hear.

Guests on the program came from a variety of sources. When we decided to pursue a certain topic or question, we would try to invite people in the know. That wasn't always easy, because not everyone was anxious to guest on a program where they would have to handle my questions and/or the questions and opinions of my listeners. There were superior types who claimed that open line listeners were riff-raff and not worthy of the time it would take to hear them out! At other times, people were grateful to go on the air to either answer questions or hear the opinions of the people. This took place in my studio or on the telephone.

During spring, some publishers would release new books, but it seemed that the largest number of books on a variety of topics were released in the fall. Publishers would have authors campaign across Canada, where they would do radio and television and newspaper interviews. Some authors addressed service clubs or professional groups. Others would appear at local bookstores or department stores, where they would preside over sales of their books and autograph the books. There were times when I would go along and act as the master of ceremonies, as I did with Pierre Berton and others at Eaton's or the Book and Brier.

The point here is that authors write about topics or people or events. Placing them at the disposal of my audience would produce opinions and questions. There were a number of people in the city who acted as public relations agents for the publishers. They would usher the writers around the various media outlets in the city and any other appearances in an exhausting round of interviews and bookstore activities.

Articles in newspapers or periodicals also provided lots of topic ideas. My first assistant, Cathy Grant, would perform miracles by looking and finding people connected to those articles and booking them for the show. When people gave Cathy a hard time I would step in and try to resolve the problem. Sometimes I was successful and at other times I was just as unsuccessful as my top-notch assistant.

There were times when we stuck our necks out and went after "big fish." These were the people who generally refused interviews or only appeared on major network shows. Quite often, we were rewarded for our boldness. We hosted some big names, such as actor Harry Morgan, who played Colonel Sherman T. Potter on M.A.S.H., actor Jack Lemmon, Bing Crosby (who became an annual guest), and cartoonist Charles Schulz (creator of *Peanuts*), to name a few. Harry Morgan asked me if every other boy in Canada was named Lorne because many Canadian men who appeared in American show business were named Lorne, such as Lorne Greene, of *Bonanza,* and Lorne Michaels, of

Saturday Night Live. I assured him that it was a coincidence and that I had not heard of any baby boy named Lorne for an eternity.

There was always the matter of getting an "exclusive" in terms of authors or celebrities. When I began my program on CKCK and later on CKRM, I couldn't demand exclusivity. In the case of CKCK, it was the first time that they had programmed open line, while the competition had been in it for a few years. Before too long, when we became the dominant program, we started to insist on being exclusive or at least first to have the celebrity on the air. Your audience numbers were always very useful when you pressed the issue. Agents for the publishers didn't like the exclusivity issue or "come to me first." Ideal for them was when they could trundle the author and/or celebrity from one radio station or television station to another and hit all local media and the newspaper on the same day. In other words, it would turn out to be "Pierre Berton Day on all Regina media." If I could get all of my guests first, I didn't care where they went after me. I didn't want to be second to anyone.

Naturally there were those who didn't like me and tried to get past me with a possible guest but I always tried to make certain that the publisher knew my audience numbers. There was a couple here who promoted musical shows; I would try to assist them by featuring the coming show on my program. However, they once directed a guest from me to a competitor. They and other such giants of thought never again got an assist from me even though some begged.

When I first went to CKRM, my former radio station informed the people at the Regina Inn's Stage West that the station would not accept any of their headline performers unless they got them first. Since I was just building my audience in the new place, I decided I would change tactics, temporarily, and agree to take the performer second. This decision had a positive effect on the people at the Regina Inn because soon I had first choice. You have to understand that the battle for audience in a multi-media market is a very real one. Advertising is sold on the basis of audience numbers and allied factors. With national advertising, audience numbers are particularly crucial.

There was a hack working in the provincial administration who initially was not helpful when I first went to CKRM. Through some string-pulling, we were able to remedy that. With advisors such as that, it is no wonder that that government is remembered as less than stellar. This individual went to his reward in the Senate and his name has come up a couple of times during the seemingly endless controversy surrounding the upper house. It will be interesting to see how all this shakes down. Stay tuned.

My competitors tried to steer potential guests away from me. I guess we realized that we would have to get up early and stay late if we were going to win. For my first week at CKRM, my first guest was Premier Allan Blakeney. I also had as a guest one of the Apollo astronauts who walked on the moon. Another early guest was the controversial former Regina Chief of Police, Arthur G. Cookson, who by then resided in Calgary. He had written a book about his life and particularly the very controversial days leading up to his departure from his job and from the city. How did we manage all that? I had ways!

Early in my time as host of CKCK's open line program, CJME placed local lawyer Tony Merchant opposite me on their own open line program. Shortly after he started, they moved his starting time to a half hour before me. Naturally, we followed suit. Tony, who can be controversial an hour before he wakes up, tried to engage me in an on-air back-and-forth slanging match. This was all relayed to me by my assistant. He even tried to get personal with me. I had never met the man. I ignored his bait and I wasn't prepared to loan him my larger audience.

Eventually, the law society gave him an ultimatum: either he practice law or broadcast, but not both. He was wise enough to choose law, where I'm sure he has made much more money, though controversy still stalks him. I get along well with Tony and his wife, Senator Pana, is really a very pleasant lady. I should note that Rawlco Radio's current talk show host, John Gormley, who was a classmate of my youngest son at law school, has always been positive and courteous with me..

I must say that I was somewhat startled by a couple of developments when I began my time at CKRM. My former station had hired Michael Wood to host the open line at CKCK a month or two before I decided on my comeback. Shortly after I returned to the program format my competitors released their new host. It was assumed that they didn't believe the man could compete, even though he was a former broadcaster who came to Saskatchewan to work in the Thatcher government. It all seemed a bit hasty to me.

The other surprise was when CKCK seemed to be phasing out their open line. The station seemed to be on a death march, to what turned out to be its eventual demise. The late George Young was their open line host; he was released at a time when I thought he was handling things reasonably well. The surprise was that when he was released, he came to me and asked if I would help him find a job. Here we were—competitors, not doing each other any favors—and here was George asking me to give him a hand up. I told him that I would give it my best shot. It wasn't difficult. I went to the Devine provincial government and they quickly made available an information job somewhere in government. At the time, George was in the early stages of a serious illness that eventually took his life. I never heard from him again.

We tried to make federal politicians, particularly the Prime Minister's office and members of cabinet, aware of our existence and we offered a standing invitation to them whenever they were in the area. Our constant contact paid off in many ways.

I should also note that listeners made suggestions through letters and telephone calls; we accepted many of them.

It would have been very easy to take our daily journal and fill an entire month with topics and guests, but that would have moved us away from any hope of being current. It was really a problem when we would book a good guest for a particular date, only to have all hell break loose over some issue locally, provincially, or beyond. When we had four and a half hours at our disposal, we could do a little tweaking here and there, but it could be difficult to cover all bases.

I was on the air with a guest and a particular topic when we learned that Pope St. John Paul II had been shot. The fastest medium in the world can't afford to sit and twiddle its thumbs. It's a red alert, but you can't leave your guest and topic and show them the door. Somehow we were able to accommodate all of these situations, minds racing at high speed to find the answers.

What we tried to do at all times was to create a situation where listeners believed that if something was happening or someone had something to say, you could rely on us to have it quickly and, most of all, accurately.

One of the most annoying practices (which didn't crop up often) was when an interest group or individual would go to our management or even our owners, asking them to direct me to place said group or individual on my program. I didn't knuckle under and I remember only one heated discussion with one superior. The final decision about who or what topic was featured on my program was mine. Suggestions were always welcome but not always accepted. It can't be any other way.

RATINGS

SOME BROADCASTERS CALL THEM SWEEPS, WHILE others refer to them as ratings. The document that contains all these numbers is referred to as "the book." These are the audience numbers that are vital to the radio station's program and sales departments. For the salespeople, good numbers give them something of an added advantage, particularly if audience numbers place the station in the leading role in a multi-station market (such as a city), but even for single station ratings, which are often in competition for advertising fees with other stations down the road. If you can hear it, it competes—and, to some degree, with community television and newspapers as well. It's all about the advertising dollars and the competition to get as many of them as possible. Some businesses are interested in the ratings while others base their purchase of advertising on the basis of the results they get from that particular station. National advertisers pay close attention to ratings.

Needless to say, program departments are also vitally interested in audience numbers, because these tell the station if the present program formula (which includes music, news, sports and promotions) is catching an audience and whether that audience is growing or standing still. The writing is often on the wall if audience numbers are declining.

The book can indicate how a station is doing at all times of the day, the age range of the audience, whether the audience is mainly male or female (and what this ratio is), and the number of radios in use at particular times of the day. It also provides total numbers of listeners within cities and out of town. The younger listener who is upwardly mobile, who buys appliances and has a mortgage and a growing family, is more interesting to the advertiser than the old folks, for obvious reasons.

Some people have received ballots once or more times. Some people have never seen a ballot. That doesn't mean a thing. The results are more likely to be accurate than not. Survey rules are intended to forbid any gimmicks that would increase listenership during the survey period, but there are ways to circumvent the rules, though it is more difficult to do these days than in the past. There are penalties.

I have always said that your success in the rating race is what you do six months before the survey period rather than at a contest or giveaway during measurement time. I think even the most jaundiced observer would agree that even though polls are, at times, inaccurate, the accuracy rate is quite high. I see nothing but steady improvement as technology becomes more sophisticated. Like all science, it was clumsy and hit-and-miss in the beginning, but growth and accuracy has come a long way.

NAME DROPPING

I HAVE USED THE TITLE "NAME DROPPING" FOR THIS section because I think anyone who didn't know my background and working record would think that I was blowing smoke if I told that person that these people found their way to my microphones and radio and television studios. Day after day, week after week, month after month, and year after year they came. The great, the small, the brilliant, and some of the unfortunate. I was impressed by some and I was amused, entertained, and angered by others. Some were barefaced liars while others were deep, dedicated professional people with ethics to burn.

Lining up guests for a radio show is not an easy thing. Not every public figure is anxious to be interviewed and the additional factor of telephone calls from the public at large puts a chill on those who consider being guests. The anonymity of callers is another concern for potential guests. Some felt that they would be at a disadvantage and vulnerable to any irresponsible charge by an anonymous caller. I would tell them that the average listener, who might not ever call the program, would listen to the exchange between guest and caller and quickly conclude whose argument they believed. Most people are fair and reasonable. Tallying up the number of good calls and negative calls was not very good poll-taking. These are merely the people who got through to the program. Politicians or their staff members tended to keep score.

I use as an example George Hees, who was a minister of the Diefenbaker cabinet. He came to my program on one occasion and told me he had another appointment and would have to leave the show early. I hated these times, because what do you do with twenty or thirty minutes "left over," with people wanting to speak to the guest, who just abandoned ship? Anyway, we launched the discussion knowing that Hees would have to leave early.

After a brief interview, we opened the lines, with the first caller taking a nasty shot at Hees. The second caller followed with the same tone and so did the next and on and on. Not one complimentary call. At our first commercial break, Hees, obviously thinking he would get some positive calls and save the situation, said he would now stay until the end of the program rather than leave early. It only got worse! Caller after caller jumped all over him, only for Hees to lose his temper and call one caller "a dumb cluck."

Days of clouds and rain made callers grumpy and so did a severe cold spell that lasted a week or two. Regardless, callers often made the show.

I'm grateful to all the "names" who found their way to my studio. We always tried to present top-notch guests and I think, for the most part, we did.

ROBERT LEITH (DINNY) HANBIDGE

If Mr. Hanbidge wasn't the most popular Lieutenant Governor in Saskatchewan's history, he was at least among two others also deemed most popular. I'm told that Archie McNabb, who I didn't know, was one. The other was Lynda

Haverstock, who I do know. Ms. Haverstock kept up a punishing pace. She is beautiful in appearance and manner. Not long after I began my program, in 1967, I realized that the Lieutenant Governor would occasionally call the program. I recognized his voice and there was a pattern to his calls. He usually called when one of his political cronies was my guest. The questions were not partisan and usually included a little humour. His Honour would always ask, "Lorne, do you know who this is?" I would say yes and he would chuckle and then hang up. The funny part about it all is that my guests would never ask me to identify him.

I interviewed Mr. Hanbidge for television and I believe that the reel of film found its way to the Provincial Archives. I remember that interview because the queen's representative began to talk about his embarrassing moments as Lieutenant Governor. Once, in a formal receiving line with royalty on hand, he noted that he was losing his cummerbund. At the end of its slide, it lay on the floor encircling his feet. My camera crew was turning purple as they struggled to keep from bursting into laughter. At the end of our work, Mr. Hanbidge offered all "a cigar and a drink of scotch!"

Lieutenant Governor Hanbidge served for some seven years in a term that is supposed to end after five years. He told me that the problem was that he was left hanging and didn't know when the term would end.

In July of 1974, I was somewhat startled by a call from one of the Hanbidge daughters. She and a sister were in Regina taking care of their father, who had only days to live. They told me that "Dinny" had asked them to ask Lorne Harasen if he would consider visiting him before the old gentleman's time ran out. I told them I would be honoured to do so. On the afternoon of my visit, I was led into his bedroom and found him lying on top of the bed covers wearing pyjamas and a very smart dressing gown. He was quite weak, so I didn't stay too long, but I thanked him for his friendship and public service. He passed away not long after that visit.

Dinny Hanbidge served as Mayor of Kerrobert, was an MLA in our legislature, a Member of Parliament, and finally served as Lieutenant Governor. He was a friend of John Diefenbaker and would laugh at himself when he, a Tory, would read the Speech from the Throne and refer to the NDP government as "my government." He was a staunch fan of the Saskatchewan Roughriders because he played for the team's forerunner. I can see him now, in fur coat, a cigar clenched in his teeth, walking with his pal Tommy Nelson, heading for the west gates at Taylor field.

Mr. Hanbidge even borrowed something from one of his predecessors, Lieutenant Governor Archie McNabb, when Princess Alexandra and husband Angus Ogilvie were welcomed to the legislature. Dinny closed his remarks by saying, "Next time, bring the kids!" McNabb had made the same invitation to King George VI and Queen Elizabeth when they toured Canada many years before.

MR. ELLIS

It is a common name but one of its users did not do common work. It is a name that has been used by hangmen in Britain and Canada to protect their identity. One day I began to think about the men who carried out this task and the fact that it had been a long time since anyone had been hanged in Canada. It seemed clear that capital punishment was on its way out.

We were able to find out that a sheriff in Ontario knew who our Mr. Ellis was and was prepared to find out if he would do a live interview. The sheriff got back to us and said that Mr. Ellis was prepared to do the interview with certain conditions. We could not call him. He would call us. He would do the interview from a phone booth. We would have to pay him a day's pay because he needed to absent himself from his work. His employer and his family didn't know about his "sideline."

I was always a little nervous about the "don't call us, we'll call you" arrangement but I decided that it was worth taking a chance. Mr. Ellis delivered on all of our needs.

He felt that he was performing a public service and was concerned that capital punishment was apparently on its way out in Canada. He explained how he tested the trap door of the gallows and the procedure to test the weight capacity of the rope. Obviously, he needed to prepare that based on the weight of the condemned person.

He was somewhat quiet-spoken and seemingly of average intelligence. As I recall it, none of the callers gave him a particularly bad time, because a substantial number of Canadians, at the time, were pro death penalty. When we reached the end of the program I thanked him and he was gone. I should have asked him how he was going to spend the rest of the day, since he couldn't go back to work or go home. He probably went shopping.

KEN CURTIS

At first glance, this name may not register. Ken Curtis had a long and varied entertainment career but he was probably best known as "Festus," the sidekick of Marshal Matt Dillon in the very popular western television series *Gunsmoke*. You may recall that the marshal's first partner was Dennis Weaver, who played the role of "Chester." Weaver decided to strike out on his own and really didn't hit it big with anything. Along came Festus and the rest is history.

Believe it or not, Ken Curtis replaced Frank Sinatra as the vocalist with the Tommy Dorsey Orchestra. I heard Curtis sing and I can assure you that he was a fine singer. For a while, he was part of the western vocal group known as the Sons of the Pioneers. Another member of the group at the time was Leonard Slye, who later became very wealthy playing a cowboy named Roy Rogers. I was a Gene Autry fan as a kid, because he needed only one gun while Rogers needed two.

Ken Curtis was a perfect gentleman. I did the afternoon portion of my show from the Regina Exhibition and he was one of my guests. He answered questions from members of the audience and slipped in and out of character through-out. He had some nice things to say about me and he was a delight to work with.

EDGAR BERGEN

We were happy to be able to book Mr. Bergen for an hour one morning and I invited the late Johnny Sandison to join me as a guest interviewer. Johnny and I were collectors of vintage radio shows from what has come to be known as the golden years of radio. I think you could refer to any age as radio's golden age, because radio has changed and kept up with the times.

Bergen came on the phone and, even though he was well along in years, his voice was strong and he spoke the same immaculate English that we remembered from those Sunday evenings when he was selling the products of Chase and Sanborn.

As we were coming to the end of our interview, I tried something that I had not warned Bergen about. I simply asked if Charlie (McCarthy) or Mortimer (Snerd) were around. Without missing a beat, wisecracking Charlie came on the phone, followed by the hopelessly stupid Mortimer.

The never-ending mystery surrounding Edgar Bergen's great success was that he was a ventriloquist. You have to see a ventriloquist work in order to appreciate his skill but Bergen was on radio where you could only hear him. He made the odd cameo appearance in movies. Charlie was always chiding Bergen about his moving lips when it was Charlie who was talking! Yes, Candace Bergen is Bergen's daughter. She once wrote that she had to compete with Charlie for her dad's attention!

ALVIN (OLD CREEPY) KARPIS (KARPOWICZ)

He was a thief, he robbed banks and trains, and he kidnapped William Hamm Jr., of the Minneapolis-St. Paul Hamm's Brewery family. Karpis was born in Montreal but eventually moved to the United States, where he joined some of the big-name gangsters and became public enemy number one. He rubbed shoulders with such criminals as Al Capone, Ma Barker, John Dillinger, and Bonnie (Parker) and Clyde (Barrow), who he said were homely and dumb as posts. They were not the glamorous types played by Warren Beatty and Faye Dunaway in the movie *Bonnie and Clyde*.

When Karpis was finally caught, he was sentenced to life in prison. He was released from Alcatraz after twenty-five years and extradited to Canada. Much of his time in prison was spent in solitary confinement. He collaborated in the writing of two books about his adventures. Parole regulations in the United States do not permit criminals to write and profit from their memoirs. Not so in Canada.

When Karpis arrived at my radio studio he was wearing a suit and tie that had seen better days. Certainly not the pin-striped double-breasted suits of gangsters in the tele-visions series *The Untouchables*. He was stooped over a bit and he was courteous and not overly loud of voice. Old Creepy really looked like your "Uncle Mike" rather than a glamorous crook.

He was quite placid and the only time storm clouds came to his expression was if he thought that you were trying to find out more about his son, who I believe was a carpenter with a family living under another name in the United States. The other name was J. Edgar Hoover, former F.B.I director. Karpis said, "I made that son of a bitch!"

Karpis described the scene when he was captured. He said that he was sitting in his parked automobile when it was suddenly encircled by several FBI agents with guns drawn and aimed at him. Karpis noted that Hoover, who took personal credit for nabbing him, was peeking around the corner of a building a safe distance away from the scene of the arrest.

I found a place for the former public enemy number one on my daily call-in show and my weekly television program. We were both scolded by my radio listeners, he for being an ex-gangster and me for having him on my show. They were not in a forgiving mood that morning, even though Karpis was contrite and said it was a wasted life.

A few years ago my wife and I were in San Francisco and decided to take a tour of Alcatraz, which has long been out of service as a prison. In one section of the prison there were sketches of some of the celebrated inmates who were guests of that cold and dingy place surrounded by water. One of them was Alvin Karpis, sitting right next to Al Capone.

I entered one of the solitary confinement cells, which were without contents of any kind and turned pitch-black inside when the door was closed. As it turned out, there was a former inmate selling a book when we visited the prison. He told us that when he was placed in solitary confinement, in order to keep from going mad, he would tear a button from his shirt and fling it in the cell and then crawl on his hands and knees trying to find it. When he found it, he would repeat the exercise.

Alvin Karpis wrote to me twice in 1971, when he was staying at the home of friends in Spain. He thanked me for treating him in a positive way. I still have the letter and postcard. I don't think I answered him but as time goes on I wish I had written to him.

His biggest problem was adjusting to life outside of prison. Karpis was imprisoned in the 1930s and spent over a quarter-century behind bars, substantially in solitary. When he was released, one of places he was curious about was a supermarket. He was simply baffled by what he saw. Quite a change from the corner grocery store when he was a boy. Not long after he wrote to me, I received the news that Alvin Karpis, public enemy number one, had committed suicide. He just couldn't adjust. Truly a wasted life.

W.O. MITCHELL

Canada's Mark Twain was a frequent visitor who came so many times that his autograph in his latest book was something like "Regards to Lorne and thanks...again." He had the distinction of having once called me "a son of a bitch" on the air. . W. O. frequently forgot that he was on the air or that the microphone was turned on. I was kidding him about something and he laughed and said, "Oh, you son of a bitch." After I told him that he had done this he refused to believe it. Once I convinced him, I asked if he would autograph my book accordingly. He refused. I told him that each morning hundreds of people in my audience did the same with malice in mind. Mitchell finally relented and wrote, "Regards to Lorne, my favorite sonova bitch. W. O. Mitchell." At the beginning of our interviews I always paused while he fired snuff up his nostrils. I once took him to a Roughrider football game; the Riders won against Montreal. Near the end of his life he was very dependent on his wife, Merna. He was a dear man.

EUGENE WHELAN

In 1986, Eugene Whelan wrote a book titled *Whelan*. His autograph read, "To Lorne, a good digger, a good broadcaster, a very human person. With my best wishes. Hon. Eugene Whelan P.C." I'm reminded of a telephone interview I once conducted with Mr. Whelan. I can't remember the primary theme of the interview. It was a situation in which I thought he said something startling but I wasn't sure. "Did he say that?" I thought to myself. "Surely not!" Besides, time was very short and I couldn't pursue the matter with him. As soon as the interview was concluded, I went to the tape of the interview and listened to the section where I thought I was hearing things. Yes, indeed, I had heard him correctly. I heard Eugene Whelan, Canada's Minister of Agriculture, say, on my program, "A cow is only human!"

JOEY SMALLWOOD

He was in the area visiting Pere Athol Murray. Pere, one of my frequent listeners and a good friend, always referred to Smallwood as the only living father of Confederation. Smallwood signed his published memoirs (titled, somewhat presumptuously, *I Chose Canada*) with these words: "Lorne Harasen. With kind recollections of our work together on one of democracy's most important remaining vehicles...the open line. Joseph R. Smallwood."

ROBERT BAIRD MCCLURE

He was the first layperson to serve as Moderator of the United Church of Canada. A delightful individual, he had spent most of his life as a doctor in the poor regions of the world, where people were in desperate need of his skills. Dr. McClure was not afraid to express an opinion that often-times qualified as controversial.

The one thing about McClure's visit to my program was that we didn't receive one telephone call. I was flabber-gasted! I was so bowled over that when McClure was back in Regina a year or two later, I immediately booked him for another appearance. Would you believe it? Not one call! I concluded that the audience was prepared to leave the asking of questions to me. They would listen to the humani-tarian doctor's colourful and often controversial answers.

His biography, written by Munroe Scott, was entitled *McClure: Years of Challenge.* Dr. McClure autographed the book: "To Lorne with happy memories of the battle of the microphone, as an amateur to a veteran."

SIMMA HOLT

Many will remember Vancouver journalist Simma for her newspaper work and frequent appearances as a guest on television panel shows. She came to my program some ten years after a previous visit to promote a book: *The Other Mrs. Diefenbaker: A Biography of Edna May Brower*. Simma signed my copy, "To Lorne who 10 years later still asks tough and stimulating questions. You have not become stale as some do. Thanks so much for sharing Edna with your listeners. Sincerely Simma." The interesting thing about "the other Mrs. Diefenbaker" is that she lies in the Saskatoon cemetery directly across the river from the Diefenbaker Centre, where Dief lies buried next to Olive, the second Mrs. Diefenbaker.

CHARLES LYNCH

The late Charlie Lynch was one of this country's top political journalists. He could also qualify as a Canadian humourist and he could play a mean harmonica! He was a war correspondent who landed on Juno Beach in Normandy on June 6, 1944, just behind the troops. Lynch returned to Normandy many times, including in 1989, when I also covered a pilgrimage of D-day veterans.

There is a scene in the movie *The Longest Day* in which a correspondent brings along a cage full of pigeons for the purpose of taking dispatches across the English Channel to England. Instead of doing that, the birds would circle the beach and head straight for Germany. The correspondent who inspired that scene was Charles Lynch, who, after the last pigeon did what all the others had done, shook his fist at the fleeing bird and shouted, "traitor!" While not advocating war, Lynch said it was unfortunate that more Canadians had not experienced the unifying spirit that the war had created in Canada. He also noted the lifelong friendships that were started among military personnel.

In his book, *A Funny Way to Run a Country*, Charles Lynch wrote: "For Lorne with thanks yet another time. May there be more! Charles Lynch."

STEPHEN CLARKSON & CHRISTINA MCCALL

These two authored a two-volume set of books entitled *Trudeau and Our Times*. The set may be the best thing written about Trudeau. I'm sure they didn't leave anything out. For me, they wrote: "This copy of *Trudeau and Our Times* is inscribed for Lorne Harasen during our lively phone-in discussion on CKRM with best wishes from Stephen Clarkson and Christine McCall." When they returned about four years later with the second volume, they wrote, "This copy of *Trudeau and Our Times* is inscribed for Lorne Harasen with many thanks for a stimulating hour of conversation and love–hate phone calls. Stephen Clarkson and Christina McCall."

DON CHERRY

We crossed paths long before he became a part of *Hockey Night in Canada*. He guested on my radio show and he was the main speaker at one of the Optimist Sports dinners where I was honoured to be the master of ceremonies. Cherry gave a reasonably interesting talk but what I appreciated about him is that he remained in the room after the banquet was over and visited with the patrons. He did so until all were gone. That was in contrast to **FRANCO HARRIS**, running back of the Pittsburgh Steelers, who appeared at an earlier sports dinner sponsored by the same Optimist club. Harris delivered a short talk that made no sense and once the dinner was over he disappeared with his fat fee and was never heard from again. The only observation of any interest he made to a few of us was that he was amazed that George Reed was able to take the beating that running backs take and take it for thirteen years.

GEORGE REED

Not only did George take countless punishing hits by opposing defensive teams over more than a dozen years, he served the community in countless charitable ways. He got out of a sickbed once for me for an interview and then again long after he retired. At the time, he was living in Calgary and was in Regina for his charity golf tournament. I wanted to interview him for a football feature I was doing during Rider game broadcasts. He invited me to come to the golf course the next morning. The next day I took tape machine in hand and went to the Wascana Golf and Country Club. I searched high and low and couldn't find him. That was fine with me; I knew that he was busy, with people tugging at him from all directions. The next morning after my broadcast, our receptionist called my office and said "Mr. George Reed is here to see you." I thought to myself, "That is classic George." That just summed up the way this man of honour operated. You just don't forget that kind of thing.

I have said many times that I was grateful that I saw most of the games that George Reed and **RON LANCASTER** played. Ron Lancaster was available like George but in a different way. His idea of an evening out was to go to a high school basketball game or a hockey game. I guess the one thing that I remember over his brilliant play as Rider quarterback was his work with young people. Ron was a teacher at Regina's Central Collegiate for a number of years. It was not unusual to see him at the neighbourhood rink cheering on a team of five- or six-year-olds by their first names. Ron was also one of the coaches of a baseball team my youngest son was a member of one summer. The kids were in their early teens but they were fun to watch because they had good coaching.

Ron was an unpretentious family man who just happened to be the legendary quarterback who piloted the Saskatchewan Roughriders to their first Grey Cup championship. Later, as a head coach in Hamilton and Edmonton, he also tasted Grey Cup champagne. In the middle of those on-field activities, Lancaster served as a colour commentator on football telecasts for the CBC and again served with distinction.

WAYNE & SHUSTER

Both spent an hour with me one morning in 1969. As they were on the air, Shuster was mostly the straight man, while the funny man was Johnny Wayne. Shuster sat calmly smoking his pipe while Wayne paced back and forth in the studio. They had a contract with an oil company and Wayne was particularly concerned that the advertising during the show not include advertising for a competing oil company.

RENE LEVESQUE

You were startled somewhat when you met him for the first time because he was particularly short in stature. Meeting Pierre Berton for the first time had a like effect in an opposite way; he was well over six feet and big in every sense of the word.

Levesque was accompanied by a newspaperman from Montreal and while I talked to him, Levesque, like Johnny Wayne, couldn't sit still and paced back and forth in the studio. The man who became a high-profile separatist and served as Premier of Quebec was a chain smoker. I recall he didn't say so per se, but he was not a fan of Pierre Trudeau (who was a strong and able federalist).

XAVIERA HOLLANDER

The world-famous prostitute guested twice on my show. Once by telephone and then, surprisingly, when she was in the city promoting a recording or book of some kind.

Truly, she wasn't much to look at and her figure was less than enticing.

During one of our commercial breaks she wondered what I would be like in bed. I assured her that for her that would remain a mystery. The "Happy Hooker," as her book was titled, and I were roundly criticized by callers for being on the radio. Still, some callers used the opportunity to ask questions, like the woman who called and wanted to know what the role of a madam was in a brothel. Some who called the show and wrote to me accused me of being her pimp. I asked the critics if they remembered the several moderators of the United Church, the bishops, the priests, and the ministers who appeared on my show. None could remember. One critic, a woman, called me two or three days later, to tell me that the Happy Hooker's book was in our public library; "and it's out!" I asked her how she knew that and there was a long pause and then she quickly hung up. It was the only program that I hosted in over three decades in which members of the public came to the station to have a look at my guest through the studio glass.

JIM JORDAN (FIBBER MCGEE)

There was no doubt who we had on the telephone when he answered our call. It was the loud, strong voice of everyone's favorite know-it-all, who over the years had contributed greatly to the sales of Johnson's Wax, his sponsor. He was well along in years but the voice was unmistakable! Molly (Marian was her actual name), his wife, had died some years earlier and Jordan missed her greatly. It was generally noted in the Los Angeles entertainment community that Jordan and Molly loved each other very much.

At one point in our interview, Jordan said, "Did you say you were calling from Regina?"

I answered, "Yes, indeed."

"I know Regina," radio's Fibber McGee retorted.

"How so?" I asked.

He replied, "We went through Regina on our way to Saskatoon for Chautauqua in 1930." Chautauqua started in 1874 in a New York community of the same name. It was an adult education movement featuring lectures, plays, and musical performances.

Some time before the *Fibber McGee and Molly* show was launched, the couple were part of a radio serial known as *The Smackouts.* He played a grocery store owner who, it seemed, was always "just smack out" of everything.

SID CAESAR

This was one of those bizarre experiences as a result of which open line hosts lose their health and die before their time. On this particular morning, my guests were CBC announcer and host **HARRY BROWN** and then the great comic genius Sid Caesar. Brown was my first guest and when his time was up I invited him to stay and meet Caesar, who was appearing at a local dinner theatre.

There seemed to be some delay and I asked my assistant what the problem was. She checked and reported to me that the television legend would only come to the foot of the stairs to our building and no further. Trying to coax Caesar past the front door was his brother, who, I guess, was his guardian. I was on the air not knowing what was going on or if Sid Caesar would ever climb our indoor stairs to talk to me.

He was eventually talked into coming into my studio but the moment I saw him I knew that this interview was going nowhere. To use the slang term, he was "spaced out" on something. I tried to ask some questions but all I got in return was unintelligible mumbling that neither I nor Harry Brown (who is now deceased) could understand. I quickly thanked him and his brother and Sid Caesar was gone. I understand that he was hospitalized in Regina for a time but nothing more. I had looked forward to meeting this great talent but instead I was given yet another example of the difficult lives of some performers. They are paid to perform often when they are unwell, exhausted, or rendered mentally unfit. Pills to stay awake or sleep and often alcohol don't help.

I saw Sid Caesar on a television tribute show a few years later. He performed well, which I was glad to see. Sid Caesar died in Los Angeles on February 12, 2014.

TOMMY DOUGLAS

Charming, lethal in debate, the memory of two elephants. This was one of the few public figures I encountered in my work who was never a problem. Not only did he remember your name but he remembered the name of your cameraman. Tommy always seemed to be available for an interview and he simply didn't pout if he received a headline or a story that may not have been the most flattering. As a kid who grew up in Saskatchewan, I quickly learned that he was someone you soon learned to respect. When he died, I'm sure there was no one who could show that Tommy Douglas personally profited from his time as Premier or any office he held. It simply didn't happen. After all, a national survey conducted by the CBC in recent years named Tommy the greatest Canadian.

WOODROW LLOYD

Woodrow Lloyd was a serious and, I'm sorry to say, humourless man who made a gigantic contribution to Saskatchewan. He might be remembered as the man who was left with piloting through Medicare during the last of that unsavory time but I think his greatest contribution was renewing and modernizing education in Saskatchewan. He also had something to do with giving teachers a much-needed "better shake" than anyone before gave them.

Woodrow Lloyd didn't have time for the light things that sometimes win elections and I once saw him react angrily to the remarks of a Regina Press Club speaker (where all were fair game) and storm out of the gathering. Of course, there was also the serious problem of his growing a beard at a time when there was still a preoccupation with hair in society.

Some might deny it, but if it wasn't hair, it might have been the cozy feeling that Mr. Lloyd seemed to have with the far-left Waffle movement. The Waffle nearly split the NDP. The group wanted a more leftist, purely socialist-nationalist party. Lloyd thought they should be kept as a source for ideas.

To have gone on to service in the United Nations after leaving politics was quite in character for Mr. Lloyd. It's unfortunate that he died after serving for only a very short period of time.

ROSS THATCHER

Ross Thatcher's leadership of the Saskatchewan Liberal Party was, for Liberals, the best prospect in decades. He was a convert from the CCF/NDP and he came on the scene when Saskatchewan Liberals were anxious to retire a provincial government that seemed to be a tired government.

I got along well with Mr. Thatcher. He was quite good to me in terms of interviews and getting into newsworthy events. When he took that constitutionally questionable trip to Santa Fe (New Mexico) to arrange the pro-rationing of potash production because prices had dropped, Mel Hinds, of the *Leader Post,* and I were the only newsmen on the executive jet loaned to the Premier and some members of cabinet and senior government officials. The rules of the game call for federal governments to make country-to-country agreements and not Premier-to-Governor negotiations but that didn't matter to the impatient Premier. He wanted things done NOW.

There was a rumour created, I suspect by his political opponents, that Ross had a drinking problem. I was in his presence at small and large functions and saw no evidence of that. His problem was that he was a severe diabetic and, coupled with fatigue from days, nights, and weekends in his office, he was often a bit unsteady.

During the 1968 Canadian Premiers Conference, which Mr. Thatcher hosted at Prince Albert National Park, we learned something about Ross Thatcher that was known by very few. A reporter from a Montreal newspaper asked the Premier a question at the daily news conference. He asked the question in French. I wondered if that might prompt an answer that might not be "diplomatic," at a time when things were starting to become a little touchy regarding Canada's French fact. Without hesitation, Mr. Thatcher responded in French. I later asked the Montreal newspaperman about the quality of Thatcher's French. He assured me that it was very good. Apparently the Premier lived with a French-speaking family, where he picked up the language while attending McGill University in Montreal. He graduated with a commerce degree at the tender age of eighteen.

I must say that one of Mr. Thatcher's greatest assets was his wife, Peggy. She was a wonderful lady.

ALLAN BLAKENEY

This was a highly intelligent man who, I found, didn't change whether he was just a member of the legislature or Premier. As a Rhodes Scholar from Nova Scotia, Allan Blakeney's service to his adopted province of Saskatchewan included senior public servant, MLA, cabinet minister of several portfolios, Leader of the Opposition, and Premier.

In the NDP leadership convention that elected Mr. Blakeney, Ross Thatcher was afraid that the young and handsome Roy Romanow would be chosen leader. Thatcher breathed a sigh of relief when Blakeney was the choice. Needless to say, the Liberals under Ross Thatcher were handed a crushing defeat under Blakeney and the NDP.

It was said of Blakeney that his intellect made him a match for Pierre Trudeau and indeed he was. It was quite sporting watching these two mental giants sparring over issues vital to Canada's future. Mr. Blakeney could also hold his own in legislative debate. He had a habit of rubbing his hands together vigorously when he scored a debating point.

When I was moving to another job, I wrote to Al Blakeney and thanked him because I couldn't remember him ever denying me an interview request. He replied in writing, saying this was so because I had never made an unreasonable request. Whenever he came to do my open line I would have a pot of tea, his favorite drink, ready for him; he would consume it by the end of the hour. Late in his term, I was somewhat startled one day when he drove up to the radio station in the same old Chrysler that was used by Ross Thatcher.

When Mr. Blakeney retired and took up a teaching position at the University of Saskatchewan law school, I urged my son Paul, then a law student, to take the former Premier's class if he could squeeze it in. He did so and spoke highly of the experience.

There are often games between politicians and media. These were either golf or softball or hockey. The one I remember best was a hockey game with Allan Blakeney and Cy Macdonald, a cabinet member in the Thatcher government, on the same line. Both were impressive. I can't remember if Blakeney played on Cy's left or right wing!

GRANT DEVINE

As we did with all our Premiers, we invited Mr. Devine to make several appearances on my show. This he did. These were generally upbeat sessions. He was easy to work with and handled himself in a reasonably competent way.

There was a great deal said and written about the Saskatchewan voter dissatisfaction with the NDP that paved the way for a Conservative landslide of record proportions. I would suggest that, rather than dissatisfaction, the Devine

Conservatives' promise of tax-free gasoline did more to elect them and point the province to financial disaster.

It was often stated that it was really Deputy Premier Eric Bernston who ran the province, with Grant Devine being the front man or public relations guy. I remember once arranging a meeting with the Premier for Paula MacTavish, of Foster Parents Plan (a third-world development agency for which I was a board member and sponsor). The government of Saskatchewan for many years made some funds available for international development work. We wanted to make certain that the government continued to support these measures and to assure them that our group, unlike some development organizations, did not engage in "politics" of any kind.

What was interesting about the Foster Parents Plan meeting was the number of "other" people who sat in on the meeting and the staff member who sat right next to what appeared to be a totally exhausted Devine. You would have thought that the staff member was there to catch the Premier if he nodded off. It was an example of the great burden that our elected people must carry. It was a useful meeting.

Eric Bernston called me to his office one evening to see if I might be interested in taking over building and running Saskatchewan's pavilion at the Expo in Vancouver in 1986. I was only lukewarm to the idea. Gordon Staseson, a Regina businessman and community activist, took the position and did an outstanding job (as he usually does with anything he touches).

There is no doubt that in future the heavy oil upgrader and the Rafferty-Alameda Dam will be recognized as the main positives of the Devine years. This is hardly enough when you weigh it against the number of people in that government who were charged and convicted (including some who were jailed) and the near bankruptcy of the province.

ROY ROMANOW

I have known Roy since 1957, when I was reading early morning news at Saskatoon radio station CFQC and Roy was a part-time high school sports broadcaster at our rival, CKOM. He went on to law school and got involved in politics and, as they say, the rest is history.

When he was first elected to the legislature, Romanow would ask some of us in the press gallery when we were going to interview him. Eventually all of us got around to interviewing him many times, but the more we wanted to interview him, the more cautious he became. That was true when he guested on my program and it remained that way until he announced his resignation and retired.

Roy, no doubt, had plans for programs and projects, but when he checked the province's piggy bank he found that Saskatchewan was in deeper financial trouble than even he had anticipated. The province had fourteen billion dollars of debt. The need to reduce the province's debt became his mantra for most of his years as Premier.

There has always been speculation about the kind of socialist Roy was. Some were convinced that Roy was really a Liberal in NDP clothing. Others thought that he was further left than he appeared. I always thought that he was a moderate who didn't have much time for political labels. His friendship with former Prime Minister Jean Chretien began when Romanow, Ontario's Attorney General Roy McMurtry, and Chretien, who was a federal Justice Minister at the time, pulled together some constitutional amendments that enabled Canada to bring home the constitution from Great Britain. René Lévesque, who was not part of brokering that deal, was livid.

Romanow had two basic faults: he wanted to be everyone's friend and he didn't want to hurt anyone. In politics that is a pipe dream!

I was invited to dinner one evening by Garry Aldridge, Romanow's Chief of Staff. Aldridge wanted to know if I might be interested in a career change that would put me in government service. I told him that I liked Romanow and would be interested in what he had to offer. This was followed by lunch in the Premier's office and before long I was employed in Executive Council as Communications Counsellor for several government departments, agencies, and Crown corporations. The money wasn't quite as good as in the broadcasting world but the job enabled me to take a voluntary executive position in a church-related organization.

In broadcasting, you cannot be away during audience rating times. You can't even die. The government job enabled me to earn a living and serve my church. I rather suspect that my not being on the air during an election campaign reduced the hell-raising that election campaigns prompt on open line radio.

In the early months of 2000, I gave notice that I would be leaving government service after four years and retiring. On my last day, the Premier invited me to his office for a farewell and a couple of small gifts. I thanked him for the experience and wished him well. I am sure that his wife, Eleanore, who wanted nothing to do with the political spotlight, was delighted that Roy was coming home to live in the city he loved.

In February of 2001 I received a letter from Roy in connection with his decision to leave politics. He had some nice things to say about me and I have kept and framed the letter.

CHARLES COLSON

This was someone who was named President Richard Nixon's "evil genius." Colson was a member of Nixon's White House staff and when the charges were all sorted out, he earned himself a jail sentence that lasted only seven months. He was mainly convicted for stealing the papers of the psychiatrist who treated Daniel Ellsberg, who had been a thorn in the side of the Nixon administration (they wanted to besmirch his character).

While Colson was in prison, he became a born-again Christian. His passion became the rehabilitation of prisoners—who, he claimed were part of the futility of prisons in terms of rehabilitation. He said the constant rise of crime demonstrated the need for a program that included the Gospel of Christ. He was in Regina to promote his approach to prison rehabilitation of inmates.

Colson said the approach of the Nixon administration was to reward friends, punish enemies, and adopt a fortress mentality. He described Nixon as the finest intellect he had ever met, uniquely gifted in foreign policy.

Colson said Gerald Ford didn't lose the presidency because of his pardoning of Nixon (which he stated was the compassionate and decent thing to do). He described the continued abuse of Nixon in the press long after Watergate was over and done with as "sadistic."

One caller to the program described Colson as a "pool hall psychologist" who, he claimed, were ten cents a dozen.

IAN PAISLEY

I must admit that when I first heard the bellicose Rev. Ian Paisley, I couldn't believe that such a creature still existed in the world. His ranting and raving about the Roman Catholic Church, of which I am a member, prompted me to wonder where this guy was coming from, when our Queen has visited the Vatican and Christian denominations have united in joint efforts in social action.

Paisley headed a locally constructed Presbyterian church, where he was named moderator. He had also been a Unionist Member of Parliament. He took the position that the church should be totally founded on the basis of Scripture.

During Pope St. John Paul II's address to Europe's Parliament, Brother Paisley, of loud voice and six-foot-four-inch frame, shouted to interrupt him and referred to him as "the anti-Christ." People in charge quickly hustled him out of the chamber and respectful behavior was established again. He was booted out of the chamber several times before and after.

As a Roman Catholic, I had always wanted to meet this curious example of intolerance. Lo and behold, the opportunity presented itself in 1982, when Paisley tried to get into the United States but was denied the opportunity when the State Department took away his visa. He took refuge in Canada and agreed to talk to me but told my production assistant that he didn't want to talk to my listeners.

I guess we didn't get off to a good start when I noted that two Popes had toured the United States but that he was persona non grata. Paisley responded that House Speaker Tip O'Neill and the Kennedys, well-known Roman Catholics, were to blame.

In the closing minutes of the interview I asked Paisley to take some calls from my listeners. He declined because "it was so arranged." I told him that he could change the arrangement in a flash. "No," he said, that was his policy; he promptly hung up the telephone. Only Paisley and one other interview guest hung up on me, that I recall. The other was the famous American atheist Madalyn Murray O'Hair.

MADALYN MURRAY O'HAIR

I think I interviewed her twice. The first time was after she was able to lead a successful campaign outlawing prayer in American public schools. The second time was after her son William publicly broke with his mother and declared himself a believer in Jesus Christ. He also claimed that his mother was a hypocrite who loved Christmas, always put up a decorated tree, and reportedly would sneak into churches during Christmas season in order to hear yuletide music. The son also accused his mother of using American Atheist Association money for her own personal purposes.

Something that always struck me as she would talk and answer questions was that her voice sounded like what you might imagine would be the voice of a witch or evil spirit. It was hard and without warmth or empathy.

Madalyn Murray O'Hair, a younger son, Jon, and William's thirty-year-old daughter, Robin, were murdered and their bodies were hacked to pieces on September 29, 1995. One of the people involved (some thought more than one person did it) was David Waters, who just happened to be the office manager at the American Atheist headquarters.

I must say that I was not surprised that Paisley and O'Hair hung up on me, but what the heck. Nothing ventured, nothing gained!

JAMES IRWIN

He was the eighth man to walk on the moon. Irwin was the lunar module pilot on Apollo 15, which space buffs may remember as the Apollo shot that carried with it the lunar rover, the jeep-like vehicle that enabled the crew to travel some distance from the lunar module's landing spot and also aided in rock-gathering beyond an immediate area.

Irwin pointed out that training for the space flight was intended to cover every possibility. No sooner did Apollo 15 enter outer space than there was a problem with the water supply for the crew. All of sudden, Irwin noted, they needed a plumber and none had been trained for the task, so they did what they could.

The experiences and effects of outer space had different effects on the astronauts. Buzz Aldrin, the second man to step on to the moon, had emotional or mental problems particularly when they returned to Earth and had to contend with media pressure and a seemingly impossible round of special events. Aldrin also ran into major marital problems, which ended in divorce.

For Irwin, his landing on the moon prompted a religious experience. He said, "I felt the power of God as I'd never felt it before." Irwin told me that this sense of God's presence was so strong that he often found himself looking over his shoulder as he moved about the moon.

This Apollo 15 astronaut worked quite closely with the evangelical churches. He established the High Flight Foundation, which sponsored retreats and Bible study sessions. One of his projects was leading an expedition to Turkey in search of information about Noah's Ark, which some explorers believe ended up in that country after the flood ended.

CHARLETON HESTON

We received word that Charleton Heston (who portrayed Moses and Ben Hur in the movies) was shooting a movie in British Columbia. We were able to get some time one morning and it was a delight. The movie was titled *Mother Lode.* Most interesting was the fact that the actor's son, Fraser Heston, was directing the movie. Not only that, but Fraser had married a Canadian girl and received landed immigrant status in this country. It should be noted that the baby placed in a basket and floated down the Nile River to be picked up by the Pharoah's household and made an Egyptian in *The Ten Commandments* was also the infant Fraser Heston.

In discussing the need for actors to broaden their "range" and not be typecast, Heston said he was still proud of the movie *Ben-Hur.* In another earlier interview, he said the movie *Number One* (in which he played aging quarterback Ron "Cat" Catlan) was the worst movie he ever made. It was not successful at the box office. Heston said only football players liked it.

COLIN THATCHER

I only interviewed him once and that was when he was Cabinet Minister in the Devine government. He was on the executive jet when his father went to New Mexico to try to get support to reduce potash production.

Whenever I was in Vancouver, I would drop in on Jack Webster, local open line giant to say hello. Almost always, he asked me to slide in behind a microphone to talk about goings-on in Saskatchewan, since a large number of B.C. people transplanted from Roughrider land.

On one occasion, Jack wanted to know about the defeat of the Thatcher government. Before we started, I asked Webster to put a tape on the machine to record the discussion. I told Jack that I would play it back on my show because if I said it in Vancouver, I would say it in Saskatchewan. The main thrust of my analysis was based on Davey Stuart's explanation that "if we didn't offend a particular group it was probably because we had not met them!" Count on Davey to tell it like it was.

After I aired the tape, I received a nasty letter from Colin, in which he made some charges that were nonsense. I didn't respond until some months later, when he ran for Vice President of the Saskatchewan Liberal party and was defeated. I guess the devil made me do it because I couldn't resist the temptation to strike back. My note basically said that I thought the Saskatchewan Liberal Party showed consummate good judgment in not electing him to a vice presidency. He quickly replied with a card in which he only wished me a sarcastic "Merry Christmas."

When I moved my program to CKRM, Colin would call the program from his tractor or combine and express opinions on a wide variety of topics. He expressed his views very well. After a long while, I thought I would say something to him that would indicate that I knew it was him who was calling but in a way that wouldn't be picked up by my listeners. He stopped calling immediately.

I didn't hear from him again until he was serving in Grant Devine's Cabinet. His assistant called me to tell me that Minister Thatcher had just returned from a very good selling trip in Europe. If memory serves me, I think it involved uranium. I said, "Who did you say wanted to come on the program?"

The reply was "Mr. Thatcher."

"Sure," I said, "let's do it tomorrow morning."

Colin arrived on time and we visited in my office before we moved upstairs to the studio, where the minister handled himself like an experienced politician. At the end of the program I thanked him and said goodbye. It was only a matter of days later that Colin Thatcher was arrested and charged with the murder of his wife.

HENRY MORGENTALER

This man would be recognized as probably the leader in the fight for abortion rights in Canada. However, a lady with ties to Regina, Eleanor Pelrine, wrote about the subject long before anyone had heard Morgentaler's name. There is no question that Dr. Morgentaler has been the fearless leader for a very long time. He was courteous and all business when he came to my studio.

Frankly, I doubt that this question will ever be solved. The positions on both sides are such that resolution seems a long way away.

JOE BOROWSKI

He went on a hunger strike, personally financed his opposition to abortion, and lived with threats like the ones on the other side that threatened Dr. Morgentaler. Borowski was a principled man who was prepared to resort to any measure that was moral in order to fight abortion, which he believed was one of the modern day evils. Borowski took every opportunity, whether an interview or speaking role, to fight abortion.

Once, when the late Joe Borowski was being upbraided for being critical of the judiciary, the former Manitoba

Highways Minister said, "What is a judge? A judge is a lawyer who used to be in politics!"

GEORGE BEVERLY SHEA

"Bev" Shea (Billy Graham's crusade vocalist for more than sixty years) was born in Canada and took American citizenship in the 1940s. Mr. Shea's father was a minister in the Wesleyan Methodist Church in Canada. I interviewed America's favorite gospel singer during one of my Christmas shows after Bing Crosby had passed away. It is estimated that George Beverly Shea recorded some five hundred vocal solos on something like seventy albums and ten compact discs. Having been heard on recordings, radio, television, and Mr. Graham's crusades all over the world, this singer of sacred songs was probably heard by more people than any other singer of religious music. I think many would agree that one of his most popular hymns was "How Great Thou Art."

Bev Shea had a great sense of humour. His sense of humour came up for scrutiny when he told me about one of the Christmas decorations he made in his home. He had Santa Claus stuck in the fireplace chimney. You could just see a pair of red trousers tucked into a pair of cowboy boots hanging above the place where the flames were located.

I once asked someone in the Billy Graham Evangelistic Association if I might have an autographed photo of Mr. Shea for my gallery of guests. I was told that their vocalist didn't do that because he felt that his God-given voice should only be used to praise God. He didn't consider himself a celebrity or entertainer. Bev Shea died in 2013 at the ripe old age of 104. He was buried in a casket made by inmates in the Louisiana State Penitentiary.

E.K. (TED) TURNER

The term "Farm Leader" is bandied about with reckless abandon, but it fit Ted Turner perfectly. I know because I worked closely with him for a number of years. As President of Saskatchewan Wheat Pool, he had a punishing schedule that kept him in the Pool board room or up in the air on his way to farm-related meetings or consultations with government. In all matters, the individual farmer and his family was his primary concern.

I think the word "integrity" describes Mr. Turner's modus operandi. During the two-week annual meeting of Saskatchewan Pool, he sat with the delegates from his district rather than at some head table. Maymont was where Ted farmed and it was the district that sent him on to be a delegate, director, and executive. I dare say that Saskatchewan Wheat Pool would still be operating if Mr. Turner had been President at the time the farm co-operative faced stormy times.

Ted Turner has collected recognition and honour that speaks to his life of service and good citizenship. He has received the Order of Canada, the Saskatchewan Order of Merit, an Honorary Doctorate from the University of Saskatchewan, was named Chancellor of the University of Saskatchewan, and spearheaded the campaign for the new College of Agriculture Building at the University of Saskatchewan.

A dedicated member of the United Church, he is also very dedicated to the Rotary Club and its ideals. For a man who took up golf later in his adult life, it was just like him to set his age as a target for his golf score. Needless to say, he achieved it.

JIM REEVES

This country singer with the pear-shaped tones was a cherished friend who was on the way to being a pop star when the light plane he was piloting went down in a severe summer storm that took his life and that of one of his band members, Dean Manuel.

Manuel was a very nervous flyer; he would down a quart of bourbon before and during the flight. At the time, Reeves was no longer a member of the *Grand Ole Opry* and had just starred in a movie in South Africa.

I first met Jim Reeves in August of 1960 when I did a guest/host shot on *Mr. Deejay U.S.A.*, which was a program carried on WSM Nashville Tennessee. The program that preceded *Mr. Deejay* was a live two-hour show known as the *Friday Night Frolic;* it took place in a large studio that had room for an audience of several hundred. When that show was over some of the performers would come to the *Mr. Deejay* studio for an interview. That is how Jim and I met.

I wrote the liner notes on one of Jim's RCA Camden albums entitled "Good 'N' Country." I once found it on the Pickwick label in Conway Twitty's record shop in Nashville. How that came about I don't know, because I was contracted and paid by RCA. Needless to say, I bought it. I still have it and have never seen another one.

I have read some scurrilous things written about Jim, but my experience with him was exactly the opposite. He was called "Gentleman Jim" and I never experienced anything but good taste and articulate speech that revealed a fine mind. His word was his bond. Some years after his death, my wife and I were in Nashville and dropped in on **MARY REEVES**, who was still running some of Jim's enterprises. It was a very pleasant interlude which was topped off with Mary taking us to dinner. You could say this was in the style of Jim!

PIERRE ELLIOTT TRUDEAU

I interviewed him once during the campaign for the Liberal leadership and at least three more times when he was Liberal Party leader. For one thing, he was what I considered a true Liberal. One of the problems in this country is that there are many in the Liberal party who are conservative and many in the Conservative party who would be more at home with the Liberals.

The leadership convention in 1968 that elected him leader was probably the most interesting story I ever covered. I shared Sam Ross's booth, which just happened to be directly above the Paul Hellyer and Robert Winters sections. Trudeau's section was not far away. We heard Hellyer shout, "Go, Bob, go!" and that usually nasty, white-booted Judy LaMarsh shout, "Let's not elect that bastard!" when it was clear that Pierre Elliott Trudeau would be the leader.

When it was over, it was worth your life to be identified as a media person in Ottawa hotels by those who opposed Trudeau. "You were the bastards who elected him!" They would back you into a corner and hurl invectives at you in the most unparliamentary of words. Less than a half-year later, when Trudeau gave the Liberals their first majority government in years, Saskatchewan politicos attending the Canadian Premiers Conference in Waskesiu were singing the praises of the new Prime Minister. "Isn't he wonderful?" some said!

In one of his Regina appearances, Trudeau campaigned during a student assembly at Miller High School. The day before, in Vancouver, he was campaigning on a downtown street when a man started to badger him. The episode ended with Trudeau telling him to fuddle-duddle. I asked him if he felt it proper for the Queen's first minister to be uttering expletives in public. He quickly responded that he didn't utter the profanity in public but in the heckler's ear!

In another campaign, he was only willing to take my questions and not those of my audience. I partially remedied that by taking questions from my callers during the hour before the Prime Minister was to appear on my program and directing them at him in the order I received them. On one broadcast, we did a simulcast on radio and television and on that occasion he took questions from all.

You can only conclude that these changes in campaign tactics are the product of special advisors who I fear lay awake at night dreaming up wrinkles. They are a pain in the lower regions of the human frame.

Trudeau was different from anything we ever had before. He had more brain power than most mortals do. He was detested by Quebec separatists because he frustrated them. Trudeau gave his advisors heartburn when he drifted away from his script and asked Saskatchewan farmers, "Why should I sell your wheat?"

He was unlike anything we had before and I doubt we will see his like again.

JOHN DIEFENBAKER

Life with Dief was never simple or uncomplicated. I use as an example one of his federal election campaigns when he was still travelling by train. We were informed that the Chief would be stopping briefly in Regina at a particular time during the afternoon. As was often the case, my assignment included a TV camera and microphone. I checked with the rail station staff to see where his car was going to stop and I proceeded to set up accordingly.

As luck would have it, the railcar rolled past my camera by at least fifty yards. I waited while Diefenbaker looked after everyone else and then I asked him if he would come back to my equipment. "What are you going to ask me?" was his response. He knew very well that his question was improper but he was going to extract something in exchange for this little inconvenience. I gave him two or three topics that I wished to pursue but not a list of questions.

On another occasion, a very simple matter turned into a production. Dief was scheduled to come out to the television station for a taping on a Friday afternoon. I arranged for a cab to pick him up at the Hotel Saskatchewan and bring him out by a particular time because studio time is scarce and it is important to be punctual. Needless to say, the appointed time came and went and no Dief. The cab company called and said that my guest was nowhere in sight in the lobby. I called Diefenbaker but he said, "I saw no cab driver." I asked him if he was available on Saturday morning; I would pick him up at a particular time. It was settled.

At the appointed time, I picked the Chief up and we were on our way. I brought along my nine-year-old son, Greg, in the back seat. As we went along, Mr. Diefenbaker engaged my son in conversation and ignored me, which was fine. Pretty soon he had the boy climb into the front seat beside him and the topic was dogs. Greg had a couple of beagles and he was working in the show ring with the late Walter Prinz, a local purebred breeder. The Diefenbakers had a dog and there was an exchange of photos later on.

All of this became a pen-pal situation for my son and Mr. Diefenbaker. On July first, the Chief would send Greg a telegram in which he would extol the greatness of Canada. He would let the boy know when he was going to be in Regina and invited him to come to him directly without stopping in the waiting line. I drove the lad to the airport at 6:00 a.m. one morning where his pen pal was taking a light plane flight to somewhere in Saskatchewan. They had their visit and away we went.

How does Greg vote now? I don't think we have a party far right enough! If I was speaking to Dief on the telephone, I would end the conversation by saying, "Give 'em hell, Chief." He would respond, "I understand you are not reluctant in that regard either!"

Both my wife and I are grateful to Mr. Diefenbaker for the interest he took in our son.

JEAN CHRETIEN

This is a politician who very effectively uses humour in an attempt to disarm you and he disarms many. He had me laughing very quickly and likewise those who called the program. He did that with those issues that he wanted to avoid or water down. Mention Chretien to Roy Romanow and he smiles and is soon laughing. They like each other even though Chretien's attempt to draw Romanow into the federal Liberal party to run as a Liberal was not successful.

It was said of Chretien that he was not "prime ministerial" enough to be elected Liberal leader. Well, once again he proved "them" wrong. He was elected leader and then gave his party two majority governments. His previous record as a cabinet minister of several portfolios was a record of generally good administration. Jean Chretien was the Liberal's minister of everything.

JOE CLARK

I liked Joe Clark and I respected him even though he took many shots from political cartoonists and commentators. I first met him when he was a relative unknown serving as a special assistant to Robert Stanfield. Joe remained quite far in the background.

Joe respected what I had to do as a broadcast journalist and he didn't try to avoid questions or filibuster or change the subject. He played it straight throughout and we were able to deal with a number of key issues.

The last time I interviewed Joe was when he was Minister of External Affairs. Fair-minded people would tell you that Foreign or External Affairs was probably Joe Clark's finest hour. He wrote to me after that interview with some good things to say about what he termed my "even-handed" handling of the show. I have kept the letter.

I once interviewed Joe's wife, Maureen McTeer. She was very business-like and was no shrinking violet.

KIM CAMPBELL

I interviewed her once during her first and last election campaign as Conservative Leader and Prime Minister. We did a hookup from Saskatoon, where her bus waited while we talked. There wasn't anything particularly memorable about the interview. I do remember her saying, "I understand that you are something of an icon in Saskatchewan." I told her that was better than the last thing I was called.

LESTER B. PEARSON

Now, this was a pleasant encounter. It came a short time after he stepped down as Liberal leader and Prime Minister. He came to the station alone and wore a beat-up old trench coat over his suit and tie. He would have preferred to talk about baseball because that was his favorite game and it's one of mine. We talked about the issues of the day and the new work he was doing in the international world. He had one condition and that was that he would not comment in any way about the performance of his successor, even though the country was still wrapped up in Trudeaumania. Now that I think of it, he did say something about his chief protagonist in Parliament—the man from Prince Albert—but even then he just smiled and said something positive.

I got the feeling that you would need to say or ask something really nasty to change the demeanor of Mr. Pearson and that even then he would resort to a response that would not exacerbate the situation.

As Prime Minister, he didn't seem to understand western Canada, but then the West didn't send him many members.

I understand that President Lyndon Johnson once grabbed Mr. Pearson by the lapels because "Mike" Pearson said something that Johnson didn't like. If he had tried that with Trudeau he would have found himself with a shoe print on his Texas crotch!

JOHN TURNER

I interviewed him only once and really didn't get any impression except to wonder why it was that such a fuss was made about him and the Liberal leadership. In fact, I didn't see anything much in him when he first ran for the Liberal leadership in 1968. I guess everything nose-dived when Brian Mulroney tore a strip off him in that famous debate. To me, he was courteous and waffled on several topics. There wasn't much news there.

BRIAN MULRONEY

When I learned that Prime Minister Mulroney was bringing a federal/provincial meeting to Regina, I took steps to try to get him to the radio station for an interview. I was going to use something that I heard about him and CKRM as a lever or gimmick.

It seems that many years ago, when Mulroney was a young man, he accompanied Alvin Hamilton as a kind of assistant while they toured the prairies in search of voter support. They stopped at CKRM at that time and when they were leaving the station, management suggested that Mulroney send back voice reports about the Hamilton tour.

Whoever was running the station at the time must have been a Tory because that was hardly the most objective arrangement. Mind you, Hamilton and Mulroney would have been foolish not to accept the invitation.

I used that connection with the station even though ownership and management had changed a few times since. I suggested that this would be a kind of reunion for the Prime Minister. They went for it. We had hardly confirmed the Prime Minister's visit when the first two or three waves of the RCMP came to check out the building for security reasons. They wanted to check every nook and cranny. On the day of the visit, security changed the spot where Mr.

Mulroney's limousine was going to stop and let him out in front of the building at least two or three times.

There was a technical person seemingly attached to the Prime Minister's office who installed plug-ins that would enable electronic media to record whatever Mulroney would say in the interview. What irked me to no end is that even this guy was asking me what I was going to ask the Prime Minister. I mumbled my response in very general terms and managed to keep my cool.

Several minutes before the Prime Minister arrived, a bus pulled up loaded with national media, who filed into the building. By that time we had about lost control of the building. When he arrived, we whisked him into the manager's office to catch his breath and Bruce Cowie, one of our company's senior executives, had some business to discuss regarding a broadcast organization. Then we climbed the stairs and entered the studio where I worked.

It was a pleasant and politically harmless interview. I gave the Prime Minister a shower radio which he could listen to while getting ready for his day. When he stepped outside the building, a group of women working in a business across the street shouted at Mr. Mulroney, asking him for a hug. He obliged them and walked across the street and gave the hug, then returned to his limousine and was gone. I don't know how the impromptu hug went over with his numerous security types!

LAWRENCE WELK

He was corny and less than articulate with that North Dakota German accent but he was loved by countless millions and my assistant and I found him to be a prince of a man to work with. Lawrence Welk acquired at least two new fans after that day and I often think of that interview.

We made an arrangement for the mayor of Mr. Welk's hometown of Strasburg, North Dakota, to call the program, which was a pleasant surprise for Lawrence. The hour went by very quickly. Lawrence Welk was on television from 1951 to 1982. He was a loyal Catholic and his standards were high in terms of good taste and family values.

He died on May 17, 1992. I have a feeling that he didn't receive the recognition that he should have. All things considered, Lawrence Welk, in his own way, was "wonderful, wonderful!"

DAWN WELLS

Television viewers will remember Miss Wells as Mary Ann on *Gilligan's Island*. She guested on my show while she was in Regina for the dinner theatre in the Regina Inn's Stage West. She wanted to get a piece of local art that would be representative of the area and not too out of line price-wise.

I thought a visit to Eleanor Oltean's farm near Pense would meet all requirements. Eleanor was a fine painter. Her paintings of the Saskatchewan landscape were very well done. (I have two). Prices were manageable but even more than that, Mrs. Oltean was a wonderfully welcoming person. Her farmhouse was tastefully decorated and her art was everywhere. I was really taken by a painting she had of her mother as a girl. Dawn purchased one of her paintings and really appreciated the welcome.

Gilligan's Island had a very short life of three years but I suspect reruns must be on the air somewhere. Dawn Wells used to live in Nashville, Tennessee but apparently has taken up residence in Idaho, where she works in live theatre.

There was a sad ending to the Oltean home. While they were away in a warmer climate one winter not long after Wells's visit, vandals gained access to the home and literally trashed it inside. For that to have happened to those people was mean beyond words. Mrs. Oltean was the last person you would ever want to hurt. I believe Mrs. Oltean, a widow, now lives in Calgary.

MAX GAIL

You might recall this American actor as Detective Stanley Thaddeus Wojciehowicz or "Wojo" in the television comedy *Barney Miller*. Gail's character was a Vietnam veteran who gradually became a policeman with a heart who tended to see everything from a humanitarian perspective (which was not always wise for a police officer). He wrote the Sergeant's exam but failed it seven times. He finally succeeded after the eighth attempt.

When Max Gail came to my studio, he was in Regina for a gathering pertaining to aboriginals, having taken on that activity in the United States. You would not have recognized him in his T-shirt and beard. He had some very pointed views about the need to assist First Nations people, who he felt were treated badly in so many ways.

Barney Miller was apparently very popular with policemen, and ran from 1975 to 1982. Police felt that it was often closer to reality than most cop shows on TV. I'm told you can buy the entire series on compact DVDs .

ART LINKLETTER

I had the good fortune to have as a guest on my show the man who long ago proved that people are funny and that kids say the darndest things. Art Linkletter was appearing on the grandstand of the Regina Exhibition, so he came on my program from the "Ex." He was kind and cooperative with everything we wanted him to do. At the time, he was campaigning against drugs, which he said played a part in his daughter Diane's suicide (she jumped to her death through a sixth-floor window).

He had some good advice for parents on recognizing a problem and he had some pointed things to say about parental permissiveness. Linkletter engaged my live audience on everything from drugs to the good work that 4H does for farm kids.

Art Linkletter was born in Moose Jaw on July 17, 1912. He had tried for years to find out who his parents—who left him an orphan—were. On this occasion, I'm told he went to Moose Jaw to continue his search and during that visit he found the answers that he sought for so long. I'm told that it was an extremely emotional moment for the celebrated performer.

As is not the case with many show business marriages, the Linkletters were married for seventy-five years. Art Linkletter died on May 26, 2010, at the age of ninety-eight.

VICTOR BORGE

There is no doubt that Borge was an international star of great talent. He was one of my favorites. I emphasize the word "was." He arrived at my broadcast location at the Regina Exhibition and one look at him told me that this was going to be an unhappy interlude.

I don't want to get into a lengthy postmortem except to say that my hope was that I might put him in a better frame of mind. You didn't know what to expect, because he would answer some questions and others he would ignore or deal with sarcastically. I turned to questions from my audience, and his pompous, smart-ass replies embarrassed the first two questioners. Predictably, not a single further question came from my capacity audience. I soldiered on myself and then sprung him early.

In retrospect, I should have interviewed him for fifteen or twenty minutes and punted him out of there. I have had many tough interviews but even the toughest have some regard for basic courtesy. I didn't care if he wanted to make it tough for me, but my audience? Many of these people are nervous to begin with and it takes courage to stand in the middle of a live audience and face someone they like or admire.

PIERRE BERTON

You could call Berton a regular on my show. He was usually good for at least one booking in early autumn. I lost track of the number of times he was a guest on my show. You had to admire his capacity for hard work and various causes. He was a millionaire and a member of the socialist New Democratic Party. There is nothing wrong with that, though some people think it is some type of contradiction. I don't agree.

Pierre was a huge man, well over six feet tall. Always nattily attired in tailored suits or jackets with the ever-present bow tie, which he tied himself. He signed my copies and he usually had something good to say about the interview. I usually acted as master of ceremonies for his appearances in bookstores and department stores. He wrote about numerous topics but I still think his best were the railway books. His popular type of history writing is a great gift to this country.

On one occasion, Pierre walked into my studio while I was interviewing former B.C. Premier Dave Barrett. I invited Pierre to join us and he did. Barrett later stated that it was the best open line show on which he had been a guest.

Pierre was never afraid of controversy. Some will remember decades earlier, when he wrote in *MacLean's* magazine that if his daughter wanted to be sexually active he hoped she would do so in a bed and not the back seat of a car. The reaction from Canadians was predictably nasty.

Pierre once said that his idea of enjoyment was a party with friends where there was lots of good food (his wife, Janet, and he collaborated on at least one cookbook) and copious quantities of booze. In his later years, Pierre became a diabetic.

BEN WICKS

This delightful little cartoonist made several visits to my program but the one that almost created a riot was prompted by his book *Ben Wicks Women.* He took a chauvinistic approach in the book to demonstrate some of the ridiculous ways that women have been oppressed by men and even by some women. Examples include that secretaries are excellent coffee-makers and servants, office women, and so on.

When Ben arrived at the station, I suggested that he take the position that he truly believed all that chauvinist nonsense. Ben was always ready for a little fun so away we went. It didn't take long for the switchboard to explode with angry women demanding Ben Wicks's head. My late friend Judge Ken MacLeod of Queens Bench Court was on his way to Saskatoon listening to the show and figured out the ruse. He said he laughed so hard that he had to pull over to the side of the road and stop the car. Knowing Ken's sense of humour, I could see how that happened.

Needless to say, Ben and I came clean at the end of the interview and pointed out how ridiculous some of society's attitudes can be. Ben autographed my copy of the book with these words: "To Lorne, A wonderful interview...and why not, he's a man...Ben Wicks. October 1978."

CHARLES SCHULZ

My listeners and I spent a wonderful hour with the creator of Charlie Brown, Snoopy, Lucy, and all the rest of the *Peanuts* gang. Charles Schulz was very down-to-earth and didn't play celebrity, yet that comic strip is really enjoyed all over the world. Books, television shows, toys, clothing, and movies made Charles Schulz a wealthy man beyond even his own expectations. The money was nice but Schulz likes the fact that he produced something for the enjoyment of millions of people.

Charles Schulz was a hockey fan and as one of his indulgences he had built in his backyard in California a full-fledged hockey rink, complete with its own Zamboni ice-cleaning machine. Who uses this rink? Why, Charles Schulz himself! He told us that he simply loved the sport and laces on the skates whenever he can.

Laurie Artiss, one-time sports editor for the *Regina Leader Post,* had by that time ended his journalistic career and become an entrepreneur with a major involvement in pins, promoting curling, particularly at the international level, and retailing curling equipment and accessories. Laurie had obviously been listening to the show and called the program. After some preliminaries, he asked Schulz to consider making one of his characters a curler. Mr. Schulz said he really didn't know anything about the sport.

Some years later I noted some photos of Laurie's home when he lived in Calgary. Lo and behold, their yard ornament theme was taken from the *Peanuts* comic strip.

ATHOL MURRAY

There is a book about him as well as a movie. He came to the Regina Archdiocese on loan from Ontario. He never went back and is buried on his beloved campus of Notre Dame of Canada in Wilcox, Saskatchewan. Monsignor Athol Murray was best known by those who loved him as "Père." There are enough stories about his exploits; I will tell only one.

I hosted an open line show once a week on CKCK Television besides my daily program on radio. On one occasion, my guest was Quebec separatist Pierre Bourgault. We usually took a break for the late news and then returned for a final segment of a half hour.

I should have realized that Père, who I knew listened to and watched my programs, would be seated in front of a television set in that messy office of cigarette butts, papers, dirty cups, and probably a glass of scotch, seething as Bourgault spoke of his plans to wreck Canada. I got so absorbed in running the show that it just didn't occur to me that Athol Murray, who would not tolerate those who would betray his beloved Canada, was waiting to welcome Mr. Bourgault to Saskatchewan.

When the show director informed me who was waiting on the line, I immediately snapped to attention and thought, "Mr. Bourgault, grab your hard hat!" As closely as I can remember his words, Père opened with "No goddamned separatist is going to destroy my country. I had boys who I lost in World War II defending Canada and no goddamned separatist is going to squander their sacrifice." Bourgault tried to debate but didn't get very far. The next day on my radio show a woman called to say that if anyone else had used that kind of language, I would have cut them off. I replied that she was probably right.

Père would write to me in his distinctive scrawl in pen and ink on Notre Dame stationery. I have kept some of those letters. I have spoken at the school on several occasions and I once taped one of Père's calls when I had Paul Martin senior as a guest. I sent Père a copy where the two extolled the virtues of Canada and Père's oft-repeated call for a national dream. He would be pleased to see how more and more Canadians believe in this country and the way that July first is celebrated by more and more people.

Athol Murray was a very close friend of the Hill family of Regina. I think he spent most Christmases with them. The Hill Family took Notre Dame College under their wing after Pere died and typically, because of their ways of doing things, the school is thriving and has a student waiting list.

Canada and God were two of Monsignor Murray's priorities. After all, as he would say in speeches and sermons, "God is almost as good a quarterback as Ronnie Lancaster!"

MAURICE (ROCKET) RICHARD, GORDIE HOWE, BOBBY HULL

This would make an effective threesome for your team! Rocket didn't want to take calls because he wanted to be able to see the person talking to him. Those burning eyes that used to freak out rookie goalies were a question or statement away all the time. Colleen Howe managed Gordie's enterprises (other than playing the game). Gordie, the superstar from Saskatchewan, remains the same affable, uncomplicated guy that he has always been. Bobby Hull is one of those people who combines a very high degree as a hockey player with a friendly manner that matches his playing ability. His engaging personality wins friends for him and the game.

Outside of the Rocket, who had always been a bit of a pernickety time bomb, Gordie Howe and Bobby Hull have done thousands of interviews and have answered all the same questions many hundreds of times but they still do interviews because of their love for the game. I was delighted to have them visit my show.

DR. OSWALD HOFFMANN

I dare say that outside of Lutherans of the Missouri Synod this name may not ring a bell, yet I include it because Hoffmann was the best preacher on radio that I ever heard. I specify radio because that medium's challenge is great; all that the listener gets is the voice.

In my first couple of years as a junior announcer in a small thousand-watt station, I signed on the station on Sunday mornings. In those days, half-hour religious programs followed one after another until almost noon. Many were less than good in terms of production and on-air presentation. Radio stations took them because they accepted the top advertising rate. If the stations wanted to discourage them, charging the top rate didn't work.

The Lutheran Hour was the exception. It was professionally produced and it had the best preacher: Dr. Oswald Hoffmann, who worked out of St. Louis, Missouri. He always had something worthwhile to say and he delivered it powerfully. Dr. Hoffman was the speaker for *The Lutheran Hour* for thirty-three years, starting in 1955. The program was heard in most of the English-speaking world.

Some years ago, when I was still at CKCK radio, I was informed that Dr. Hoffmann was coming to Regina for some function. I immediately set out to make arrangements to have him guest on my program. He agreed to do the program and we had a pleasant visit before the program and during. Billy Graham and Bishop Fulton Sheen were outstanding preachers but I think Dr. Hoffmann was a touch better.

Hoffmann died in 2005 at the ripe old age of ninety-one. He and his wife had four children: three sons and one daughter. Two of their sons are ordained Lutheran ministers. You can still catch many of Dr. Hoffmann's sermons on the Internet.

WAYNE GRETZKY

The St. Louis Blues of the National Hockey League made Regina the site of one of their training camps and we soon learned that one of their exhibition games would see the Edmonton Oilers as their opposition. That meant that Wayne Gretzky would be in the Edmonton lineup. I immediately set out to try to get an interview.

The Oiler office indicated that time would not allow Gretzky to come to the station but that they would arrange for an interview at the Agridome (as it was known then). I informed them that I intended to bring along my thirteen-year-old son Paul as a co-interviewer. Paul was playing minor hockey at the time and was very interested in all NHL players but particularly Gretzky. I suggested that he draw up a list of good questions and that we would alternate asking them.

In his usual good-natured way, The Great One went along with the idea during a break in the team's morning workout. One of Paul's questions was how the superstar felt about summer hockey schools for kids. Gretzky didn't hesitate to respond by saying that he was opposed to them. He said youngsters should be doing other things in the summer rather than lengthening the minor hockey season.

We concluded our interview and Gretzky went back to his workout. Paul still has a copy of the interview. What is Paul doing now? He is a partner in the Regina law firm Kanuka Thuringer.

JOHNNY CASH

I had occasion to interview him once and MC one of his shows. He was very obliging but through the interview he snorted and sniffed, which led me to believe that he was on something. During the show there was a bottle of vodka in the dressing room, which belonged to someone. As everyone knows, Cash went through a very difficult time, which could have cost him his life, much less his career.

I met June Carter in Nashville in 1960. At the time, she was a *Grand Ole Opry* comedienne and did some singing with the musical Carter family. At one time she was married to country singer Carl Smith, who ceased to record or perform after a long string of hits in the 1950s. He was one of those entertainment retirees who stuck by his word and stayed retired.

Johnny always credited June with saving his life and she clearly did. It seemed that they were meant for each other; after June, died Johnny followed not too far behind.

GLENN DOBBS

He was a Roughrider for only about three years but his effect on the province has never been topped before or since. Dobbs actually ushered in the modern era of the Riders. He played the game like a superstar and he topped that off with a pleasing personality. At one point Saskatchewan was known as "Dobberville."

I interviewed Glenn Dobbs several times and never once did he say anything negative or nasty about the city of Regina, the province, or the people. On his last appearance on my show there were calls from Ron Atchison, who Glenn referred to as that "big hound."

Sully Glasser called and Dobbs named him "the little scooter" and then Hall of Fame referee Paul Dojack called and Dobbs said American football officials could learn something from Dojack about "getting on with the game." Glenn Dobbs stood six feet four inches but he made an even bigger contribution to football as a pastime in Saskatchewan.

PATSY CLINE

The late country singer with a voice capacity that could be heard unamplified in the next county, Patsy was far bigger in death than she ever was in life. I met her in Nashville in 1960. While taking a break during a live radio broadcast, she came directly to me as a visiting broadcaster, in search of my opinion. She wanted to know if I thought she should change her recording label. There I was, a radio "veteran" of about four years at the ripe old age of twenty-two, being asked by a recording star if she should switch recording companies. Heady stuff indeed. I was scared to death.

Patsy was under contract to one of the Decca subsidiaries. While she didn't tell me, I thought that she might have been courted by Columbia records, which, at the time, was building an impressive list of country performers.

I took the safe way out and suggested that she stick with her present label, that something good was bound to happen soon. Her concern was that she had not hit the charts in a big way for almost four years. Fortunately for all of us and not long after my "advice," Patsy Cline hit on several songs that have become country standards.

One of the problems that female country performers had to live with in the early 1960s in the conservative U.S. South was that men were the stars and women were mostly the supporting cast. They just didn't make the money or have much clout when they bargained for themselves.

Patsy lost her life on her way back to Nashville in a light plane after performing at a benefit for the family of a country music disc jockey who had died.

JOHN FISHER

They called him Mr. Canada because of his popular national radio series. He broadcast stories about this country from every region and he quickly became a modern patriot at a time when Canadians were not that big on flag-waving. Fisher's contribution to creating a greater awareness about their country among Canadians cannot be overstated.

Prime Minister John Diefenbaker appreciated Fisher's work and moved quickly to appoint him Chief Centennial Commissioner for Canada's celebration of its one-hundredth birthday. Unfortunately for Mr. Fisher, the government changed and the new government named Judy LaMarsh Minister of State, with the Centennial Commission being part of her portfolio. The tension and backroom battles were named by some "The John and Judy Show" after an evening radio soap opera of the same name. The big anniversary was a success in spite of the politics.

Fisher once described LaMarsh to me as "mean and unfeeling." One increasingly gets the impression that in that case there might be enough evidence to convict.

GLEN CAMPBELL

Almost from the first time I heard and saw him perform, I was a fan. First and foremost, his material was fresh and for the most part without category. It wasn't country even though it seemed to be related. It wasn't folk even though the message and tempo were often uncomplicated.

I was a fan long before I saw him perform. The opportunity finally came during a trip to Las Vegas. Campbell performed at the Frontier, backed by a complete orchestra with a lush-sounding string section. Seeing Campbell as an instrumentalist (he was a studio instrumentalist) added another dimension to his shows. He was really a virtuoso with stringed instruments.

His introduction was stupendous. With the curtains drawn, a narrow screen came down the centre of the stage. Backstage, Campbell sang lyrics that were given a series of pictures on the screen. The tempo of the song continually increased until finally Campbell stepped through the screen. He sang everything from country to ballads to Frank Sinatra.

I was able to meet Campbell some years later when he performed at the show lounge at Casino Regina. He looked tired and wrinkled but he did justice to his hits. A tumultuous marriage and violent episodes with drugs took a superbly talented human being into a decline that could only be described as unfortunate or disastrous for an amazing musician and millions who appreciated his art. I understand he is ill with Alzheimer's and is no longer able to perform.

PRINCE PHILIP

The Queen's husband has always been a special interest of mine. For the most part, we have seen him as a silent attendant to Her Majesty, hands behind his back, on tours that must be excruciatingly dull for someone who has seen and done it all.

I met him personally during a visit to Regina during Saskatchewan's one-hundredth anniversary. At the time, I was a member of the Saskatchewan War Memorial Committee, which was building a memorial structure on the grounds of the legislature containing the names of all from the province who gave their lives in war. At first, we wanted the Queen to turn the first sod for the World War II memorial. We were told that because the Queen was over eighty years of age and had a very exhausting schedule, she could not walk the long block to the site of the memorial. We were offered the Prince. Actually, I thought that was a better idea for that particular purpose.

I was selected to be one of the two who accompanied the Prince to the memorial site. As we walked along on that rainy day, I thought I would engage the Duke in conversation regardless of any rules that prevailed about only speaking when being spoken to. I thought, "This is my country, settled by my forebears and defended by members of my family. I will speak any time I want to a visitor to my country" (even though he was more than a visitor). I said, "Sir, is it true that an American tourist once asked you why Windsor Castle was built so close to the airport? (The castle was built one thousand years before there were airports). He replied, "Yes, absolutely." I think he enjoyed that.

Our Philip didn't seem to know what a sod-turning was but once instructed he performed the task with dispatch. He wanted to look through the World War I structure but one of the aides quickly came to his side and said the Queen was waiting for him to accompany her to the next function. As he walked away, he turned and said, "Send me some pictures." We did and he acknowledged them.

JEAN BELIVEAU

The passing of Jean Beliveau in recent times reminded me of my Jean Beliveau story. I remain a staunch Montreal

Canadiens fan and the long-time Hab captain is a major reason for my fanaticism.

I was going through a list of guests on my program over the years and noted that many Canadiens players guested on my program, including Rocket Richard, Ken Dryden, and Larry Robinson. I have also met Pocket Richard, Guy Lafleur, and Boom Boom Geoffrion, to name just a handful. The one I had not met was the great gentleman Jean Beliveau.

It was not long after that reminder that a publisher's representative called me and told me that Jean Beliveau had written a book and asked if I would like to have him on my show. "Of course," I said.

The night before the great man was to appear, my mother passed away in Winnipeg and I had to go immediately and make funeral arrangements. My colleague Geoff Currier filled in for me on the show.

Some years later, my wife gave me a gift of tickets to a two-game series in Montreal's Bell Centre. I had been to the old Forum several times and I wanted to see the new venue—which was not a disappointment.

Before leaving Regina, I contacted the Canadiens front office about meeting Beliveau. I told them about my near-miss and was told that he did not attend all games as he had in the past, largely because of ill health, but that they would try. I gave them my hotel number and I told them that I would understand if it didn't pan out. The days ran out and we returned home without meeting Big Jean.

Two days later, I was sitting all alone in my office in my home when the phone rang. I answered and the voice at the other end said, "Mr. Harasen, this is Jean Beliveau in Montreal." After I picked myself up from the floor, we had a delightful visit on the telephone. He thought the Habs were improving but that they were generally not big enough in stature. He told me that he would become eighty years old that summer.

Jean Beliveau was loyal to family, dedicated to his church, and committed to Canada.

DON HARRON

Don Harron, alias Charlie Farquharson, was a talented individual who guested on my program many times. Harron's experience as a radio actor went back to Mavor Moore's time on CBC radio's *Stage* series. Charlie was a long-time performer on Nashville's cornball *Hee Haw* show. Harron said people in the deep South just couldn't figure out where Farquharson was from but they enjoyed him nonetheless. The answer, of course, was that he was a takeoff on a rural local from Parry Sound, Ontario. One of his most hilarious books was *Old Charlie Farquharson's Testament,* which included the opening chapter "Jennysez" (Genesis) and "Exxodust" (Exodus). You can imagine the rest.

Don and his wife, singer Catherine McKinnon, made a visit to the program some years ago to promote a Christmas book. Catherine had a heavy cold and I was able to make an appointment for her with my doctor, Dr. Jack Alexander. I was grateful to Don for a favour, which was getting Charlie to be part of a kick-off luncheon for the Roughrider campaign for a million dollars (the football club's share of the Taylor Field expansion in the late 1970s).

Perhaps one of Don Harron's finest artistic efforts was the huge role he played in putting together the lyrics and book for the musical adaptation of the novel *Anne of Green Gables,* which I saw staged in Charlottetown, Prince Edward Island.

GREER GARSON

This experience came at an unexpected time and place. I was travelling with the Ross Thatcher delegation when he took the unconstitutional trip (this was federal government territory) to New Mexico to try to get Governor David Cargo to agree to pro-ration the mining of potash because an oversupply was driving down prices.

The capital of New Mexico is Santa Fe, a quaint place with architecture influenced by Mexico and the Pueblo Indians. Streets and roads were old donkey trails covered by pavement. We were told that there was a large artistic community there and that actress Greer Garson, who was particularly popular in films in the 1940s, also lived in Santa Fe.

A group of us were leaving our downtown hotel one afternoon when someone in our group recognized Greer Garson coming down the street. We bid her good afternoon and she stopped immediately and wanted to know where we were from and the purpose of our visit. The actress promptly welcomed us to her city and state. I remember Attorney General Darrel Heald (ever the gentleman) removing his hat while speaking to her. We told Miss Garson we were from Saskatchewan, Canada. Her eyes lit up instantly and she told us that she was related to a Canadian politician named Stuart Garson (who was once Premier of Manitoba and then a federal cabinet minister).

It was a pleasant little visit and all were pleased to meet the lady who was probably best known for her screen role as "Mrs. Miniver." Come to think of it, no one took a picture or asked for an autograph.

ED SCHREYER

The Yorkton Jaycees hosted a weekend gathering in September of 1965 which included Jaycees from Saskatchewan, North Dakota, and Montana. It was largely a social event, with only one or two "business" items. One was a debate on the topic of whether Canada should join the Organization of American States. I and a professor from Winnipeg were recruited to argue in favor of the idea; a Yorkton lawyer and a professor from the University of Saskatchewan were opposed.

I was given the task of picking up the Winnipeg academic at the train in Melville. My problem was that I didn't know what he looked like. The train pulled up to the station and the passengers poured out. What do I do? I waited for the platform to clear and then asked the lone figure left there if he was Ed Schreyer. He replied, "Yes, I am."

The debate judges ruled that Mr. Schreyer and I lost the debate and we all know Schreyer went on to become Premier of Manitoba and then Governor General of Canada. Some years later, when he was Governor General, Schreyer and his wife were in the Regina area and had a Sunday without any engagements. Walter Smishek, a Blakeney cabinet member at the time, invited the Schreyers and some others for an "off-the-record" day at his cottage in Kannata Valley. My wife and I were among the invited guests. During the afternoon, a number of us took a ride in Walter's boat. Passengers included the Governor General, Premier Blakeney, and some other political figures. As we slowly travelled past the main pier at Regina Beach, it was amusing watching people do double-takes (it was not generally known that Schreyer was in the area).

I must say that Schreyer never changed through those years. He was the same low-key individual that I first met years before. When we saw each other, infrequently, we usually laughed about our lack of success in debate.

JEAN LUC PEPIN

He will be remembered as a federal minister in the Trudeau government who had responsibility for the Canadian Wheat Board, among other things. Pepin came through Regina during a time when grain farmers were having some serious problems in that sector: usually transportation, poor sales, or prices. I wanted to sit him down for an interview to pursue some answers about the situation and determine if there was some light at the end of the tunnel.

I was able to book him for a television taping and I told his staff that I would probably include, as a co-interviewer, a farm leader, if any were available. Pepin's staff thought it was a good idea. My first inclination was to have someone from Saskatchewan Wheat Pool but no one was available. My next thought was to invite Roy Atkinson, the straight-talking president of the National Farmers Union. He readily accepted and drove down from his farm.

That morning, Pepin was preceded to the station by one of his assistants, who I informed that Atkinson was my guest interviewer. The assistant congratulated me for having the NFU President participate in the interview. When Pepin arrived at the station he took one look at Atkinson and went bonkers. "I was not informed!" he cried, "This is not professional." The statement regarding professionalism got my motor going and I told him that his staff was informed of my intentions the previous afternoon. "Don't call me unprofessional," I said as I started to shake with anger. Pepin backed down and cooled off very quickly, like bullies do when you don't run away from them. I could have told the minister that I was congratulated by one of his staff just twenty minutes before, but I didn't want to jeopardize the assistant's job. We went into the studio and recorded a very informative and civilized interview.

CATHY GRANT

This is a name that I "drop" even though it will not be widely known. She was my first assistant at CKCK radio and she was never matched by any of the others who came after her. I had one who didn't know how to make a long distance telephone call. I hadn't thought to ask in the interview.

Cathy came to work for me straight from Mount Royal College in Calgary. I was immediately interested in her application because I knew that she came from a good family. She settled into the job quickly and pulled off some miracles. She was still very young but she was not intimidated by the high and mighty and she used all sorts of ingenuity to secure guests and provide research material. After I left CKCK, she stayed on for awhile and then did some radio work in Winnipeg. She later married an American diplomat and lived for awhile in the Soviet Union. I understand she now lives in the United States and is a mother, an important job anywhere! She was the best!

KAHN-TINETA HORN

Some may remember this exotic name belonging to a fiery Mohawk model who had some views that were scary, to put it mildly. She had nothing good to say about white people and even suggested a diet item that Caucasians should pursue with vigor.

Miss Horn stated early in our conversation that cow's milk was poison and that aboriginal women listening in should not feed it to their children under any circumstances. On the other hand, she urged white people to continue making "nature's most perfect food" available to their kids. I concluded that the implication was that it would be one way to reduce the number of whites in society. She provided no scientific basis for her claim except to trace it back to some sort of aboriginal wisdom.

Miss Horn was a beautiful woman but she harboured some very ugly thoughts and attitudes.

LOUIS RIEL

No, we didn't have this controversial figure as a guest on the program, but whenever we raised his name there were some very strong feelings expressed both pro and con. In the early days of the program, in the 1960s, the majority of callers believed Riel to be a traitor who deserved hanging. That has changed over time, with his name now memorialized on highways and buildings.

One aspect of the Riel saga that isn't discussed very much these days is his mental health. The prevailing thought among his critics was that he was mad! I decided to do some journalistic psychoanalysis on my television show.

Adding to the local debate was a statue erected on the legislative grounds, of a Riel in his nightshirt with his genitals on display. It was commissioned, I'm told, with good intentions by the Thatcher government and produced by John Nugent.

During Canada's Centennial, the Regina Chamber of Commerce began a re-creation of the Riel Regina trial, which has run every summer since then. We filmed Riel's address to the court (beautifully portrayed by Steve Arsenych). I then had a psychiatrist who had recently come to Canada from Scotland psychoanalyse Riel. I chose him because he had never heard of Riel and didn't hold any opinions about him.

The psychiatrist went through books, medical records, and court proceedings. We blended Riel's courtroom address with my interview of the psychiatrist. When we reached the end of the interview, the newly-Canadian psychiatrist's conclusion was that Louis Riel was a paranoid schizophrenic. He also concluded that the statue, which has long since been removed, was an insult aimed by the sculptor at the government for what he thought was a politically motivated commission.

CHARLOTTE WHITTON

She was the first woman mayor of a major Canadian city. (Another woman preceded her in a small northern Canadian town.) Whitton was the mayor of Ottawa from 1951 to 1956 and 1960 to 1964. She was the one who coined the saying, "Whatever women do they must do twice as well as men to be thought half as good. Luckily this is not difficult." When she attended Queen's University she played on the women's hockey team and was said to be the fastest skater.

Charlotte Whitton never married but was opposed to easier divorce. She lived with a lady friend, which in this day and age has caused some to wonder about her sexual preferences. Whitton said and did things that caused some to call her an anti-Semite. In fact, she opposed all non-British immigration.

Charlotte Whitton was a dedicated member of the Progressive Conservative Party. When I interviewed her on television, I asked her, as a good Tory, why the party so often used long knives on their leaders. In an instant her eyes were blazing. She clenched her teeth and for a moment I thought she was going to come up over the desk to get me. She didn't but, still quite enraged, said "Yes, we are quite open, but the Liberals use little pen knives on their leaders when no one sees it!"

ROGER WHITTAKER

The British singer who made a name for himself in Canada with the hit "The Last Farewell" toured this country several times and was a big favorite in Regina. Tickets for his concerts sold out very quickly. I should note that not only did Roger sing but that he was a whistler of extraordinary ability.

I took my tape recorder to what was then the Regina Inn and to Roger Whittaker's suite. It was getting to the time when we were starting to think about Christmas, so I suggested to Roger that we do an interview about the way the Whittakers celebrated Christmas, which I would play back around December twenty-third or twenty-fourth.

I found him sitting in the living room wearing slacks and a beautiful sweater, with his beard nicely trimmed and a nice warm smile. While Bob Hope was visiting troops and never at home for Christmas, Roger Whittaker said there was absolutely nothing that "would tempt me to be away from my family at Christmas." His handlers knew that and would not book him for anything beyond the first two or three days of December. He noted that his wife, the housekeeper, the dog, and the first three children were all female but the odds had improved for him with the arrival of two sons.

Roger noted that the traditional dinner of turkey and Christmas pudding enjoyed in much of the English-speaking world is common in much of the rest of the world, including in Africa, where he lived as a boy.

He also offered a recipe for a yuletide drink that would be worthy to try, since all ingredients are available here. Pimm's (a gin-related item) is one-third of the mix and lemonade or 7Up is two-thirds. Add fruit, ice, chop up an orange, celery, cucumber, banana, and apples. Mix well. You can now conclude that you may need the whole bottle of Pimm's. Get some mint and rub it into the inside of mugs and serve.

Velma and I were invited to an after-show cast party in the greenroom at the Centre of the Arts; Roger's easy grace made for a wonderful interlude.

Roger Whittaker retired a few years ago because of some heart problems and he and his family left Britain some time ago and lived in County Galway, Ireland, and then France. He is close to eighty years of age.

ROBERT STANFIELD

It has been said that it's too bad that Robert Stanfield wasn't given an opportunity to lead a government in Canada. I'm inclined to agree, because the image largely portrayed by television was way off base. Those pictures of fumbling that football or peeling a banana at the leadership convention simply crucified the man. His slower speech didn't help. Though, as someone comically observed once, "they would never appoint Bob Stanfield to the Senate because he talks too fast for that place!" I wonder how many of history's giants would have been destroyed by television and image politics. Apparently, Abraham Lincoln had a voice that was anything but pleasant to the ear.

I found Mr. Stanfield to be a warm and easy person to be around. He had a terrific sense of humour, which I'm told made him a favorite at the National Press Club's annual dinner. He was also patient with the inevitable delays at television studios (I had no end of experience with fuming politicians and pain-in-the-neck assistants in this regard). Whether holding public office as Premier of Nova Scotia or in his private business, Stanfield was recognized as competent and successful. When I changed jobs I was pleasantly surprised to receive a note from Mr. Stanfield wishing me well.

I should note that meeting Mr. Stanfield included meeting an obscure research assistant in his office named Joe Clark.

WILL MILLAR (IRISH ROVERS)

It was always nice to take a day off from the problems of state, farm prices, and tragedies to have a little fun on the program, and fun we had when Will Millar of the Irish Rovers came to call. The Rovers were appearing at the Centre of the Arts in Regina, so I extended an invitation to the fellow who did most of the talking on their television show.

Millar was tired when he arrived at the station because he had partied late the night before but he came to life once we hit the air. He talked of his hungry days as an unknown entertainer and the pressures and misery of public adulation and mind-boggling travel. He teased elderly ladies with Irish accents and played a game trying to guess what part of Ireland they came from. He invited some of these gals to call in with Irish folk songs to aid his constant search for material he had never heard before. If they called in with a song that he knew, Millar would sing a duet with them on the telephone. He was an absolute delight.

Will invited me to drop in to the greenroom (the backstage lounge or waiting room for performers, all of which are named the greenroom) at the Centre of the Arts that evening, which I did. I think all of us have heard stories about how difficult it can be for a trio or quartet to get along over a very long period of time. They rehearse and perform together, travel together, and spend most of their time together.

When I arrived at the greenroom that evening, the performers were all in the room but each separated from the others as far away as the dimensions of the greenroom would allow. At one time, one of the Rovers lived in Prince Edward Island and the others were spread about in British Columbia.

DANNY GALLIVAN/ DICK IRVIN

They were the voices of the Montreal Canadiens for many years. Danny Gallivan was a gentleman and he was an exciting play-by-play broadcaster who invented his own terms of description. Some were the "cannonating shots," the "Savardian spinorama," and goalkeepers who got the puck caught up in their "paraphernalia." I had Danny on the phone from Montreal the day after the first game of the famous 1972 series when Canada was in shock after the Russians kicked our butts. In the studio, I had Bill Hicke and Fran Huck, who were once Habs. Danny managed to squeeze in something nice about Bill and Fran even though the topic was something else.

Dick Irvin has written books about hockey, has broadcast hockey, and to top it off is a fan of the Roughriders. Dick grew up in Regina and two of his best friends are Gerry Welsh and the late Johnny Sandison. He married a girl from Regina and his late father was a coach of the Canadiens. Dick possesses a tremendous hockey memory and he very deservedly received the Order of Canada. Dick is a good Canadian who can look back on his body of work with pride. These Regina fellows go places!

JOHNNY SANDISON

Johnny had the most listened-to early morning radio show in Saskatchewan. When you look at population figures for the southern half of the province and follow them through audience figures, when John was at his prime he simply didn't leave very much for the rest of the broadcasters in his listening area (which was substantial with the wonderful range of CKCK at 620 on the dial).

Johnny was a fireman first, following in the footsteps of his father. Then came an opportunity to get into radio broadcasting at CKRM Regina and, as they say, the rest is history. He eventually gravitated to the number-one outfit,

CKCK radio, and made a name for himself as a morning personality and a television weatherman and interviewer.

A big part of his success was that he moved about the community, which he served in a variety of ways. He spent more than half a century with Canada's Navy, starting as a Navy Cadet. He went on to enlist in the Second World War at age seventeen and served on a Corvette on the stormy North Atlantic. On his return, he stayed with the naval reserve, where he gained his commission. There were many summers during which he would go out to sea for various stretches of time.

Along with his wife, Margie, and their kids, Patty and David, Johnny loved his work. We shared a love for broadcasting and classic radio. Whenever I would have Fibber McGee (Jim Jordan) or Edgar Bergen and Charlie McCarthy and Mortimer Snerd on my show, I would invite Johnny to come in with me as a guest interviewer. I would get a bigger kick out of the enjoyment Johnny got out of hearing these radio stars of old.

I spent a fair amount of time with Johnny in the closing months of his life. When I visited him just days before his death he referred to me as "his faithful friend" and that is something I won't forget.

Johnny Sandison was a professional broadcaster and would have remained as such if he had lived to nine hundred. I don't think he was a tough salary bargainer but when he went over to CKCK Television full-time, I think General Manager Bruce Cowie addressed the matter of Johnny's income. The "Morning Mayor," as he was known on the radio, was a family man, a man of the church, and honest as the day was long. He served his country in war and he was the recipient of the Order of Canada.

When Johnny Sandison retired from CKCK TV, the station stayed on local programming all day as a steady stream of people found their way to Johnny's set to wish him well and say thanks.

CLARK MOLLENHOFF

This man guested on my show twice in 1973, once by telephone and then as a studio guest a few weeks later. Mollenhoff was a particularly valuable guest because he was appointed as Special Counsel to President Richard Nixon. Mollenhoff worked in the White House for about a year and then quit because he didn't like what Nixon, Haldeman, Ehrlichman, and some of the others were doing. As an example, he was given nine income tax returns to aid him in doing some background checks for the President's office. He was concerned because, by U S. law, income tax returns are confidential. Fortunately for me, some time after quitting, he wound up coming to Regina because he had a married daughter living in the city.

When Mollenhoff came to my studio, he filled the doorway; he was six feet four inches and he weighed 250 pounds. He was an intense person who you knew would not put up with any nonsense. A couple of weeks after Mollenhoff appeared as my guest, he got into a shouting duel with Nixon at a televised news conference because he felt that the President was ignoring him.

It is felt by some in the United States that it was Mollenhoff who coined the term "investigative journalism." Mollenhoff's background included working with Bobby Kennedy in nailing Jimmy Hoffa and the Teamster's Union. He wrote about a dozen books, which earned him a Pulitzer Prize. As well, he received six honorary degrees. Included among his books was a critique of President Jimmy Carter entitled *The President Who Failed: Carter Out of Control.*

Mollenhoff also taught journalism at the university level. He died of cancer at the relatively young age of sixty-nine.

KEN PRESTON

He was a former Roughrider player who made his mark as General Manager of the football club, particularly in the

1960s and 70s. I think he contributed most to fostering that first dynasty, in the 1960–70 period, when the team won its first Grey Cup and appeared in three others. George Reed and Ron Lancaster, among many others, were brought here during his time. When he picked up Garner Ekstran at the airport, he said he was expecting a bigger man. Ekstran, at his first practice, promptly broke someone's nose.

Preston was criticized for being too tight-fisted with money. He was because he didn't have it. Ken performed miracles with no money to speak of. I wonder what he might have achieved if he had Manager John Herrera's budget! His negotiating technique was to place his offer to players on the desk and then wait to see them blink. Ken Preston was a man of few words. I was pleased to call him a friend. His wife, Dot, was a great lady.

ARCHBISHOP M. C. O'NEILL

He was the third Archbishop of Regina. Michael Cornelius O'Neill was studying for the priesthood when the First World War broke out. He promptly put his studies on hold and joined Canada's armed forces. For displaying bravery on the field of battle, he was awarded the Military Medal. O'Neill served again in the Second World War, this time as Principal Catholic Chaplain Overseas with the rank of Colonel; he was again decorated, this time with the Order of the British Empire.

Later, Archbishop O'Neill received honorary doctorates from his alma mater, the University of Toronto, and from the University of Saskatchewan.

Archbishop O'Neill took over as Archbishop of Regina in 1948. He is probably remembered best for the growth of Catholic institutions during his time as head of the archdiocese. He was a humble, quiet, prayerful man who was also scholarly, a patriot, and devoted to his church. One of his major involvements was participation in the Second Vatican Council, which had been called by Pope St. John XXIII.

I considered Archbishop O'Neill a personal friend. I acted as broadcast commentator at Christmas midnight Mass at Holy Rosary Cathedral for at least a dozen years and the Archbishop was the presider at most of those. I took Communion to patients in the Plains Hospital for a number of years and found the Archbishop's name on the list of Catholics who I would be visiting on a particular Sunday. When I arrived at his room it was clear that he was in his last days. It struck me that I had a rare privilege to briefly minister to a man who had ministered to me and his people in such a major way for so long.

When I was leaving CKCK, the Archbishop wrote to me in his longhand, wishing me well in the future and wondering how I was able to keep my sanity in my work. I didn't have the heart to tell him that I had lost my "marbles" long ago!

ARTHUR FIEDLER

Music lovers will recognize this name as the Maestro of the Boston Pops Orchestra for many years. He paid a visit to my program while in Regina to conduct the Regina Symphony. I brought along my two oldest children, who were involved in school music programs at the time.

Fiedler was an honorary fireman and Regina was one of 270 fire departments that honored him. The Maestro was an interesting man.

He started playing the violin, which he said was a chore, so he switched to the viola, which he said was more interesting. Fiedler didn't get married until he was fifty. He told me that a recording at that time of Mozart with a "beat" was "profane" but he once made a recording of the Pops playing the Gillette Blue Blades jingle.

He told me that travelling to other time zones didn't bother him. Fiedler said, "I just set my watch to local times and sleep and eat when the local people do." He autographed for me a copy of the album of music from *Swan Lake* (which he had conducted). Fiedler had a gruff way of speaking. At the end of his Regina concert, he turned to the audience and gruffly announced, "For our encore we will play "Mack the Knife!"

RALPH GOODALE

Ralph was a guest on my program several times in his various incarnations as member of the Saskatchewan Legislature, Saskatchewan Liberal leader, Member of Parliament, Minister of the Canadian Wheat Board, Minister of Agriculture, Minister of Natural Resources, Minister of Public Works, Minister of Finance and Opposition, Government House Leader, as well as Deputy Leader of the Liberal Party of Canada. I would suggest that if he could speak French he might have been Liberal leader long ago.

I moderated the first televised leaders debate in the 1986 Saskatchewan election, at which time Ralph was leader of the provincial Liberals. Anyone who watched closely would tell you that Goodale won that debate hands-down, but politics in Saskatchewan march to a different drummer and Ralph's very effective performance didn't translate into success at the polls.

Success in politics doesn't usually fall from the sky. You have to work at it and Ralph works hard all day seven days a week. He gets up early and stays late. If you move around the community, Ralph Goodale is seemingly everywhere. The same applies to the service he provides to his constituents. If he doesn't have the answer, he will get it for you.

It will not keep me awake at night if my scribblings are viewed as those of a grit promoting a grit. I should note that in 2006 Ralph Goodale was named Parliamentarian of the Year in Canada and was celebrated as such in a major article in *Maclean's* magazine. Commenting on Ralph being tough when he needed to be, journalist John Geddes once wrote that Goodale "can take a punch!"

Ralph graduated at the top of his class from the law school at the University of Saskatchewan. He was awarded the Gold Medal for Academic Achievement. I don't think he has ever practiced any law. If so, very little. Otto Lang, a former Dean of Law at the University of Saskatchewan, no doubt played a significant role in Ralph's very early political activity and electoral success as a Member of Parliament at the age of twenty-four.

Ralph Goodale's wife, Pam, a retired teacher and principal in the Regina public school system, supports her husband in a low-key but pleasant manner. Her family is said to come from a long line of Liberal party supporters. Ralph's accolades include being named Queen's Scout when he was a boy, the highest honour in Scouting. Many think he's still a good scout!

TOM BEYNON

Tom was an offensive lineman with the Saskatchewan Roughrider team that won that first Saskatchewan Grey Cup in 1966. A Canadian, he was a very competent player and contributed a great deal to that first championship. He was a Rider for only a short time and went on to play for the Ottawa Rough Riders, where he was part of another two Grey Cup championships. It was a remarkable career in the short time of five seasons.

When Tom came to Saskatchewan, he was interested in becoming a lawyer while continuing to play football. He already possessed a mechanical engineering degree from Queen's University.

Harold Pick, a Regina lawyer, pulled some strings at the University of Saskatchewan law school, which enabled Beynon to play football and work at getting a law degree. The routine was that Tom would drive to the University of Saskatchewan in Saskatoon in the morning and then return in the afternoon for football practice. After practice, he would have dinner and then go to the courthouse to study. The next day he would repeat the routine.

After two seasons, he was traded to Ottawa by a reluctant Coach Eagle Keys. Tom's specialty is law as it pertains to intellectual property. In later years, Beynon got his master's degree in law from Osgoode Hall Law School in Toronto.

Some years ago, Tom Beynon made his services available to the Junior Football Association in Canada. He also assists young law students whenever he can. I introduced him to the Opimian Society, which is all about fine wines.

Even though Tom was also an Ottawa football player, he has a special fondness for the Roughriders of Saskatchewan and makes a point of attending player reunions here. At the conclusion of the most recent anniversary reunion of that first Grey Cup, I interviewed him about the weekend program. His response was positive but he became emotional at the conclusion of his remarks because this was likely the last time that he would see some of his teammates. Quite so. Coach Eagle Keys, Ron Lancaster, and Ken Reed would soon pass away. Others who are no longer with us include Ron Atchison, Gordon Barwell, Cliff Shaw, Jim Worden, Reg Whitehouse, Ted Dushinski, Gene Wlasiuk, Ed Buchanan, Assistant Coach Jim Duncan, and Trainer Sandy Archer.

SYLVIA FEDORUK

The first woman to be named Lieutenant Governor of Saskatchewan and the first woman to be named Chancellor of the University of Saskatchewan was Sylvia Fedoruk; her name goes back a long way with my family. Her mother and father, Mr. and Mrs. Theodore and Ann Fedoruk, were friends of my parents. According to the baby book kept very faithfully by my mother, the Fedoruks had a gift for me when I was born, Mrs. Ann Fedoruk was one of the sponsors at my baptism, and Mr. and Mrs. Fedoruk and Sylvia attended and had gifts for me at my first birthday.

Sylvia was an achiever from the very beginning and my mother constantly referred to her as a model for me to follow. The evidence was compelling. Miss Fedoruk excelled at sports and the scholarships came early and often and didn't stop until her formal education ended. She went on to receive recognition for the balance of her life as a medical physicist and an active citizen. She ultimately received the Saskatchewan Order of Merit and the Order of Canada.

Miss Fedoruk was an only child whose mother died young. She spent much time with her father, a quiet-spoken country school teacher who was very proud of his daughter.

I called on Sylvia, a former national women's curling champion, to offer congratulations and encouragement to Sandra Schmirler, who guested on my show at the beginning of her climb to legendary heights in national, world, and Olympic curling achievement.

The first woman Lieutenant Governor had a great sense of humour and despite the distinguished ladder that she climbed to the top, she remained very approachable and easy to be around. I was on the program as a master of ceremonies at some functions where Sylvia was in attendance as a main speaker or participant.

My wife and I hosted Miss Fedoruk for dinner in our home during her term as Lieutenant Governor. She arrived at the appointed time with a jar of dill pickles under her arm. The label on the home canning jar read: *"Syls Dills."*

They were actually quite good and just another example of the common touch and good humour of the seventeenth Lieutenant Governor of Saskatchewan. Her work as a medical physicist prompted a name change from the Canadian Centre for Nuclear Innovation to the Sylvia Fedoruk Centre for Nuclear Innovation.

Sylvia Fedoruk died on September 26, 2012. She was eighty-five years old.

LARRY SOLWAY

Some in western Canada may remember Solway as a panelist on a network television show known as *Flashback*. His main occupation in the fall of 1970 was hosting an open line radio show on CHUM Toronto, one of the major stations in that city. Larry Solway took a step in November 1970 that would cost him his job. He put together five programs dealing with sex and all associated matters, ranging from frigidity to impotence and including orgasm and masturbation, among other allied subjects.

As it turned out, CHUM listeners only heard four of the programs. The fifth never went to air because CHUM management felt that the series didn't meet local standards of taste and acceptability. Obviously, Solway disagreed and resigned. It should be noted that Solway used some of the best professionals on the topic, such as Dr. David Reuben, who authored the bestseller *Everything You Wanted To Know About Sex But Were Afraid To Ask,* along with a psychiatrist and others who could provide learned answers for listeners.

Some months later, Solway wrote a book with a title that I thought was classic: *The Day I Invented Sex.* The book included a transcript of the fifth program (which CHUM management blocked from going to air). Needless to say, the author toured the country promoting the book and I booked him for both my radio and television shows.

I should note that I gave Solway my opinion of what had taken place. I told him that programs on the topic of sex had a necessary place on radio and TV. My concern with the content of his programs was that the discussions about topics such as orgasm and masturbation were too explicit for the day's standards.

I once hosted a series of five-minute advice programs on FM radio with a couple who worked in sex therapy. This was many years after Solway. I remember a dentist at the YMCA tell me that he felt a little awkward with the radio on in the background discussing premature ejaculation while he worked on the teeth of a nun.

Needless to say, Larry Solway and I took a fair amount of abuse from listeners who phoned in. He for the programs and the book and me for having him on the show. We were called perverts and dirty old men and letters to me were even worse. One woman wanted know if my wife and I performed in front of my children. I believe there were also demands that I be fired. My concern then and now is that sex is a problem for many individuals and couples. All you have to do is look at the big business that pornography is. Our schools have been trying to do the right thing and to some degree the situation has improved.

KNOWLTON NASH

He guested on my program on two or three occasions; I came to respect him as a journalist and as a person and particularly as a broadcast journalist. Nash was a foreign correspondent, a manager of the CBC's news and current events department, and also served as anchor of the CBC's flagship newscast, *The National.*

Knowlton Nash knew that he wanted to be a newsman while still a boy. In fact, he reportedly had his own news-sheet of about a half dozen pages at age eight, where he would sell advertising to merchants in exchange for candy and bubble gum.

I was particularly interested in his views regarding the quality of news service these days. In his book *Trivia Pursuit,* Nash said the news media of today is awash in sensationalism. He argued further that show business values were corrupting the news and he used as examples the death of Princess Diana (which the media reported with the most minute detail) and the extensive coverage of President Clinton's sex life. Nash felt that the policy in some of these newsrooms seemed to be aimed at audience ratings rather than educating and informing the people. I feel strongly that the book should be required reading in all schools of journalism.

I watch Canadian news media and shake my head at times. The policy, it seems, is "if it bleeds, it leads." Highway fatalities, fires, murder, and so-called standoffs have priority. The standoffs never lead to very much in this part of the country but the media come rushing to the scene, thinking, hoping that this time there may be a dramatic exchange of gun fire. At least that seems to be the hoped-for objective.

The presentation of news, particularly television news, has become mundane. I refer to those two-person present-ers, often a man and woman, the style imported from local stations in the United States. The only two-man team on American networks was Huntley and Brinkley, of NBC, and they have been gone for decades. The format has long since outlived its usefulness. I wonder about the qualifications of the team. I could do without those inane little exchanges between the newscasters and the sports and weather guys. ABC, NBC, CBS, CTV, CBC, and Global all have one-person presenters and CTV and Global have single presenters (who happen to be women).

I shudder when I hear newscasts referred to as "the show!" and at the idea that broadcast journalists are celeb-rities. Knowlton Nash did journalism a favour in writing his book. When he died, on May 24, 2014, Prime Minister Stephen Harper described him as "one of the icons of Canadian broadcast news."

GALE GORDON

He was probably the finest character actor anywhere. Someone once said that Gordon was a great supporting actor throughout his career. He appeared in at least two dinner theatre plays on Regina's Stage West. He was a guest on my radio program at least twice. If the name doesn't ring a bell for you, let me remind you. Gale Gordon appeared in just about all episodes of Lucille Ball's *Lucy* series. On radio, he appeared in just about every show worth listening to; he was known as the fellow who would do a slow simmer and then explode, to the delight of the studio audience. He was Mayor LaTrivia on *Fibber McGee and Molly*, school principal

Osgood Conklin in *Our Miss Brooks*, he had a part on *The Great Gildersleeve*, and his explosions were part of television's *Dennis the Menace*. At one point, it was thought that he was radio's highest-paid actor.

Gale Gordon was a gentleman in the best sense of that word. His mustache was always neatly trimmed and his clothing was pressed and in good taste. He said he liked Regina audiences and the hospitable way he was treated here. There was a gentlemanly manner about him, nothing close to the highly explosive characters that he played on radio and television. An interesting sidelight is that Gordon was born with a cleft palate, which had to be repaired in Britain.

Gale Gordon died in California on June 30, 1995, at age eighty-nine, a matter of weeks after the death of his actress wife, Virginia Curley. They were married for sixty years. There were no children. Gordon was posthumously named to the National Radio Hall of Fame and he is remembered on the Hollywood Walk of Fame.

JACK WEBSTER

The "Oatmeal Savage," as newspaper and magazine journalist, Allan Fotheringham called him, was probably the best reporter in the country. Jack was fearless, aggressive, unrelenting, and he knew how to extract information from just about anyone. He first worked for the *Vancouver Sun* when he emigrated from Scotland but he eventually dominated on radio and television as well.

For most of their married life, his wife, Margaret, suffered from serious psychological problems. It was felt that when Margaret and Jack, at age seventeen, conceived a child and then put the baby up for adoption, Margaret's problems began. They dogged her for the rest of her life. Even when the Websters reunited with the young woman when she was an adult, it was too late for Margaret; she was too far gone to be helped.

I visited Jack in order to see how the administrative side of his work was done because I wasn't satisfied with my approach. It was a useful trip. Jack put me behind a microphone for an hour to talk about what was happening in Saskatchewan, since there were many people from Saskatchewan who had moved to British Columbia. Chief among Jack's interests was why the Ross Thatcher government was turfed out of power.

While in Vancouver, Jack asked me to assist him in bringing home one of his vehicles, a Land Rover, which he used at his farm on Salt Spring Island. I drove the car and Jack drove the Rover. He amused himself as he led the way by having me, the small-town boy, running amber lights most of the way. That was Jack. When we got to his home I was introduced to Mrs. Webster but didn't know about her problems until Jack wrote his book. Later that evening, the three of us attended a Canuck hockey game.

Jack did his first radio work for CKNW from a studio in the Georgia Hotel. Later, when he moved, CJOR built Jack a studio in Gastown. I wanted to see it and did. There was a federal election on at that time, and so once again Jack wanted me to sit in as a guest and talk politics. I was wearing a very light suit along with a lime-green shirt and a paisley bow tie. A caller wanted Jack to tell him how old he thought I was. Jack guessed that I was "forrrrtyish" and, commenting on how I was dressed, said "Harrrasen looks like a Liberal candidate on the make!"

I had a tremendous amount of respect for Jack Webster. He was honest. He sided with the little guy. He was a loyal Canadian. He only wanted to be known as a reporter. He didn't like to be branded as a showman, but he had lots of that trait, which, when combined with his journalistic talent, made for a highly effective individual. I was proud to know him.

VICTOR ERNEST HOFFMAN

I was working an early morning news run at CKCK radio in mid-August of 1967 when a story of unbelievable savagery reached my editing desk. Nine members of the Peterson family of Shell Lake, Saskatchewan, had been murdered at point-blank range by Victor Ernest Hoffman, age twenty-one, who had been released from a mental hospital just three weeks before. Only four-year-old Phyllis Peterson was spared. Hoffman later said that he didn't kill her because the youngster had the face of an angel. It was thought by some that Hoffman didn't shoot her because he simply didn't see her lying in bed between her two sisters. Hoffman also told police when he was later captured that the day before the killings that he had fought with the devil, who Hoffman described as tall, black, and without genitals.

Needless to say, once informed of the slaughter, people in the Shell Lake district were nervous that the killer had not yet been apprehended. Many of them with firearms kept them close at hand until Hoffman was captured.

Once he was arrested, it was reported that Hoffman would be arraigned in North Battleford the next day. CKCK radio had an agreement with a local flying service that they would transport our news personnel if quick and/or long-distance travel was required. I quickly booked a plane and we were soon on our way. The pilot had considerable experience and as we headed for North Battleford he kept taking generous drinks from a white plastic bottle that I thought was water. I was later told that it wasn't water...or Kool-Aid! In fact, as we flew along, the pilot suddenly swooped downward and pointed to an open piece of land in the middle of nowhere where his father was buried. I was delighted to have that information.

When we arrived in North Battleford, I made some telephone checks and soon drifted off to sleep in my hotel room, knowing that I needed to get up early in order to find a place to sit in the courtroom. I was able to get a good seat in the courtroom even though it filled up very quickly.

Canadian media from coast to coast, major newspapers from the United States, magazines, and broadcast networks all were represented in this sensational court appearance.

Hoffman was brought to the courtroom by police. The accused looked bewildered, spaced-out, and really not in tune with what was happening around him. When the judge remanded him to the North Battleford mental hospital for a psychiatric assessment, Hoffman asked, on the basis of obvious past experience, "Will I have to have shock treatments?" The judge didn't answer the question directly. Crown Prosecutor Serge Kujawa said Hoffman was "the craziest man in Saskatchewan."

Later, Hoffman was found not guilty by reason of insanity. He was sent to a mental hospital in Penetanguishene, Ontario. At one point there was talk about letting him have supervised access to three communities in the area, but the general public heard word of that and raised an outcry that terminated that idea. Victor Ernest Hoffman died of cancer on May 21, 2004, at age fifty-eight.

JACK RAMSAY

He will be remembered as the former RCMP officer who wrote a critical piece in *Maclean's* magazine in 1972 about Canada's pride and joy, the Royal Canadian Mounted Police. This was unusual because very little had been said about the force in such a general and negative way. Even more than that, it was criticism by someone who resided in Saskatchewan, the home of the iconic police force (particularly in Regina, where the RCMP are trained, and, at the end of their years, where many choose to be buried).

The criticism ranged from discipline in the force to lacking sensitivity in dealing with Natives to having to wear boots and spurs while driving police cruisers. Ramsay argued that it was difficult for members of the force to find anyone they could take their problems to without running the risk of discipline or expulsion. Public criticism didn't work because the public relations of the force (ranging from Hollywood's treatment of the force in Nelson Eddy's portrayal of an RCMP officer to the Musical Ride) contributed to an attitude among Canadians that the RCMP was above criticism.

Jack Ramsay guested on my program and stated his case in no uncertain terms. His point about the sacred cow status of the RCMP was certainly demonstrated by the reaction of listeners, who were critical of Ramsay for raising the controversy and for me for having given him a platform.

One of Ramsay's concerns was that he was unable to get a reaction or have a discussion with the ultimate power over the police force: the federal government. As it turned out, Solicitor General Jean-Pierre Goyer was a guest later on my program and I was able to get agreement from both that they would meet after the program. In fact, I vacated my office to give them privacy. Shortly after, we had a request for the tape of Goyer's appearance by G. Campbell McDonald, of the Ontario Premier's office, who wrote, "Congratulations on your open line achievement. Bringing the two antagonists together both on and off the air was a valuable contribution you have every right to be proud of."

I think the *Maclean's* article and the public discussion that followed led to some changes that have been useful for all concerned. Jack Ramsay went on to a political career with the Reform and Canadian Alliance parties and the Western Canada Concept. He was an early supporter of a union for the Mounties, an issue which has been raised again in recent times. His criticism of the way the RCMP dealt with aboriginals fell hollow when he was later charged with sexual misconduct with a Cree girl while serving with the RCMP in northern Saskatchewan. He was sentenced to one year of probation with community service.

As for the RCMP, they seem to limp into controversy from time to time, but the general public continues to support them. After I had completed two or three programs on the RCMP, a lady called me during a program and asked if I had any sons. I said I had two. She then asked what my reaction would be if they joined the RCMP. I said I would be proud. She said she felt better and hung up.

KRESKIN ET AL.

Kreskin (born George Joseph Kresge) is an American mentalist who prefers that he not be called a psychic. He was a guest on *The Harasen Line* and I was invited to join him onstage for a stunt later that evening at the Saskatchewan Centre of the Arts. I believe that what he does is a trick but he is the best at what he does that I have ever seen. Kreskin must be good because Johnny Carson's *The Tonight Show* featured him as a guest more than sixty times.

Kreskin is very charming and quickly befriends his audience and interviewers. You may feel that you are leading the conversation but he skillfully answers some of your questions while cleverly ignoring others or taking them into an entirely different direction.

In announcing the topic or guest as a psychic, the word would only be half out of my mouth and before I announced the telephone numbers the switchboard would explode. The lights would remain on for the duration of the show. If I stayed on the air for the rest of the day and night, the lines were jammed. In fact, the volume of calls on one such morning created a problem of overloading the works for SaskTel.

Some of the psychics, numerologists, et al. were good performers. Some were bloody awful! But it seemed that all were consulted after the program, where they would charge their fees and make their trip to the city highly rewarding.

I began to think about what I was doing in providing these people with a platform and I had some very great doubts. What troubled me was what some of these individuals did to gullible people who sought their services. Besides, I didn't believe in this hocus pocus, so why should I promote it? I decided to stop and not facilitate this practice any longer.

The cries of anguish by some of these folks were long and loud. I didn't care if they went to competing broadcasters. I should note that hosting open line on radio doesn't mean that the host only features things that interest him. You have to choose rather widely, which we tried to do, but I felt this was almost a matter of ethics.

I get the impression that handwriting analysts may have more to recommend them than number people or psychics.

DR. MORRIS SHUMIATCHER

This was one of the great characters in our province and one of the most brilliant lawyers in Canada. Morris Shumiatcher came to Saskatchewan from Alberta in the 1940s after the war, where he had served with the Royal Canadian Air Force as an air gunner. He had a PhD in law, which was rare in Canada. Shumiatcher was employed first as a law officer in the Attorney General's department of the new CCF government and then he became personal assistant to Premier Tommy Douglas.

One of his contributions to government service was that he put together the Saskatchewan Bill of Rights, which served as a model for similar declarations by the federal government and the United Nations.

Later, Dr. Shumiatcher left government service and faced problems in the courts, which he once said were an attempt to destroy him. It was over some investment and related financial matters. He was exonerated. He had top legal advice but observers say Shumiatcher quarterbacked his own defense from where he was sitting in the court. In the short term following the trial there were some who felt that the brilliant lawyer was ill-treated in the legal world for a short time.

"Shumi," as he was known, stayed in Regina, practiced law, and earned the respect of the community. Both he and his gracious wife, Jacqui, were very generous supporters of the arts and charitable and community causes. He designed his own suits, was one of the first in the city to take up jogging, acquired some valuable art, and wrote two books: *Man of Law: A Model* and *Welfare: Hidden Backlash.* Most significant is that he left behind his socialist encounter and embraced a more conservative posture. He frequently said, "If you are not a socialist when you are eighteen years old, there is something wrong with your heart. If you are still a socialist at age forty, there is something wrong with your head!" He also possessed an amazing vocabulary, thought to be one of the best in Canada by those who know.

Dr. Shumiatcher went after abortion laws for activist Joe Borowski by bringing some of the finest experts in the field as witnesses but they did not win their case. My friend Jeffrey Simpson, of the *Globe and Mail,* asked me to arrange a meeting with the famed lawyer, which I did. It was an interesting evening over drinks and dinner; many topics were pursued, including abortion.

I had Dr. Shumiatcher as a guest interviewer on my television show for one program with a Quebec separatist, Pierre Bourgault, and another with fiery Quebec labour leader Michel Chartrand. He had both worked up in short order, with Chartrand at one point walking off set.

"Shumi" was one of a kind, who could discuss the deepest aspects of the law one moment and the next get on the floor and play with his poodle! He was an original if there ever was one. He died in 2004.

JOE SOEHN

Joe was an art director at CKCK Television for many years and he was also an unofficial researcher for me (I did have an official one). This came about because Joe was a voracious reader of newspapers, periodicals, and almost anything else in print. He would circle clippings of such publications as the *New York Times* and drop them off at my office.

Was Joe eccentric? Well, let's see. He didn't ever learn to drive a car. He would often go downtown, sit on a bench, and watch people. He was writing a book about psychology without ever having studied the subject. At vacation time he would go to the university and monitor classes. Each year he would go the Department of Education and ask the receptionist if he could see the changes that would be made in the curriculum in the coming year. He got quizzical looks but eventually they would do as he asked. Joe made it a point to attend the annual meeting, required by law, of the Catholic school system even though he was one of only six or eight attendees.

Joe Soehn was notorious for not looking after himself. He didn't like doctors and he refused to see dentists. Joe's wife died long before her time and left him with a number of children. One day when Joe didn't show up for breakfast the kids went to his bedroom and found him in a coma. He was taken to hospital in a diabetic coma. He didn't realize he was diabetic and probably ignored the symptoms. Joe spent a month in hospital recovering from his brush with death. I picked him up when he was released and stopped at the pharmacy before I drove him home. I would be willing to bet that he didn't always take his medication or get refills regularly.

There was a reunion in Joe's hometown of Fox Valley that he decided to attend. He bought his bus ticket and was on his way. Joe told me that he went to the community hall and had a tremendous time renewing friendships and visiting. He decided to call it an evening and left the hall for his mother's home. He walked and walked and soon realized that he had forgotten where his mother's home was in the village. No, he wasn't drunk. Joe didn't want the embarrassment of going back to the hall to ask for directions so he continued to walk until he found his mother's house.

Was Joe Soehn eccentric? I'll leave others to decide, but he was a special friend. I was grateful for his interest and for being a good sounding board.

EARL CAMERON

Long-time listeners and viewers of CBC news will remember the very staid and unflappable image of Earl Cameron, who first read the *National News Bulletin* on CBC Radio starting in 1944 and then on television from 1959 to 1966.

Cameron was born in Moose Jaw and started out as a teacher. He got the broadcasting bug during a summer job at his hometown station, CHAB radio. It was his voice that announced the D-day invasion to the country on June 6, 1944.

His voice was authoritative but in a positive manner. You felt you could trust him. This was in contrast with the "Voice of Doom," Lorne Greene, who read the radio news before Earl Cameron. In like manner, there were contrasting presentations when Cameron succeeded Larry Henderson on television.

The CBC had a period of time when it seemingly couldn't decide if newsreaders should be staff announcers who also read commercials and other programs or if newsreaders should be journalists. The broadcast unions also got into the debate.

For Earl Cameron, as a staff announcer, his income from commercials was significant; apparently he was prepared to give that up in favour of the broadcast assignment. The CBC finally decided that their newsreaders should also be journalists and an unhappy Earl Cameron was replaced by reporter Stanley Burke (it turned out to be a short-term appointment for Burke). There was also some discussion along these lines with Lloyd Robertson, who was attracted to the privately owned CTV Network, where he was given a role in putting together the national news.

Many will remember that Canadian humourists Eugene Levy and Joe Flaherty once created two news characters named Earl Camembert and Floyd Robertson—about guess who? It all was done in good fun.

I was pleased to host Earl Cameron on my radio show. He was in Regina for a United Way event. In person, he was nothing like his TV image. He walked into my office sipping a Coca Cola and really spoke like one of the boys from Moose Jaw. During the program we began to talk about the idea of a woman reading the national news. The response from most women callers was that this was no job for a woman. Earl just smiled.

Earl Cameron died in 2005 at age eighty-nine. One observer called him Canada's first noteworthy television news anchor. Knowlton Nash said Cameron was as Canadian as wheat and added that even if the news was bad, Cameron's presentation style assured you that everything would be okay.

LYNDA HAVERSTOCK

Young women could not do better than adopting Lynda Haverstock as their role model. She is highly intelligent, dedicated, is not afraid of hard work, and she has all the social skills that define a strong and capable woman.

Lynda was a teenage mother who had left school and raised her child. She later finished school and then went on to university, where eventually she earned her doctorate in psychology. This is a measure of the lady, when you consider that she left high school to have her child and then returned to finish high school and go on to university to earn several degrees, a doctorate, and three honorary degrees from the University of Regina, Royal Roads University (in Victoria), and Queen's University (in Kingston).

It should be noted that one of Lynda Haverstock's good deeds was to use her psychology qualifications to develop a program for farm families in crisis. This was an absolute necessity at the time and it's the type of program that is useful when the cyclical ups and downs in agriculture demand it.

Lynda was the first woman to be named the leader of a political party (Liberal) in Saskatchewan. She was a conscientious leader who could give and take in debate. She was a guest on my program several times and I used to chide her particularly when she raised her intention to make certain that members sitting in her caucus would be squeaky-clean and make a commitment to behave and stay out of trouble. The old cynic in me argued that commitment would only last until some bozo member would do or say something politically stupid. Treating me like a vampire, she would make a cross out of her two forefingers, but smile while she did so.

Lynda Haverstock's finest hour was when she became Saskatchewan's nineteenth Lieutenant Governor. In her typical way, she got up early and worked late. If she turned down a request, it was only because it was impossible for her to fulfill it. Lynda went up and down the province making friends for herself and the office she held.

Without getting into specifics, there have been times in the past where she wasn't treated fairly or in a considerate way by some people. Regardless, Lynda didn't whine about it.

Lynda is married to Harley Olson, a former CEO and Deputy Minister, and between them they have several children and grandchildren. One has multiple sclerosis; predictably, Lynda works in aiding the search for a cure.

WILLY COLE

I have worked with all kinds of people in my half-century in broadcasting, but none who worked as hard as my friend Willy Cole, Program Director and early morning announcer for CKRM radio Regina.

Willy Cole hails from Selkirk, Manitoba, which is located just north of Winnipeg. He played junior hockey in Manitoba with considerable skill. No one knows the trouble he has seen as a fan of the Toronto Maple Leafs!

Willy Cole's radio career has taken him to CFCN Calgary, Portage la Prairie radio, and CKRM. His day would start very early, with him bright and cheerful on his breakfast show. Very often twelve hours later he would still be around the radio station tending to his duties as program director. Weekends would see him working, on remotes Saturday and even on Sundays as well, when he should have been at home resting. Many Saturdays, Willy would also be out with his dance band; he played for many years before he retired his accordion.

With the Saskatchewan Roughriders and Regina Pats hockey club being official parts of CKRM sports coverage, Willy also patrolled the sidelines as master of ceremonies or just being involved in the promotion of the day or week.

When Willy took over the Program Director role at CKRM, the station's audience totals were not very plentiful, but with the right mix of country music (in which he was an expert) and public service, news, sports, and various promotions, the station grew in audience numbers and stature in the Saskatchewan listening community.

His stamina is really something. Despite his workload, Willy Cole has always been upbeat with a great sense of humour. Willy and I took our microphones to the 1989 Grey Cup in Toronto. We were up before dawn and broadcast throughout the day from the Harbour Castle Hotel until it was time to go to the game. We first went to a booth right next to us in the hotel and bought two caps on which we had printed "Saskatchewan Roughriders, 1989 Grey Cup Champions." How is that for faith in your team? We tucked the caps into our haversacks and headed for the game.

When Willy retired from broadcasting a few years ago they held a farewell for him in the Casino Regina Show Lounge. The place was packed. The people wanted to say thanks to a good family man and a fine broadcaster:

DAVID JOHNSTON

This name will immediately be recognized as that of the twenty-eighth Governor General of Canada. If you watch him closely, you will soon note that the man is a warm human being. He appears to enjoy his contact with people.

Shortly after he began his term as Governor General, he and Mrs. Johnston paid a visit to Regina, where he participated in a few activities, including a visit to the Saskatchewan War Memorial on the legislative grounds. I participated in the establishment of that memorial and so I was on hand when the Governor General visited it. I was wearing my Legion blazer and waited while he came down and met some of my associates. When he reached me, I told him that I called him the "smiling" Governor General. Smiling, he took my hand in both of his and asked why. I replied that he was always smiling when he was out in public. Sharon, his delightful wife, quickly chimed in that if he stops smiling, she always pokes him in the ribs.

When his Excellency's term in office was extended by two years, I felt I should write to him and tell him how pleased I—and I'm certain many Canadians—was that his time in office had been extended. He made a copy of my letter and then, with pen in hand, thanked me on that copy and said some other kind things.

Governor General Johnston came to his office with an extensive background in law and higher learning. He attended Queen's, Cambridge, and Harvard, where he was a hockey star. Johnston taught law at Queen's, the University of Toronto, the University of Western Ontario, and McGill. Johnston was later appointed President of the University of Waterloo.

His Excellency authored or co-authored twenty-four books and also served as a director of several public companies. He has received honorary doctorates from twenty universities plus the Order of Canada.

The Johnstons have five daughters and twelve grandchildren. Mrs. Johnston has a doctorate in rehabilitation science. On the domestic side, she made certain that all her daughters became fluent in French; they also went on to learn several other languages.

ROGER MILLER

He wrote and recorded such songs as "King of the Road," "Dang Me," "England Swings," "The Last Word in Lonesome is Me," and "Engine, Engine Number Nine." Miller was interested in writing songs but he didn't know how to play an instrument. He stole a guitar but turned himself in the next day. The police didn't charge him because Roger said he was joining the army. Later, he said his education was "Korea. Clash of '52." He admitted that he didn't do too well in school because he even "flunked school bus." Unknown at the time was that he was a genius.

Eventually, he learned to play guitar and fiddle. I first met Roger Miller when I was MC at a show starring Faron Young. Earlier, Roger was out of work when Ray Price released him as a member of his group. Young asked him if he was a drummer. Roger said, "No, when do you need one?" Young replied, "Next Monday." Miller quickly answered, "Next Monday I'll be a drummer." He was hired.

Either with Price or Young, Roger Miller was a backstage clown who could take the most common item or situation and make a hilarious observation or analysis; this trait later earned him the title of "Cracker Barrel Philosopher" and placed him on the cover of the *Saturday Evening Post*. Some in Nashville observed that Roger probably had the most talent in Music City and was the most undisciplined.

I asked Roger to record some promotional spots for programs on the radio station I was working for at the time. He took the scripts and modified the words in a way that was hilarious—but you couldn't put them on the air because you would lose your license in a flash.

Roger wrote clever novelty numbers such as "My Uncle Used to Love Me But She Died" as well as honky-tonk numbers like "Invitation to the Blues," recorded by Ray Price, and "Billy Bayou," which Jim Reeves performed to number one on the hit charts. He wrote the words to "Dang Me" in four minutes. "King of the Road" took six weeks. Miller was travelling in the Chicago area when he saw a sign that read: "Trailers for Sale or Rent," which he thought could be the opening lyrics for a song. Some days later he noticed a hobo in an airport gift shop and that prompted a song that hit the top of the country and pop charts.

I was sitting in with Ralph Emery during his all-night record show on WSM in Nashville on August 26, 1960, when Roger Miller came into the studio with his first hot-off-the-press RCA recording of "In the Summertime." The song wasn't a great hit and RCA dropped Miller three years later. Roger didn't have much difficulty signing with another record label. He said it took twenty years to become an "overnight success."

For a time, Roger had his own show on NBC. He guested on *The Tonight Show*. He wrote a Broadway musical based on the story of Huckleberry Finn, which earned him seven Tonys.

Roger Miller died of lung cancer in 1993. He was just fifty-six years old.

D-DAY

In June of 1989, the Department of Veterans Affairs invited me to join a delegation of veterans in Normandy for the forty-fifth anniversary of D-day. It was a working trip for me because I sent back reports for my station (CKRM) and a network of radio stations across Canada.

I had always felt that I was in tune with the military and remembrance because my father served in the army in World War II and returned safely, along with two uncles who were in the tank corps, an uncle in the navy, and an aunt in the air force. I was an enthusiastic army cadet in high school and once considered a military career.

Planting my feet in the sand of Juno Beach, where the Royal Regina Rifles and other Canadian troops came ashore, and standing in front of those rows and rows of grave markers, changed my perspective very quickly. The first grave that I visited was that of Lieutenant Hugh

Walker of Canora Saskatchewan who was part of the First Canadian Parachute Battalion. At the ripe old age of twenty-one, he died leading men in battle. The graves are maintained and kept up beautifully by the Commonwealth War Graves Commission.

The graves were the resting places of soldiers from such places as Ituna, Melville, Yorkton, Balcarres, Regina, Saskatoon, Estevan, and Kamsack, among others.

The soldiers' ages ranged from eighteen to nineteen years, and up. They were farm boys, plumbers, teachers, carpenters, and were involved in a host of other occupations. All of them were heroes.

Charlie Lynch, the Southam newspaper writer, was part of the pilgrimage. He followed the invading allies by about an hour in 1944. He came back many times since then. Lynch made an interesting observation, suggesting that despite the human losses and the cost of war, it was unfortunate that Canadians who were born after the war didn't have the opportunity to join together in a common cause the way those living then did.

I came away having learned several things. I was impressed with the gratitude of the French people, the magnitude of the loss of life, the fact that our veterans were heroes, and that the price of freedom was very high indeed.

As the service was coming to a close at the last cemetery we would visit, we noted a local woman, who came to see what was taking place. The woman told us that she had lost fourteen members of her family in the Second World War. She said that it was her daily practice, since the war, to come to the cemetery, "to pay homage to the young Canadians who came to free my country."

When we visited in 1989, it was still a regular occurrence to find explosives and fully uniformed skeletons in the wheat fields, pastures, and streams in that lovely part of France—which, a long time ago, was the killing fields of World War II.

GRANT TURNER

This is a name that may not be recognized widely but country music fans will recall a cordial gentleman who, for almost half a century, was an announcer on WSM Nashville Tennessee's *Grand Ole Opry*. I met Grant in 1960 while doing a guest shot on WSM's *Mr. Deejay U.S.A.* In fact, I spent a good part of the weekend with Grant.

I hosted an hour-long show on WSM right after a live program known as the *Friday Night Frolics*. Grant operated for me while an engineer behind the glass made certain that the program reached the airwaves in good condition.

Grant Turner was born near Abilene, Texas, in 1912. He first studied journalism and then worked in newspapers before switching to radio. He saw the actual "Father of Country Music," Jimmy Rodgers, perform at a Texas radio station and was immediately smitten by country music and radio broadcasting. Rodgers was known as "The Blue Yodeler" and, because of his first work with trains, "The Singing Brakeman."

On a Saturday afternoon, I guested on Turner's *Opry Warmup* show and then walked with him to the historic Ryman Auditorium where the *Opry* itself was broadcast to some ten million listeners every Saturday via the facilities of clear channel WSM radio. The lasting impression on me was the way Grant conducted himself as he made his way to the big country music show. He was stopped time and again by would-be song writers and would-be singers with lyrics and no doubt many would-be singers who gave Grant a copy of a do-it-yourself recording on labels that I had never seen or heard of.

In true southern gentleman's manner, he would stop and patiently listen to what they had to say and then politely say that he would listen to the recording and have a look at the work of the budding songwriters. This would continue all the way to the steps of the *Opry*.

Later, Grant Turner introduced me from the stage of the Ryman between introducing the various *Opry* stars and reading commercials for such sponsors as Pet Milk. There was a time in the 1940s, 50s, and 60s when NBC's radio network picked up a half hour of the *Opry*, sponsored by the Prince Albert tobacco company, and the announcer of choice was Grant Turner.

On Sunday after church, *Opry* comedian Archie Campbell (who went on to star on television's cornball show *Hee Haw)* picked me up at my hotel and we attended a performance of Teddy and Doyle Wilburn in a Nashville park. Later, I was dropped off by Archie at WSM because Grant had invited me to drop in while he was filling in for the regular program announcer, David Cobb. Was it another country music show, you ask? No. Grant Turner, this time, was hosting a program of classical music. Later, Grant and I went out for a hamburger and I thanked him for his kindness and friendship.

Among his awards, Turner was inducted into the Country Disc Jockey Hall of Fame and I suspect that he was particularly grateful for his induction into the Country Music Hall of Fame in Nashville in 1981. Grant Turner died of cardiac arrest in 1991 at the age of seventy-nine years. He passed away just hours after announcing a Saturday night *Grand Ole Opry*.

KATHRYN CROSBY

She was born Olive Kathryn Grandstaff in Houston, Texas. She shortened her name to Grant when she started making movies. During my years of contact with Bing, Kathryn would answer the telephone at home only rarely. It was usually the butler, Allan Fisher, or Bing himself. I first had an opportunity to shake her hand in person in May of 2003, at Gonzaga University in Spokane, Washington, where I had a part in the weekend program honouring the one hundredth anniversary of the birth of Bing Crosby.

I soon learned that this lady who didn't take up much space was strong and resolute. A shrinking violet she is not! We have stayed in contact ever since. I call her at least a couple of times a year to inquire how she is doing. There is usually a card at Christmas and for the past half-dozen years Kathryn has sent a beautiful custom-made tree ornament that definitely qualifies as an heirloom. The Christmas card is usually a reproduction of one of her paintings.

Kathryn is strongly committed to preserving the memory of Bing, her first husband, and she oversees the various business enterprises and investments that she wants to preserve for her children and grandchildren. It would shock most people to know the length to which con artists and crooks will go to try to plug into what will be a comfortable inheritance for the Crosby "kids" (who are well along in middle age). In her younger years as a wife and mother, Kathryn became both a teacher and a nurse.

Kathryn hosted the Bing Crosby golf tournament for a number of years after his death. She has appeared in dinner theatre and musical reviews and she is in demand for appearances at various functions that relate to Bing. For a while, she hosted a television talk show on KPIX San Francisco and, just prior to the economic downturn in the United States in recent years, Kathryn found a novel way of displaying Bing's memorabilia, in restaurants that would call themselves "Bing Crosby Restaurants." I was invited to attend the official opening of one in Walnut Creek, California. She is a resourceful lady.

In the year 2000, Kathryn married Dr. Maurice Sullivan, whose doctorate was in education. In fact, at one time he was the tutor of the Crosby children. In November of 2010, Kathryn and Dr. Sullivan were in a car crash that took his life. The automobile went out of control, hit a large boulder, and rolled several times. Dr. Sullivan, the eighty-five year old driver, was thrown out of the car and killed. Kathryn was taken to hospital in critical condition, where she was told that she wouldn't ever walk again.

The hospital medical staff may have thought that Kathryn Crosby would never walk again but they obviously didn't know Kathryn. Painfully but courageously, she is walking and taking ballet lessons to improve "muscle tone and strength." The remarkable aspect of all of this is that Kathryn has now reached her eighties. She doesn't set small objectives. Just like the time she led a small group of nuns to the Vatican and told someone in authority that it was long overdue that the Sisters be allowed to wear more comfortable clothing in their work. She is something!

JOHN NEWLOVE

This is the name of one of Canada's most outstanding poets of all time. He was also a childhood friend of mine in the town of Kamsack. In fact, he broke his leg jumping off a coal shed roof in our backyard.

John, who was born in Regina, came to Kamsack from the village of Veregin when we were both in grade six. His father was a lawyer who happened to be an alcoholic and his mother was a teacher. John lived in a number of smaller communities in Saskatchewan because when his father would go on a drinking binge, his mother would separate from him by taking John to another town or village, where she would seek a teaching job.

We all suspected that John Newlove was different. He usually didn't take notes and he didn't have all the text-books. Come examination time, he would cram and get very good marks. His writing in school was exceptional. In fact, it was often brilliant.

John took an unusual interest in the military and was a dedicated army cadet during his school days. He entered the Regular Officer Training Program at the University of Saskatchewan but left it after a year, telling me, "The University of Saskatchewan is the intellectual asshole of North America!" There ended the military interest.

Since poets generally need to have a separate source of income (because their poetry raises only modest amounts of money), John Newlove had many jobs, including teaching school, working as a social worker, a labourer, a radio announcer, a senior editor at McClelland and Stewart, writer-in-residence at Regina Public Library, and such places as the University of Toronto and Concordia University in Montreal.

His work has been published in anthologies in at least eight countries and translated into French, German, and Romanian. John Newlove was, for a time, an editor for the Commissioner of Official languages. His awards included the Governor General's Award in 1972.

In 1968, *Maclean's* magazine said, "We don't publish poetry and the only reason we're making an exception on these two pages is that we think John Newlove is a genuine literary rarity: a poet who speaks plainly about plain themes, in a way that is honest, direct and moving."

John developed his father's problem with "the drink" starting in high school. I led him home after one school dance. The Newloves lived just a block from school; I just opened the back door and pushed him inside and promptly left. In fact, in a newspaper interview shortly before he died, John said that his happy objective each day was to get "pissed." John Newlove died on December 23, 2003. He was sixty-five.

It was a long drop from that coal shed roof.

HENRY HAYNES & KENNETH BURNS

Most people would know these two by their stage names of Homer and Jethro. They recorded satirical versions or parodies of hit songs on the popular and country hit parades. Such gems included the "Battle of Kookamunga" based on Johnny Horton's "Battle of New Orleans" and their album *Fractured Folk Songs*.

Something that many people were unaware of was the fact that they were excellent instrumentalists. Burns (who called himself Jethro) was an accomplished mandolin player and the shorter Haynes (who was known as Homer) played a mean guitar. In fact, they recorded two instrumental albums: *It Ain't Necessarily Square* and *Playing it Straight*.

RCA's A&R man on most of their recordings was Chet Atkins, himself a renowned guitar virtuoso. Atkins was also married to Jethro's sister.

Both launched their careers in Knoxville, Tennessee, in 1936. They did some performing with another musical savage, Spike Jones, and his City Slickers. Along the way Homer and Jethro played on Don McNeil's *Breakfast Club*, Chicago's *WLS Barn Dance*, had guest shots on programs such as the *Grand Ole Opry*, and did some touring in the United States and Canada. They first recorded on King Records but they were long-time performers for RCA Victor Records.

Burns and Haynes served in the U.S. Army in World War II. They served in separate army units but united again as a team after the war. They made several appearances on Johnny Carson's *The Tonight Show* because Carson, who was quick on the retort himself, liked the quick comebacks from the two comics. Their various forms of recognition included a Grammy Award.

It was interesting that even though Homer and Jethro played hayseeds they never dressed as such. It was tailored suits and not bib overalls. Homer also liked to chew gum as he sang or spoke.

Homer (Haynes) died suddenly in 1971. Jethro (Burns) took his partner's death quite hard. He didn't do much work for awhile but returned to active duty and played some jazz festivals for a time. He died in 1989.

Homer and Jethro were inducted into the Country Music Hall of Fame in Nashville, Tennessee, in 2001.

BILL CAMERON

He was the first real news director I met and worked for. The people who have that title are the ones who run the newsrooms in radio and television. Much of what they do in electronic media is the same as in print media, in terms of searching for information and reporting, but the disciplines are very different because one has to do with space while the other is conscious of time.

Bill worked in the newsroom at CFQC Saskatoon under a very tough taskmaster named Godfrey Hudson. There were long hours and some very tough rules. While some wondered why the rules needed to be so tough, the CFQC newsroom was winning awards for broadcast journalism. The point that needs to be made is that the awards were coming from American sources. Unlike today, there was little or nothing in the way of news awards in Canada. Certainly not in broadcast journalism.

As examples of rules, Bill Cameron's rule was that no lead sentence in a news story should be longer than twenty words and no other sentence longer than thirty words. He counted them. You would receive a memo reading: "Lead sentence in second story in the 7:45 a.m. newscast is twenty-one words long. Close but not close enough." All of this, of course, is about discipline, because broadcast time is limited when you write and report. Bill didn't want you to quote from a newspaper or magazine because "we are the fastest news medium in the world and shouldn't be quoting the slower print medium." It was acceptable to say the story was from a "news source." Cameron didn't like to use jargon or technical terms. You used simple words that everyone understood. Teletype copy had to be edited, particularly the British United Press wire (which was a newswire written in newspaper style), but even the Broadcast News newswire (which was written more in broadcast style).

Bill Cameron and Assistant News Director Ian Bickle (a former colleague of mine) wrote beautifully for any type of news medium. It was a talent that you couldn't help admiring. Both wrote for broadcast and print; they were a pleasure to read or hear.

Bill went to work as Government Information Director when the Ross Thatcher government was first elected in 1964. Bill Cameron and Jim Moore took me to lunch one day and offered me the Cabinet Press Secretary job. I thanked them but told them I was happy where I was, as Radio News Editor at CKCK Radio.

From government service, Bill Cameron went to work for CBC Saskatchewan in their newsroom. He died long before his time. We lost an ethical, dedicated, and very professional journalist in our province. I think I still have some of his memos. It was quite an education.

SORRY, WRONG NUMBER

I usually answered calls to my program, whether local or long distance, myself. I needed help from the main control room when the volume of calls was so great that we risked losing them while waiting for the next commercial break. The program operator would take the call, tell the caller what line they were on, and then put them on hold. Some callers would get tired of waiting and would hang up.

One day when I was fielding calls I took a call directly and put it on hold. When the turn came up for that call, I asked the person where he was calling from. He replied, "Calgary." I asked, "What's on your mind this morning?" He then proceeded to talk about something that didn't make sense to me. I asked him to tell me who he was calling. He gave me an answer that confirmed for me that this was a wrong number. I asked him if he had any idea whose number he reached. His answer was that he had no idea. I told him he had reached an open line radio show in Regina and for the last number of minutes he was actually on the air for a station that covered the province and spilled over into Manitoba, Alberta, North Dakota, and Montana. There was a pause for a number of seconds and then he said, "Oh gawd!" He quickly hung up and we returned to those who knew what we were doing and wished to comment. Can you imagine him trying to tell the people in his office or his wife where his morning telephone call took him?

ANITA BRYANT

She was an attractive pop singer who at one time was crowned Miss Oklahoma. She is probably remembered as one who stridently opposed gay rights. I interviewed her in later 1978 and our callers supported her unanimously. My audience at that time was reticent and shy about talking about most things sexual but any reference to homosexuals and lesbians was certain to bring hysterical demands for my head. Around the same time, a Winnipeg Unitarian Minister married two men; if some of my listeners could have reached him they would have hanged him on the spot.

"Paper Roses" was probably Anita Bryant's best-remembered hit. She recorded some forty hits, which made it to various places on the pop charts. She was selected as a spokesperson for the Florida orange juice producers and one of her assignments was to sing the "Battle Hymn of the Republic" at the graveside service of President Lyndon Johnson.

Anita Bryant's world started to come unraveled when she strongly and very publicly opposed a government bill that opposed discrimination on the basis of sexual orientation. She had not felt much opposition when my office invited her to share her views with my audience. Bryant immediately accepted any opportunity to express her views publicly.

It should also be noted that she opposed divorce until she had one of her own. This added to the problems beginning to mount over her views about homosexuality. The Florida orange juice people dropped her as a spokesperson and evangelical groups stopped subscribing to her ministries. Some bars stopped serving screwdrivers (which included vodka and orange juice). Instead, some offered a drink called "the Anita Bryant" (a rather uninviting mixture of vodka and apple juice). Some radio stations stopped playing her records. It should be noted that homosexuals themselves were concerned at the time about keeping their identities a secret because they feared for their jobs and were afraid that they might be persecuted.

I understand that Bryant now lives in Oklahoma, where she, with a second husband, has toned down her fundamentalist views on life. There is no question that her public posture cost her money and peace of mind.

MAYOR HENRY BAKER

This was a politician from head to toe. It was not easy covering him. His actions included steps toward being re-elected. He almost always would play to the gallery during Council meetings. During estimate time, he would vote for more and enhanced services and when the time came to set the tax rate to pay for all those goodies, he could be counted on to vote against it. I know because I was there.

For a good part of the time that he was mayor, councillors belonged to slates, which operated like political parties. The CVA (Civic Voters Association) was the avowed opponent to Baker. Baker himself ran on the RCA (Regina Citizens Association) ticket. The RCA was composed of some New Democrats and Liberals. The CVA tended to appeal to some Liberals and Conservatives.

Henry was an interesting study politically. I am told that Ross Thatcher tried to entice Henry into running with the Liberals in Regina in 1964. According to the cloak and dagger story, they were to meet in a secret place and discuss how badly Thatcher wanted Henry. Henry didn't show up for the meeting so he ran for the NDP and won his seat.

Holding two jobs, that of mayor and member of the legislature, began a major discussion in the city about Henry's ability to do justice to either office. He, of course, argued that being in the legislature gave him an inside advantage in pursuing the needs of his city. His opponents tried to unseat him but just never succeeded. I guess you could say that he was moonlighting with a cheque and pension as an MLA in addition to his mayor's salary.

We learned later that Henry Baker didn't attend his CCF caucus meetings and generally didn't subscribe to anything approaching solidarity or caucus discipline. He was a lone wolf. One graphic example involved the Homeowner Grant, which the Thatcher government introduced. On a particular afternoon, the official Opposition CCF was laying on the heavy artillery, with the Homeowner Grant locked firmly in their sights. They argued that it wasn't equitable and that it was highly political. Imagine, a government accused of doing something political.

Then it was Henry Baker's turn to get up and speak. I can hear him now. He said, "Now, about that Homeowner Grant; it was my idea and I should be credited for the idea. It should be increased." Right there and then, Opposition Leader Woodrow Lloyd turned his chair to face Baker with a look of absolute incredulity on his face. Here was the Opposition laying on the licks and here was one of its own members breaking with caucus solidarity.

During my years covering City Hall, I had a modest little television show called *City Hall Beat*. Whenever Henry was my guest, prior to the start of recording the Mayor would talk continually to the cameramen, asking them "to make me look good." He had this idea that the floor crew could actually improve the appearance of the guest. I found out later that he was very sensitive about his profile being shown. I don't know what the hang-up was.

The other thing that Henry Baker wanted was to have the entire program played back for him in the control room. On one occasion, he watched what we had recorded to the end, thanked us, and left. About four hours later I was stretched out on my chesterfield at home when the phone rang. It was Henry. He said, "That program was no good for me. The cameramen shot my profile throughout." I guess he left the television station and reached a boiling point over that time and called me. It took a while, but I got him to cool down. Henry was not above calling management if a reporter wrote or broadcast something he didn't like. At times, he would call me. I particularly remember one time when he called and threatened me. He said, if you can imagine, "I made you and I will undo you!" I thought it was hilarious and said so. I guess he liked being the mayor of Regina and anything that might threaten that needed to be dealt with.

As mayor, Henry Baker was everywhere: funerals, anniversaries, and grand openings. You name it and he was there. Strangely, when he was defeated a couple of times, he would disappear like a phantom until the next election, and then you saw him about town again.

Henry handed out cuff links for men and brooches for ladies. He handed them out by the bushel. In fact, he gave me a pair of cuff links with the city crest when I was leaving CKCK. I still have them and wear them at times.

Henry Baker was an ideal public relations man but he also fancied himself an administrator, economist, engineer, and what-have-you. The problem was that he would inject himself into all areas of operation. He favored the co-commissioner system, which gives the mayor and top administrator equal power. The city manager system gives more power to the manager; Henry opposed it. Somewhere, the mayor needs more power than a councillor. He needs to do more than just chair council meetings. I think the public expects that.

The impressive Council Chamber at City Hall is named after Baker and so is a scholarship.

HAIR

The rebellious 1960s provided interesting times in so many areas. LSD, love-ins, flower power, Vietnam. All of it was a bit frightening for the older generation, who wondered if societal chaos was just around the corner.

Entertainment included some of the new way of doing things. In particular, I remember a musical titled *Hair* that included, wonder of wonders, a nude scene. Earlier in the show there was a brief exchange between cast members, in which one asked the other, "Who is your hero?" with the other replying, "Lorne Harasen!" Needless to say, the theatre audience enjoyed it. I guess as the show went from town to town they would ask for the name or names of local controversial residents. It was a clever little item.

Now, the much-heralded nude scene in *Hair* saw the curtain open. There was the cast, set up in a human pyramid, totally nude. You got a look at them for a few seconds and the curtain closed. It was entirely harmless.

In my review on television the next night, I said I went home after the show, went to my bedroom, took off all my clothes, and stood in front of a mirror and said there is no way that is worth ten dollars!

There was another listener complaint that also related to nudity. This was an opening for a television show known as *Here Come the Seventies*. It opened with a nude young woman with a nice figure, her back to the viewer, walking into a lake. She walked until she disappeared under the water.

There were some lady callers who were not happy with such a display. I would usually tease them or play straight man. I told one woman that when the program came on, I would run to the back of my television set to see if I could get a look at the woman walking toward me!

JIM MCLEOD

Jim was, for many years, a peerless newscaster on CKCK Radio and Television. His authoritative voice, his delivery, his pronunciation, and his good English were all a part of his broadcast approach. In addition, whether on radio or television, Jim came to work dressed like the professional he was. Bow tie, suit or jacket, slacks, a neatly trimmed mustache, shoes shined, and everything about him ship-shape!

For many years, his cohorts in the newsroom would try to see if they could divert his attention while he was on the air and cause him to break up or laugh. There was no way! It's an old game in broadcasting. There was only one memorable such time for Jim.

Jim would edit out any copy that contained slang or even moderate profanity. If he didn't have time to read over some copy before going on the air, he developed the capability that some of us had of being able to actually look ahead a couple of lines while verbalizing the earlier words. During an election campaign, a politician observed that he had discovered a "chink in the armour" of an opponent. Now, the *Funk and Wagnalls* dictionary reveals three definitions for the word "chink." One of them is a small crack or crevice and another is an offensive way to refer to Chinese. Jim, ever the gentleman, was editing as he went. He reported that the politician had found "a Chinaman in the armour" of the opponent. Jim immediately realized what he had done and laughed so hard he couldn't finish the newscast. In fact, he would laugh about it just telling the story many years later.

Jim McLeod was offered the national newscaster's job when the CTV Network first went on the air. Among his reasons for not accepting was declining health. Listeners or viewers were not aware that he was in almost constant pain, due to an arthritic spine, and also from the side effects from medication he was taking. There were days when I wondered how he could work.

During his years at CKCK Radio, Jim hosted a science program and another show where he reported on stories from provincial weekly newspapers. He also hosted a Saturday morning musical show for a time called *Hello Saskatchewan.*

Jim McLeod didn't believe in God. He didn't push that with everyone around him; it was simply his opinion and that was that. I understand that he once hustled a minister of religion from his hospital room.

I visited Jim in his home a short time before his very untimely death. One of his hobbies was photography. He took close-up shots of flowers. Though very ill, he developed some beautiful enlarged pictures in his home lab, which he gave to me and which I shared with my friend, CKCK Program Director Doug Alexander.

I don't know if they make broadcasters like Jim McLeod anymore. Pity!

THE PREMIERS, ERNEST MANNING, ALBERTA, JOHN ROBARTS, ONTARIO, ALEX CAMPBELL, PRINCE EDWARD ISLAND & ROSS THATCHER, SASKATCHEWAN

Did I have them all on the program at once? Yes indeed and it was one of the most pressure packed episodes in my working life. Not the Premiers themselves but the circumstances surrounding that program.

They were all in attendance at the 1968 Canadian Premiers Conference in Prince Albert National Park. At the beginning of the meeting I asked a member of Premier Thatchers staff (who shall remain nameless) to set up two or three Premiers that I could interview for my Thursday program which was 25 minutes long at the time. He assured me that it would happen.

The evening before I contacted the Thatcher aide to learn who he booked only to be told that he didn't have time to book anyone. Wonderful! Now what do I do? The reality was that I had to make it happen myself. Their meetings were closed to media.

We only had a news conference at the end of each day.

I knew that the Premiers had breakfast in the dining room of a small hotel in the Park. I got permission from the hotel management to remove the bed and furnishings from a room at the top of a flight of stairs. I then set up a table and the microphones and recording equipment. As the Premiers came in I asked if they would climb the stairs to my "studio" after they finished breakfast. Premier Manning said he would and so did the Premiers, Robarts, Thatcher and Campbell. Campbell was a straggler and so I asked him to come up to the room where I would have already started the program. This he did.

After about 25 minutes the ever impatient Premier Thatcher started to shuffle his feet which told me that they (he) needed to leave for their meeting.

I thought that I had solved all my problems but a new nail-biter presented itself. As I was feeding my interview down a broadcast line it suddenly lost contact with the radio station and we didn't have time to spare. Suddenly after some anxious moments we regained contact. The receiving end had time to rewind the tape and get it to the main control room with about a minute to spare to airtime.

For the sake of your health you don't want many days like that.

THE RHYTHM PALS

For decades Mike Ferbey, Marc Wald and Jack Jensen entertained Canadians on radio, television, recordings, exhibition grandstands, night clubs, stock shows and you name it. Their close harmonies with songs from just about every genre made them popular performers. Mike and Marc were originally from Saskatchewan and Jack was a British Columbian.

The Pals were probably best known from their Tommy Hunter Network television shows. When CBC dropped the Rhythm Pals from the show they were keenly disappointed and felt that Tommy should have spoken up for them.

I took time on my CKRM morning show to salute one of their entertainment milestones when Mike, Marc and Jack were in town for some shows. Included were telephone calls of congratulations from such people as Tommy Hunter, Juliette and Al Cherney.

Mike and Jack retired ahead of Marc who soldiered on as a single until 1987. Mike Ferbey died in 2003 while Marc Wald and Jack Jensen died within months of each other in 2012.

SID BUCKWOLD

The former Mayor of Saskatoon and Senator was a gentleman in the best sense of that word. Sid would take comical swipes at Regina but it was never nasty. He was an ethical businessman and people who worked for him had nothing but good to say about him as a boss.

Many people felt that it was unfortunate that Sid Buckwold, a Liberal, wasn't elected to higher office in senior government.

Sid happened to be in Regina just days before the Liberal leadership convention in 1968. I was going to be covering the convention and I knew Sid was going as a voting delegate. I knew him well enough to ask him who he was going to vote for from that lengthy list of leadership hopefuls. Without hesitation he told me that he was going to vote for Mitchell Sharp on the first ballot because he liked him and felt that he was competent but felt that Sharp would not win the leadership. Buckwold's next choice was Pierre Elliott Trudeau.

History records that on the day before the start of the convention Mitchell Sharp pulled out of the leadership race and said that he would be supporting Trudeau. Obviously now Sid Buckwold was voting Trudeau.

On the flight to Ottawa there was a stopover in Toronto. As we were walking into the terminal there was a newspaper stand and the headline on the paper read that Mitchell Sharp quit the leadership derby and was throwing his support behind P.E. Trudeau. Cliff McIsaac, a member of the Thatcher cabinet, looked at the headline and grumbled "We better get there and vote for a Liberal!" I don't know if he realized I was walking right behind him.

After we got to Ottawa I checked into my hotel which I would swear was somewhere on Baffin Island. A late booking on my part. In fact I was told by the hotel that I would have to share the room with someone because hotel space was limited. He never showed up but the hotel made me pay for him. Can you believe it!

Once checked in I then went to the convention site to check things out. I was sharing a booth with our Ottawa Bureau Chief the old war horse, Sam Ross. We were right on top of the Hellyer and Winters sections which would prove to be an interesting location later on.

Suddenly I noticed Sid Buckwold taking the stairs up to my location. There was a look of exasperation on his face. He told me that he wanted to make a statement. In it he said that he was ashamed that people calling themselves Liberals were calling Trudeau a communist, a coward who didn't fight for Canada in World War Two and worse.

I thought his reaction spoke volumes about Sid Buckwold the good man. I wrote my story and sent it back to Saskatchewan. Sid went on to see his man win regardless of dirty campaigning against him.

Sid once wrote to me and said the Harasen line was "the most responsible open line I know." I kept the letter.

I should note that the names I have dropped here are only a small representation of the total number. There were countless others, such as the Hispanic girl who came to the program to ask that people boycott California grapes while the workers tried to get a living wage. The reception she got from some caused her to weep on the air. Michael Meeropol, his name changed for his protection, was the son of Julius and Ethel Rosenberg. Meeropol, as a small boy, saw his parents go to the electric chair for passing American secrets to the Soviet Union. There was Ma Murray, a B.C. small-town weekly newspaperwoman who suddenly developed a hearing problem if you asked her a question she didn't want to answer. They all either made me laugh, feel sorry for them, admire them, or loathe them; there were many who gave my spirits a lift.

We didn't have names to drop every day. On those days I carried the conversation myself, stimulated by a topic. Some days I expressed an opinion and had to defend it. Other times I would carefully avoid expressing an opinion and still had callers who said they agreed with me. You see, merely raising a topic meant, for some, that I was in favour!

Wayne and Shuster

Governor General David Johnston

Don Cherry, son Paul and Butkus the dog

Pierre Trudeau at Miller High School

Kathryn Crosby

Roughrider Ray Elgaard

Lorne: Boy Announcer

Tony Peña — St. Louis Cardinals

Jim Reeves

Arthur Fiedler, Boston Pops

The Chief and son Greg

Patsy Cline

Premier Ross Thatcher (middle)

Guy Lafleur and Steve Shutt

Roger Whittaker

Fly-in Fishing

We've been married for almost 60 years

Gordie and Colleen Howe and Bobby Hull

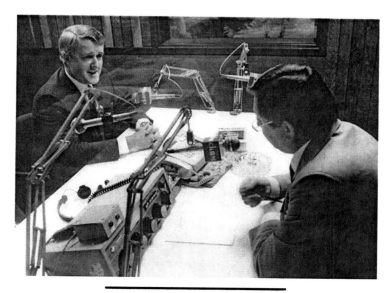

Prime Minister Brian Mulroney

Young Johnny Cash and Young Lorne

John Candy and son Paul

Glenn Dobbs- Roughrider Legend

Prime Minister Kim Campbell

Jazz great Oscar Peterson

Pierre Berton

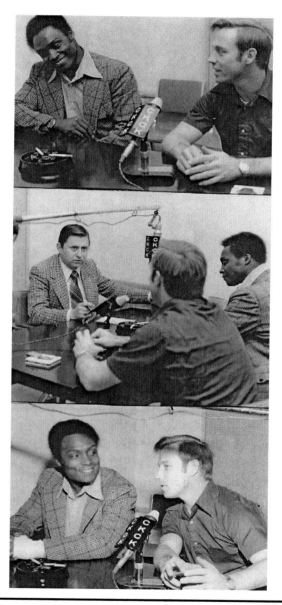

Ron Lancaster and George Reed guest on the Harasen Line

INTERVIEWS

RENÉ LÉVESQUE

The first thing that struck me when I was introduced to René Lévesque was his height! He stood five feet three inches. There must be a psychological lesson in that. Perhaps his great ability as a television communicator made him seem larger than life. (I think I must have experienced the same feeling in the other direction when I first met Pierre Berton and found him to be a giant of a man, well over six feet.)

The Quebec separatist had a very appealing manner about him. It isn't hard to understand his success in achieving power in that province. Lévesque related to people very easily and instantly made you feel comfortable. While he was far from simple, there wasn't anything complicated about him. In print, his words would ignite. Yet in conversation, most things he said sounded eminently reasonable. At times, that smirk or shrug made him come off like a bit of a smart-ass, but a pleasant little smart-ass!

Lévesque was a restless chain smoker and most times he looked like he could use another five or six hours of sleep. I thought he was a candidate for a physical breakdown but I suspect his mission kept him going.

I interviewed him twice, once by telephone and once in person in my studio. This interview was featured on *The Harasen Line* on May 15, 1968. Pierre Elliott Trudeau had just been elected leader of the Liberal Party and had called his first election. It was also more than two years before the October Crisis of 1970. Lévesque was still nowhere in terms of clout or power, but the things he said at that time make for interesting reflection. Then, as now, I fear that ignorance and intransigence, and their product, bigotry, made Lévesque and his mission more successful than it needed to be.

May 15, 1968

Harasen: If I may come to the point to begin with, the kind of support and the kind of things that are happening in Quebec, and particularly the support that has been rallying around you, truthfully scares the hell out of people like myself. Is there a reason for me to feel that way?

Lévesque: I don't think so, except if you're kind of naturally afraid of change, because a lot of people, mostly older people, but sometimes not so old, are afraid of change even if changes are required. They're scared, so in a case of a person like that, yes, because we think, we deeply believe, I think there is support rallying, and I'm not exaggerating. I don't mean we're a majority right now but eventually we hope to be, and there is support rallying around a position which is mine and putting an end as far as Quebec is concerned, to the hundred-year-old federal system, but that's not necessarily the end of the world.

Harasen: Well, I think I'm anything but afraid of change, but I'm a little dubious about the possible loss of Quebec to Canada or vice-versa.

Lévesque: Well, I mean, what kind of loss? Supposing we have a different political system and we still live side by side in the same...after all, I don't go to...you're calling from Regina, I think? I want to make sure about that; you didn't give me much time to prepare. I don't go to Regina very often and you don't, I suppose, come to Quebec or Montreal very often, but we can still exchange, we can still be, in fact in many ways, much better friends than...we're proposing also and we hope that it eventually can be accepted, better partners in a free relationship, than in something which quite a few in Quebec and even outside Quebec, an arrangement that many are fed up with. You know, supposing you have something which is one hundred years old, one hundred and one now, Confederation, it isn't because it's old that it's bad, but it isn't because it's old that it's a sacred cow either. Whether you...you know...you agree on amendments...after all, nothing is eternal...or want to get a new deal completely, that doesn't have to breed hostility or scare or things like that, if it's done democratically.

Harasen: What sort of sovereignty do you visualize for Quebec, Mr. Lévesque?

Lévesque: Well, in the full sense of the word sovereignty, in other words, that Quebec decide on its own priorities, decide on how it should spend its own tax money. By the way, sovereignty for Quebec would mean for a lot of westerners that I heard complaining in the last few years, that they'd stop paying equalization payment to Quebec and a few other things. So in some ways you'd be rid of the problem of Quebec. On the other hand, we'd still be neighbors side by side, exchanging...everybody buys and sells, you know...to and from each other. And in many ways, you'd be rid also of all this B and B problem, which I think is also a pain in the neck to many people.

Harasen: I know that some of these questions that I'm asking may be mundane to you and may have been asked of you many, many times.

Lévesque: No, but I'm trying to deal with them as quickly and honestly as I can.

Harasen: One of the concerns that is expressed frequently, and I notice that last weekend, a labour leader differed with the view, but there has always been doubt expressed about the economic viability of a separate Quebec.

Lévesque: Well, I've got no doubts myself because I've worked with economists for six years in government and I have great respect for economists, but I know darn well, you put five of them in the same room with the same question, you'll get five answers. You know, economists have a problem and most experts have one too. Anything they can calculate, in other words, any column of figures they can slap you with, they'll give you, and usually in a pessimistic way. But they always forget one thing, which is that when a population, just the same as a man, has drive and ambition, that's a factor you can't put in figures and it changes the whole calculation. In other words, if Quebec should have to start alone, which we were not proposing, you have to read the details of our position to know that. But if Quebec should start completely alone, it would also start as well equipped as any country that started off in the twentieth century, that's for sure, any small country, and with a resource base, and now our education is being revamped. We have good relationships normally with our next-door neighbor, the United States, and the same in Europe, with or without General DeGaulle, and, except if we argue that Quebecers are more stupid than anybody else in the world, which I won't buy, there's no reason why economically as otherwise we can't make a go of it. But our proposal is that we find some arrangement with the rest of Canada, if the rest of Canada wants to go on, so that we have a more intimate relationship economically, to mutual advantage if we so desire, on both sides.

Harasen: What form of government do you visualize?

Lévesque: Form of government?

Harasen: Yeah.

Lévesque: Well, we're not up to that yet, we're still rallying support. We had a sort of preliminary platform which was voted, you know, the end of April. And this just puts the question, either a reorganized parliamentary system, in other words, something a little less broken up in nineteenth century pieces that the present departments, or possibly some sort of presidential system, you know, along the American lines, but it's still a question mark to our members.

Harasen: You mentioned something about having a modest army and a control of media. What did you mean by that, first of all the army, secondly media?

Lévesque: Well, first of all, let's get rid of the army, okay? Modest army—I think that was mostly very quick news reports. What we voted on was to get out, if Quebec becomes sovereign, to get out of all military entanglements like NORAD, which we were sold a bill of goods on while they were getting excited about Trudeau. They signed for another five years, no discussion, and no debate, probably something like two hundred million dollars a year for something which is as dead as a dodo! So this kind of thing we think we should put a stop to if we ever get our Quebec self-determination. No NORAD and no military NATO! Some Atlantic community might come up, but let's stop wasting resources that are needed for real priorities, on keeping up with the Joneses, which is practically all we're doing with those twenty- or twenty-five-year-old arrangements. A modest army would remain in the sense that at least during a transition period we have a few thousand guys from Quebec who are in the Van Doos, and a few other units, plus a few very marginal industries that shouldn't be closed down, so you have to maintain that until you find out what your position would be. As far as media, you know the control of media. Is that what your question was?

Harasen: Yes, that's right.

Lévesque: Well, this is, I think, I'm sorry to say, but bad reporting if it was put that way. What we tried to describe was something more or less along the lines of CBC or, even better, BBC. In other words, the control of media, which means the airwaves especially, are a public property and should be better watched and organized than they are now with the Board of Broadcast Governors and all the hassle you've had for the last ten years with the two Fowler reports and Judy LaMarsh and a lot of other nincompoops playing around with it, not counting Pickersgill. But it doesn't mean government control. It means a set-up where airwaves are free as far as opinions and information is concerned but where you don't build a racket on the exploitation of airwaves, as we've seen too often in Canada.

Harasen: Well, as a former journalist and as a broadcaster, I can understand and I think you know what the situation is, and I think that perhaps you might appreciate the position of the media, but I wonder about a bureaucrat having something to say about this.

Lévesque: No, that doesn't mean bureaucratic control. It means something like this. The *Montreal Star*, you know, the paper in Montreal which you probably heard is not exactly radical or socialist! A couple of years ago, talking about that, and I kept that editorial very carefully, said one thing and I quote just about, at least substantially, what they said, and that's a conservative paper basically—that the only businessmen who can tear up their contracts and go back on their word have been the broadcasters, especially, who have permits that are renewed, as you know, full of regulations that were never respected and in many cases were practically torn the moment they were signed on. In other words, they give their word they are going to respect the public and then the only thing they are interested in is to make as much money as possible every second of the time they can sell. Things like that—when you have regulations, they should be respected.

Harasen: Let me ask you for, in a word or two or even a sentence, for each of these gentlemen which I shall name, your view of their assessment of the Quebec, if I may call it, Quebec situation. First of all, John Diefenbaker.

Lévesque: Well, Mr. Diefenbaker...you mean as far as Quebec is concerned?

Harasen: His understanding of the situation.

Lévesque: Well, I don't think he understands Quebec very much. But I can't blame him because he came into public life, especially as a Prime Minister, rather late in life, from a western background, and I think it won't be a surprise to you or any of your listeners in the West if I tell you that I don't know very much about the West. You're far away and vice versa. Anytime I go out west I find great misinformation or non-information about Quebec and that may be unfortunate but it's a fact, and I think Mr. Diefenbaker reflected that a bit.

Harasen: How about Lester Pearson?

Lévesque: Well, Mr. Pearson was closer, I think, to some understanding, because, well, first of all, he had a long career in Ottawa and that's just about next door to Quebec. That should have helped him, and apart from that, I think the Liberal party, through no great merit, was always stronger in Quebec, as you know, than the Conservatives... you know, during the last fifty years, so that gave them at least a chance to find out from their own caucus. The use they made of their knowledge, I don't want to comment on, because I might be bitter.

Harasen: How about Pierre Trudeau?

Lévesque: Well, Trudeau is a different case. I don't know. What do you think of Trudeau?

Harasen: Very interesting!

Lévesque: That's for sure!

Harasen: Incidentally, he said not too long ago that you have started insulting people. You haven't insulted me on this program.

Lévesque: If Trudeau said that, he was a bit nervous. I suppose that was before he became leader.

Harasen: Yes, as a matter of fact, just before.

Lévesque: No, I don't think I've...well, it can happen, you know, it's always relative that you say something about someone, he feels insulted. On that basis I should feel insulted about twenty times a day, but life is too short! I don't feel I've insulted persons. Trudeau, as far as I'm concerned, I know him from way back. I'm not a close friend of his but we had occasion to work together. He's a very competent intellectual. He's very sincere, I think, and his career proves it, about civil rights, personal rights. In that sense he's close to Mr. Diefenbaker's forte, you know, the rights of the individual. That is something admirable. On the other hand, economically and socially, Trudeau, I think, has no policy at all and hasn't found time to have ideas about that that are substantial in any way. And as far as Quebec is concerned, if he doesn't change his mind, he was a rigid, traditional, status-quo man. He's a poison!

Harasen: Do you think Canada will go along with him on the twenty-fifth?

Lévesque: Well, I don't know. The funny thing is that parts of Canada...through a lot of mass media propaganda, which, after all was—it was a real happening that convention they had, you know, with miniskirts and everything. A lot of English Canada bought Trudeau as a sort of...I haven't got the right expression...but they bought Trudeau under an illusion. I'm being brutal about it. They bought Trudeau because he looked like the man that could keep Quebec quiet. Well, they may be in for a big surprise eventually, but...and I'm sorry because this would be a sort of disappointment which might breed bitterness, but Trudeau has no roots in Quebec, really. He might have roots in this election in the sense that there's not much opposition among the Conservatives up to now anyway. And there's an old Liberal tradition that he may play on but he sure as hell won't stop Quebec from developing and pushing the present, you know, the present development of Quebec to its logical conclusion, and you know what I think that is.

Harasen: When is this sovereign status, this sovereign state going to happen?

Lévesque: I don't know. As soon as possible. We're working like hell so it doesn't wait till the year 2000, but...

Harasen: Five years possible?

Lévesque: Well, you know, with our system you can't put it in years. You go by elections. We'd say two elections from now should make it clear. That could come out more or less as five years. The first election we think we have a good chance, if we don't make too many mistakes, and we're not too stupid, we have a good chance of getting something close to the balance of power or maybe grabbing it the first time. The second time should tell the story.

Harasen: What do you say to people who call Réne Lévesque a separatist?

Lévesque: Well, I say it's too bad that word, especially in English, that word is used so easily because it is normally used as a sort of closing-up of your mind. You know, you say "separatist" and that's the end of that. On the other hand, politically, I suppose I have to admit I'm a separatist because I want to separate Quebec politically from Confederation, so what the hell I should worry about semantics.

Harasen: We're told that there's a considerable amount of internal strife in the organization that you are heading, that people feel you are not pulling fast enough; there are others who feel you are going too fast.

Lévesque: Look, there are some guys that say Lévesque is becoming very conservative so he's getting old, and other guys say that I'm a rabid socialist, so as long as I get guys shooting at me from two extremes, I'll just try and creep along in what I think is a reasonable direction so that Quebec can follow.

Harasen: It has been suggested that these designations, the labels, left and right, are now outmoded.

Lévesque: They're always so subjective. I mean, you're always left of someone and right of somebody else in politics. You very seldom hear or read honest evaluations of people on that score.

Harasen: Let me ask you about this recent flurry about Gabon and the Paris Education Conference. What did you think of it?

Lévesque: I think, basically, whatever you think of the political aspect, you know, or the wear and tear that it gives Ottawa and Quebec as far as civil servants and a lot of people running around nervously with files about the whole thing, and Leger coming back and going back and all that madhouse, I couldn't care less about. The basic problem is this, and it's another example of a rather antiquated arrangement. There are two cultural groups in Canada. Call them nations if you like or don't call them nations if you can't stand it, and ours is French. Now, there are relationships that were very normal for Ontario. There was an Ontario House, for instance, in London I think, way way back in an Ontario immigration policy were even paying transportation for British immigrants to keep the British components weighted enough.

Every time Quebec, and during the years I was in government I know it was the same thing, every time Quebec moves there's a sort of majority backlash that says, uh, uh, uh, they shouldn't do that and they shouldn't do this. They shouldn't go to Gabon; that was an educational thing. They shouldn't go to Paris. Well, Jesus almighty! I mean, if they can't stand that, they've got surprises coming up in the next few years. This is a normal, basic, healthy requirement along the way to whatever shape Quebec takes eventually. We're a French society. We're developing. I remember when I was a kid, a lot of English friends of mine used to say, "Oh, you French Canadians should get rid of your old educational system, you know, you're breeding nothing but priests, doctors, and lawyers." Now we're doing it and the normal development is that we want to take over our own affairs. I don't see why the hell when Quebec wants to discuss educational affairs in French it should go through a guy like Paul Martin, whose French sounds like it's out of Windsor through Detroit, or some other guys in Ottawa who don't know from nothing! I mean, this is a basic, healthy requirement for a population which is getting competent people now, developing exactly the way we were told to do, and it's something which is a spill-over of this educational revolution and is going to go on. I mean, it may make some nervous Nellies wonder, but it means that they really stopped thinking about 1867!

Harasen: A great deal was made about the renewed pride in Canada and so on during Centennial year..."O Canada" and the new flag and so on. Do these things mean anything to René Lévesque?

Lévesque: No, I'm sorry, they don't. If you mean do I feel...

Harasen: Does your chest swell with pride?

Lévesque: I haven't got that kind of chest, you know, that would swell that much. No, I'm sorry. Look, the flag was being something that was talked about very passionately when I was about seventeen or eighteen, working towards my junior BA...you know, we have that French system, so that was about twenty-five, thirty years ago. At that time, the simple mention of a flag other that the Union Jack would make the rest of Canada go absolutely stark raving mad. Well, that was thirty years ago; I was excited then. When the flag came up, I don't know, two years ago, after two months or three months of debate, I though it was a very passé thing and in the meantime, for what it's worth, Quebec gave itself this fleur-des-lis thing. I don't swell my chest very much but I like the fleur-des-lis and I couldn't care less about the other one. You know, this is the tragic thing...it's like a love affair. Fifty years ago, thirty years ago, a lot of things in Quebec would have been accepted, but when it comes thirty years too late, what can you do? Feelings change.

Harasen: Ross Thatcher once said at a recent conference that if there were a hundred problems in Saskatchewan, the hundred and first would be national unity. What do you think of an assessment like that? I don't know if he feels that way now.

Lévesque: It confirms me in something I've always thought but it's none of my business: one of the sorriest mistakes that Saskatchewan ever made was bringing Mr. Thatcher out of retirement! He may be a good promoter in small things, but let's say, as a statesman, he leaves a lot to be desired.

Harasen: You obviously don't hold him in very high regard.

Lévesque: From what I know of him. Personally, I don't know him, so I have great respect for him personally, as for everyone I'm asked about, but politically, from what I've read or heard of him or about him, well, I can't say he's exactly a man I look up to very much.

Harasen: I'm going to end the discussion on that note, Mr. Lévesque, and this may sound like a euphemism; I'm not going to wish you luck but I hope the end result is good for you and for Canada.

Lévesque: Look, whether we are right or wrong in your eyes, I hope to God you believe one thing, that the only thing we're trying to work on, and you accept that or not, is, first of all, that in my case I'm a Quebecer, I work for Quebec. According to my judgment and other people's judgment, we're doing it the right way. Democratically, we'll find out eventually but immediately after that, we hope to God that as neighbors, partners and everything else, what we bring up may be eventually, as a solution that will be good for both of us. Thanks again for calling.

Harasen: Thank you for talking to me, Mr. Lévesque.

JACK LEMMON

I have always regarded actor Jack Lemmon as a genius. His sense of timing and ability to get "inside" a role made him a world favourite. In 1955, Lemmon won the Oscar as best supporting actor for his part in *Mister Roberts*. He was nominated for the best actor award on several occasions, in the almost twenty years that followed, without success. Many thought he was robbed when he failed to get the nod for his role in *Days of Wine and Roses*.

In early 1973, Jack was talking up a picture in which he had starred, *Save the Tiger*. It was a serious dramatic role with a message. We contacted his office and asked if he would like to guest on *The Harasen Line* via long distance, and he agreed. Little did I realize when he talked to me on March 7, 1973, that the following year he would be nominated and finally win that elusive Oscar as best actor for playing Harry Stoner in *Save the Tiger*. Watching the Academy Award telecast, I felt good when he walked up to the podium to receive his much-deserved and long overdue award.

The memorable thing about Lemmon's appearance on my program was the gracious and pleasant way that he handled my questions and those of my listeners. He was even extra-kind to the "Gee whiz, I'm talking to Jack Lemmon!" callers. He was a superstar in every respect!

Harasen: Jack, one of the first things I suppose we should get to is the enthusiasm that has surrounded *Save the Tiger*, one of your latest releases. They tell me that it puts an end to the image of Jack Lemmon as comedian rather than Jack Lemmon as superb actor.

Lemmon: Well, I hope so. Wait a minute. I don't know if that's good. But anyway, no, I guess probably because I haven't done a drama in ten years since *Days of Wine and Roses*. I guess probably a lot of people get in the habit of sort of pigeon-holing you, which I think is not the problem of the public. It's really because of Hollywood itself, which tends to do that.

Harasen: Do you find yourself in a position where if the public expects you to do a particular thing, or like you doing a particular thing, that there's an obligation to continue in the comedy roles ad infinitum?

Lemmon: No, I don't think so. I think that if you do something well, no matter what it is, hopefully the public will accept it, but this has opened bigger than practically any film I've ever been in. As a matter of fact, it is bigger than any film because it's broken the *Godfather* records in New York and California when it opened and those were the all-time records.

Harasen: Tell us a little bit about it: the plot, the social comment, and I'm also curious about the selection of the title.

Lemmon: The tiger is a simile in the sense that, at one point in the picture, it's just a passing little thing. There isn't a great point made out of it, in other words, just because it is the title, but there's one little scene where I'm walking down the street and a fellow is trying to get people to sign a petition to "Save the Tiger," as he says, because there's only 540 of them left. He says, "I think they're worth saving, don't you?" And I say, "Yeah, I do," and I sign it.

Well, the simile really in the author's mind is that Harry Stoner, the character I play, is a dying species also and he might be well-worth saving. Now, the reason that he's a dying species is that he's a fellow who's beginning to crack up under the pressures of living and existing in business today in our society. He's not exactly a prototype. He's just one segment of our society and he begins to behave in a rather odd way because of the enormous pressures that are being put on him.

Eventually, he practically cracks up and ends up facing the decision of whether or not to burn his factory down, which is not a very pleasant thought, and commit a felony to collect the insurance and stay alive economically, because he spent his entire life for materialistic ends only, you see. In other words, it's sort of a misuse of the American dream, which does happen to many of us, I think, and very, very slowly we've reached a point where we rationalize our behavior and our ethics and our morals and the point being that decent men can end up doing indecent things if they're not careful and that our society, unfortunately, does condone possibly a little too much of this behaviour and we all sort of dance around the law a little bit, some people more than others.

But slowly, over the years, Harry Stoner, from a very idealistic young man coming out of the Second World War, has reached a point in trying to become successful where he's really compromised all those ideals that he had. In other words, basically what was really an honest, decent man has ended up doing indecent things.

Harasen: Tell me, Jack, how do you feel about a particular medium of films being used for social commentary?

Lemmon: I think it's great purely and simply because I also realize or believe that there is room for all kinds of films. I think that, you know, some people who might be overly idealistic in a way would have the pendulum swing too far the other way and say, "You know, films are not an entertainment medium. They're an art form and they should only be used for social comment." That's ridiculous! There's room for all kinds of films and I think that a film like *Tiger* is a terribly valuable one but I'd hate to see every film coming out being a "message film" and basically this is not a message film. It's a dramatic story and a whale of a good one but secondarily and in the background, there is a social comment that is made. In other words, it has to stand on its own, in my opinion. If someone's going to come in and plunk a couple of bucks down to see it, then they doggone well should see a good dramatic story, not just a message that I could mail out, you know, in a letter or something.

Harasen: What do you say to those who might criticize this as another one of those attacks on all those things that made America great?

Lemmon: Well, there's nothing you can do if someone were to be silly enough to do that because it isn't an attack on what made America great. The point being, it's an attack on what keeps America from being great if we're not careful. There's a big difference there. In other words, I think it's sort of silly to say our society is perfect. We must never ever find any fault with it because obviously it will never be any good if we were to do that. We have to continually find fault and try to better ourselves and keep reminding ourselves of our morals and our ethics and our ideals and not be dissuaded from that. Certain people might feel that way but fortunately very, very few, so far anyhow.

Harasen: Jack, I'd like to go back to that comment you made about Harry Stoner being one of a dying species. In other words, the fellow who went through the Second World War, went to war for his country, came back, went into business, built up a business, a home, a family, did it by spending a lot of time away from the family, perhaps had to bend or test his own moral code of ethics a little. You say this is a dying species. Now, what is he going to be replaced with?

Lemmon: He's going to be replaced, I think, with a younger generation that is questioning some of our behavior in society and I'm with them. I agree with them! It's an interesting thing, just to digress for a second; I went all over the country and out to Toronto also and everywhere I went in about ten or twelve major cities from coast to coast and in between, wherever possible, which was in all but one city, I think we played for as many college students as we could get in one place and then we'd sit and rap for hours afterwards. I would say without any hesitation that ninety-nine percent of them went absolutely ape over the film for the simple reason that they agreed. They didn't agree with Harry Stoner any more than I do.

What they agreed with is not only the dramatic story, as I said which is prominent and comes first, but the secondary social comment that is made that if you have nothing but materialistic goals in mind, if that's all that success means to you; if nothing means anything except the car, maybe a pool, two cars, the private schools, in other words, money; if that's the only goal in life, if that's all success means, then it's a wrong ideal. It's a misuse of the American dream, and that is what the kids are criticizing and I agree with them.

Harasen: Jack, is it possible that maybe Harry Stoner could clean up his act and modify things a little and still continue?

Lemmon: He could. Yes. That's what's fascinating about it. This is why it's a very controversial film, because we've even had people fighting in the lobbies of theatres afterwards in several instances—you know, some defending Harry Stoner, saying "Well, he was forced into it by society and it's all society's fault." Well, that's not true. It's a combination of a society that can and does allow these kinds of pressures to exist without reminding us of other ideals that I think are more basic and important, plus the particular character of the individual. In other words, not everybody is going to be forced into a position of committing a felony in order to stay alive and making that choice. In other words, if Harry does burn the factory down, it doesn't mean that everybody put in that position in our society would do it. There are others whose principles would never allow them to do such a thing. That's the dichotomy, that's the interesting thing, because we're made up of all kinds of people but here are an awful lot of Harry Stoners and there are little parts of Harry Stoner in everybody that ever went out in the jungle that ever went out in the business world.

Harasen: Well, I can hardly wait to see it. We'll again remind our listeners that it's entitled *Save the Tiger* and

I think it has a relevant message. Now, Jack Lemmon is an actor of considerable ability, a great talent. Now, I'm curious because you talked about the fact that there has to be a good story as well when you put your $2.50 down at the box office. You have to have that. There are a number of people in the acting profession who have involved themselves very extensively in social and political action: Jane Fonda, on the other hand, John Wayne, on the other side of the fence, and so on. Do you get involved in social or political action or do you merely restrict yourself to your profession?

Lemmon: No, I do, Lorne, but not to the extent, let's say, of Shirley MacLaine or Jane Fonda. I haven't been that adamant about it as far as politics go. Up until a few years ago, although I've always been basically a Democrat myself, I have refrained really from vehemently coming forth for various candidates for the simple reason that I felt that just because I was a motion picture star, let's say, sort of a celebrity personality or whatever, that if I had any influence on other people, why should I assume that I know so much about politics that I should sway their votes, since it is not really my field. However, in recent years, as my concern, probably like most of us as a citizen, became more and more. Due to the pressures and the problems of our world and our society domestically, let alone throughout the world, I have come out on behalf of various democratic candidates in recent years but I have never really gone from city to city or been quite as vehement as some others. As far as other social issues go, I've been very vehement mainly on pollution, which I think is the number-one problem: pollution in all its aspects. In other words, I've been very ecology-minded and have been for quite a while and I do everything I possibly can to make people more aware of it.

Harasen: If John Wayne or Jack Lemmon or Joe Namath takes a particular position on a social or political question, do you think they have the power to sway people in this day and age?

Lemmon: There is no doubt about it. How much I don't know, but I do know there is a certain power there, which I think is good depending on what you're doing. When you're taking a sociological issue such as pollution or something, I think it's wonderful, or for instance, the help we can give to various charities or to raise money for good causes. That's a marvelous thing and I think that if you're fortunate enough to have a career such as I've had, if you can give something back in that way, then I think it's almost beholden that you do it. And if you feel strongly about something like that, that you know perfectly well is for the good of all of us, then I think it's great. That's a different thing than a personal political opinion. When it gets into an issue like that, I think that you definitely can help a great deal. There's no question on the millions and millions of dollars that have been raised with the backing of various celebrities and stars that have really helped get it going and get it off the ground.

Also, I know that there is response there because a number of years ago, I started to do a series of one-hour documentaries on pollution and at the end of the first show that I did, which was based mainly on air pollution, I requested everybody that was listening to me to write their particular constituents and to tell them to start forcing legislation and that if they were to get just a form letter back from their senator, their governor, etc., they should keep the form letter to remind them never to vote for that person again when election time came up. That if he was going to try to just give a form letter back, then forget it! And what happened was that the then-senator in California got ten thousand letters in forty-eight hours urging him and demanding that he start forcing stronger legislation over air controls and pollution controls, so, therefore, I know that there is an immediate reaction.

Harasen: My guest has been actor Jack Lemmon. The movie is *Save the Tiger*.

JIM GARRISON

The Jim Garrison story on *The Harasen Line* had an unusual beginning. On the last day of 1967, I asked my audience to call in with their nominations, like *Time* magazine, for Man of the Year. Chauvinism still alive! As you might expect, the nominations included the Prime Minister, the Pope, provincial politicians, and an assortment of sports and entertainment personalities. I kept a tally. Strangely, the relatively unknown name of New Orleans District Attorney Jim Garrison came up again and again. The interest, of course, was his theory that Lee Harvey Oswald was merely a "fall guy" in an elaborate conspiracy to murder President J. F. Kennedy. At the end of my program, the result, by a wide margin, was Jim Garrison for Man of the Year, at least among my listeners.

This unusual choice of a relative unknown made me curious enough to follow it up. It seemed logical to me that if a substantial number of my listeners were interested in Garrison, it wouldn't hurt my program to cater to that interest. I began to make telephone calls to the New Orleans District Attorney's office. I called two and three times a day for more than two weeks. On some days, I would go back to the office at night to try again. Nothing! I've seen secretaries run interference for their bosses but none could hold a candle to Garrison's staff. I was usually told that he was either before the grand jury or that he was on the telephone. One afternoon, his secretary told me that the D.A. was before the grand jury and would not be back for at least three or four hours. Being a bit suspicious, rather than calling back in three or four hours, I called back in fifteen minutes. As I suspected, fifteen minutes later Garrison was on the telephone. The message was clear. I wasn't going to get Jim Garrison this way.

I made contact with a New Orleans radio reporter and asked him to have Garrison call me or provide a number where I could reach him. One evening, a day or two later, I was covering a meeting and unavailable. He did leave two telephone numbers, one for his office, which was useless, and the number of a private club that he frequented when he wanted to hide for awhile. I tried for about another week without success. I went back to the office one evening planning to throw in the towel if I failed once more. I dialed the club number and asked for the elusive New Orleans District Attorney. "Just a moment," was the reply. The next sounds I heard were the big, booming tones of Jim Garrison, who welcomed the opportunity to discuss the shocking events in Dallas, Texas, on November 22, 1963. Garrison insisted that his interpretation was "the way it was"! His was not a theory, he said. Fact or fiction, it was perhaps the most sensational of all my interviews. Certainly it drew more audience response in letters and telephone calls than anything I did before or after.

The interview was aired on January 23, 1968, and, by popular demand, was re-broadcast the following Sunday morning. I'm told the schools and university classes listened to the interview and many people admitted to taping it. There were countless people who called to encourage me, thinking that I was single-handedly trying to solve the Kennedy assassination. "Keep it up, we're behind you," they would say.

Garrison's claim that Montreal was used as a base of operations, prior to the Dallas drama, was picked up by the Canadian Press. It was reported widely, from the Nassau and Bahamas *Tribune* to a reporter for a French language newspaper in Montreal who tried to get me to give him Garrison's private number. I declined to do so. That year, the Regina Men's Press Club, as it was known in more chauvinistic times, gave me an "Excellence" award for the interview.

I tried to get Clay Shaw, who was the brunt of some of Garrison's charges, to give us his side of the story, but he declined because some of this was already in litigation. I quit trying after 1970. I was unable to obtain a return engagement with Garrison before he vacated the District Attorney's office.

At the time, there were many people who asked what I believed about the Kennedy assassination. Some thought that I might be a disciple of Jim Garrison. I don't believe all of Garrison's theory or conclusion but I also do not believe the Warren Commission's whitewash either. Garrison's useful contribution was that people were prompted to think about the question rather than swallowing the "official" conclusion. What prompts my doubt is that the Warren Commission came to its conclusion very quickly. I understand that some members of the Commission missed meetings and contributed little or nothing to the exercise. I guess the assassination was a black mark for the most powerful country on earth and a country that thinks it's the cradle of democracy.

There was a movie produced about Garrison's work entitled *JFK*. Kevin Costner played Garrison.

Harasen: First of all, Mr. Garrison, before I get into the questions about your investigation and so on, how does it feel to be named the "Man of the Year" by the listening audience of a Canadian radio station?

Garrison: Well, I can tell you, Mr. Harasen, it's a very pleasant surprise because there seem to be a number of areas in the United States where, I guess, I'm regarded as kind of a fraud for not accepting the Warren Commission, so I'm very delighted.

Harasen: Mr. Garrison, what are your theories about the assassination of President Kennedy?

Garrison: Well, we don't have theories. We've found out that an element of the Central Intelligence Agency executed the President. I'd call it an execution because it was essentially government-sponsored and that's the main reason that vital evidence is being hidden for seventy-five years by President Johnson, who is the chief beneficiary of the assassination. That's the main reason that every major government agency is trying to conceal the facts of the assassination. So, if you want to call it a theory, that's my theory except that happens to be the way it was.

Harasen: What part did Lee Harvey Oswald have in it?

Garrison: He had nothing to do with the killing of the President or with the killing of Tippit (police officer). He did not shoot a rifle or a revolver at any time. He was not even on the sixth floor of the Book Depository when the President was shot and he was not even near the Tippit scene. As a matter of fact, a number of witnesses at the Tippit scene strongly insisted that Oswald was not the person who shot officer Tippit, but, of course, they were not called to testify because the Warren Commission did not want to hear anybody who did not support their particular fairy tale. Oswald was a goat, a victim, a patsy, if you will, who was selected a long time before.

In other words, it was a carefully worked-out plan and it began with the selection of a person who could be grabbed and then eliminated and who presumably would satisfy the American public and the world that this was the man who did it. The reason he was selected was because his visit to Russia, which he did in the service of the United States, made it look as if he was a Communist. So all they had to do was to follow up and create a picture of a Communist and make it acceptable and this was done. I'm quite sure the President of the United States is perfectly aware that Oswald had nothing to do with it. Then Oswald was eliminated forty-eight hours later and supposedly the case was closed. That's the way it was done. He was just a complete victim.

Harasen: As an American citizen, Mr. Garrison, where does the problem lie? Have we got a problem with justice or a problem in government?

Garrison: That's a very, very good question. The answer would be in two parts: that we have a problem in government as a result of which we have a problem in justice. We have unfortunately arrived at something I never thought would be here. To be blunt about it, we have a form of fascism now in this country. I think it's fair to say that it began on November 22, 1964, when you have, for the first time, I think in our history, a coup d'état in which one man was removed to make way for another. Only this time there was excellent cover and for the first time in history, I think, you had elements of an intelligence service handling it so they had cutoffs and red herrings and every sort of devious cover. But I think that I would be less than honest if I didn't say that unfortunately my government has now fallen heir to the mantle left by the Third Reich. I know these words may sound strong but they're accurate and true, so I say them to be perfectly accurate, to call our country now the Fourth Reich, except it's a little bit more dangerous because like carbon monoxide it's insidious because you can't see it or smell it. We don't have the jackboots and the uniforms and the other things, but the massive control of the press and the massive power concentration, in one place, in one person's hands, used ruthlessly, exists today. That's what we have and I'm going to fight it and the only way they can stop me is to kill me.

Harasen: You've been accused of being a publicity-seeker and some people have suggested that you're a nut.

Garrison: Yes, that's right. Anybody who comes across the truth in this case, immediately they have to be branded as a nut. For example, when Sylvia Odio (witness) saw Oswald with two other individuals, well, she was a nut because they wanted Oswald to be by himself. And so it goes in this case. Of course, they have to do that. They will do whatever they have to do. Several months ago, I was, according to one national magazine, tied in with organized crime, although my office has never lost a major case in six years. Last summer, all the television networks were telling the people how I intimidate witnesses and offer heroin to witnesses and things like that. So this is just the latest phase. They haven't even mentioned that I flew in combat in France and Germany and was decorated, but that's all right. I'd rather not give them the dignity of a reply. I just keep moving ahead. These are signs of desperation. This is because they know we found out who did it and how.

Harasen: Let me ask you this, are roadblocks being thrown in your path and do you feel you'll be allowed to finish your job?

Garrison: Are roadblocks being thrown in our paths? I guess they are! Every phone call we make from any of our houses or the office is monitored, tape-recorded, a voice-activated tape that's flown to the Justice Department, if you'll excuse the expression, in Washington. In fact, that's why you catch me here. I have to come here to make my phone calls at night and move around to different hotels to keep from being monitored. Witnesses are being harassed. Every now and then when we find our way to documents or papers which are valuable to us, we find that the government has been there first and they've been destroyed. Roadblocks is an understatement, but I don't think they can really stop us because once you find out what the truth is and once you see the picture, then if you just work a little harder you overcome the roadblocks.

Harasen: Let me ask you about the reaction of the people in your own city. How do they treat you? Has the treatment changed at all?

Garrison: Oh no. They know here, see, I've been District Attorney about six years, and they know here that we have never, for example if you take murder cases, we have never had a defendant walk out with an acquittal and it's not that we're unfair or anything, but it's just that we don't go to trial unless we're prepared. They know the kind of office we have and they know I would not charge a man except for one reason, except that we have a good case against him. So, I'd say the support in the city would be somewhere over eighty percent. Most of the people in the country, I think, I'd have to put it this way since I have no way for sampling by a poll, but I'd say a very large percentage of the people in the country are in favour of an inquiry and since this is the only inquiry, I'd say they're in favor of this.

But what we have developed as a result of this, what I call fascism, concentrated in Washington, is alienation between the people and the government. It's an inevitable result of any form of fascism and Nazism because the government is operating independently of the people and it's pursuing its own objectives. For example, it doesn't matter in the use of napalm in Vietnam. I'm sure that most Americans are not in favour of using the napalm on other human beings and increasingly they're not in favor of the war, but it doesn't matter whether they are or not because now this government can do whatever it wants. But I'd say in balance, we have a great deal of support in this country but you would not know it from reading most of the newspapers because the major newspapers, for the most part, and the major television networks, at least NBC and CBS, are the kept press. They are part of the official establishment.

Harasen: Mr. Garrison, one of my callers suggested that perhaps the Kennedy family is financing your quest.

Garrison: No. We have almost no financing and that's why we're broke half the time. They're not financing it. But I don't blame them. I'm sure they have had continual reassurances from Washington that this is just some sort of publicity thing and I'm sure that the New York Times and the other papers that they read have made it appear that way, so I can't blame them if they have some doubts. We have not heard from them. I don't blame them at all but I think that they will learn in time, as will everybody in the country, that we just plain found out what happened. Now, about that, I don't claim that we're great investigators. The point is we tried and apparently the federal government didn't try and simply by trying, we found out and it's a pretty large element of the Central Intelligence Agency of the United States.

Harasen: Mr. Garrison, let me ask you this. I think you answered that in this last question. Have you had any dealings at all with any of the Kennedys? Have any of them contacted you?

Garrison: No. But again, I must emphasize that I don't blame them. You can imagine, you have an opportunity to see with detachment the kind of announcements that come from Washington now. The exaggerations concerning the casualties in Vietnam, the new lies and one new lie leading to three more, so you can imagine what they're being told and I really don't blame them.

Harasen: Is Lyndon Johnson finished as a president? Will he ever be the president after November?

Garrison: Oh, I think with the concentration of power that he has, he's liable to be president indefinitely. But I don't want to try and be a soothsayer, but I think that we've reached a point, at least at the present time, I don't even know if the clock can be turned back, where there's so much power concentrated in Washington, that it looks like it will be very difficult to beat. It's almost irrelevant whether he's popular or not. On the other hand, if the federal government is not able to obstruct our trial, and they've been trying very hard, and the facts come out, it may be that the apathy of so many Americans may change when they see what the government's been concealing from them. But again, I can't make a predication about that because there is so much apathy, but again apathy itself is a facet of fascism. If you recall in Germany, the people in Dachau, when they walked by the crematoriums, gave very little thought to what was happening even though they could see the smokestacks. The government cultivated the apathy and we have a cultivated apathy here so I can't predict whether there will be a popular response or not. All I can say right now is that this is not the democratic government it once was and we have assumed some imperialistic and fascistic aspects since November 22; I would say beginning on that day in 1963.

Harasen: I just want to ask you a couple more questions, Mr. Garrison. You have a Canadian witness taking part in the hearing. Can you tell us anything about him? How did he get involved in the case and who is he?

Garrison: Well, the interesting thing about Mr. Giesbrecht is that he gave his version of what he saw sometime before it even occurred to me that anything was wrong. I really can't criticize the average person who accepted the official fairy tale, which is what it is, a complete fairy tale, because I too believed it for so long, but Mr. Giesbrecht happened to be sitting at a table in Winnipeg and he overheard two persons discussing the assassination with obvious intimacy. One of these was David Ferry, quite apparently, and his description of the occasion and dialogue was published in the paper in the spring of 1964. So there is no question about the fact that it's true and it turns out that it fits exactly things that we learned quite separately.

Harasen: Will 1968 be a year of solution for you? Are you going to bring it to a head this year?

Garrison: If you speak of solution, I hate to use the word because it sounds like an Agatha Christie murder mystery, with no reflection on her, in which the detective walks into the living room and says "I've solved the mystery. Shut the door and I'll explain it to you." But it is nevertheless true that as far as finding out the essentials of what happened and many of the key people to that extent, '67 was a year of solution. 1968 will be a year of resolution, I think. I can't conceive of their postponing the trial again and again. I'm sure that the American press, by the time it reached you, for example, has made it appear that we've been holding the trial off, but we tried to get the case to trial four months ago and the defendant moved for continuance. But, I understand that most of the world hasn't even been told that. We're going to push very hard for trial on February 13 because we want to resolve this trial and get it over with.

But I think the probability is that there will be a combination of postponement attempts by the defendant and strong interference with witnesses, with our office, from the federal government. Whether we can survive that, and I mean every possible implication the word has, in '68, I don't know, but I know that we will be pressing for resolution of it.

Harasen: Just getting back to the Canadian involved again. Have you talked to him at all? Have you had much to do with him?

Garrison: Oh, yes. A number of times.

Harasen: Has he been to New Orleans at all?

Garrison: It hasn't been necessary to have him come down here. One reason is that the things he heard and the things he described even as they were described in the Canadian paper in 1964, fit too closely, too many points, for there to be any question at all about it. As to the group, as to their modus operandi, as to what they did, we'll probably be meeting with him shortly before he was used, but there is no necessity for a trip in this case. We have such a limited staff for this and so little time that we're concentrating on other areas.

Harasen: So, in other words, his work is done?

Garrison: His work is done and it's obvious that he's telling the truth and with a great deal of accuracy.

Harasen: There were no other Canadians involved?

Garrison: Hmm. I can't say that. I've never said this before, but you and the people listening to you have been awfully considerate supporting us, so I may as well tell you something that hasn't been told before. The Central Intelligence Agency, the elements which assassinated President Kennedy, used two cities outside of the United States for their base of operations. They used Mexico City and they used Montreal.

Harasen: That's very interesting.

Garrison: Yes, the CIA is set up that way. This prevented the average...for example, at the working level of other federal agencies, it would be harder for somebody to stumble across what they were doing. But again I want to emphasize that it isn't the whole agency, necessarily. It's a clique, individuals, particularly those who previously had been working in connection with Cuba and most of them are interrelated with extreme right-wing organizations and reactionary. I don't mean right-wing like conservative. I mean further over so that it's essentially Nazi and individuals of Nazi persuasion in Texas helped in the effort.

Harasen: Was Montreal a jumping-off spot for a long time?

Garrison: No. Montreal wasn't a jumping-off spot so much as a control base and so was Mexico City. I don't want to pretend to speak with too much certitude as to what went on there. We had nobody there listening, for example, to conversations at the time because we didn't know anything was going to happen. It was the same thing in Mexico City. But everyone involved in the case, before any major move, had to either touch base at Mexico City or Montreal. So obviously, there was some form of instructions and control coming from Montreal and Mexico City. At the same time, I want to emphasize, it was distinctly an American proposition, and distinctly Americans involved, with the possible exception of a few Latin Americans, who were brought in by the Americans. I referred to them before, but it was American-controlled and the idea that "my God, I'm an anti-Communist, I don't want this to be a Communist state," but the idea that any Communism is involved in this just has nothing to do with the facts. It's a fraud which was created by this element of the CIA and is now being perpetuated by the entire United States government. There's no question, for example, that now President Johnson and key people in the federal government in the United States know that Oswald had nothing to do with shooting the president and they know perfectly well that the men who killed President Kennedy are alive and unbothered but they couldn't care less. As a matter of fact, the men who played key roles in killing President Kennedy are, as a practical matter, on pensions and receive regular amounts of money, apparently as far as we can find, from the United States government, probably through some of the Central Intelligence Agency funds. For example, just to give the type of fund, the Cordell Hall Foundation, and things like that.

The Central Intelligence Agency, in this country, has penetrated so many private businesses and so many foundations that you never quite get your hands on it. You just bump into a foundation or fund or something. But that's how they funded the operation. Now, others further back who assisted in a minor way or witnessed to something fundamental, have been taken care of by being given jobs at Boeing, Chrysler, the National Space Authority, not that these organizations necessarily know what they did. But it's perfectly accurate to call the assassination of John Kennedy a government-sponsored operation and if there was any question about it before, certainly Mr. Johnson's left no doubt about it since.

Harasen: On that note, Mr. Garrison, we're going to conclude a most interesting conversation. In conclusion, I can only hope that your conclusions or the conclusion of your work will be good for everyone concerned.

Garrison: That's very kind of you and I do appreciate your interest and I want to assure you and all the listeners in Canada that we'll never give up and we'll never step back an inch.

BING CROSBY

The Bing Crosby connection has been a very enjoyable contact in my working life which endures to this very day.

I came home for lunch one day near Christmas in 1966 to be told by my wife that one of my competitors had tried, on the air, to reach the Bing Crosby residence and then tried to reach the Holy Land. He failed on both counts. I thought that to be rather odd. If he had been successful it would have been a wonderful example of spontaneous radio but the chances of that happening were slim and none. My "spontaneous" adventures were always carefully planned! I vowed that next Christmas my listeners would have Bing Crosby!

I made contact with the Crosby office and made my request early. I worked through Bing's brother Larry who handled media matters for the entertainment titan. I happened to say to Larry that Bing was as much a part of Christmas as Santa Claus. Larry said, "Tell him that" which I did.

Listener reaction was strong with requests that I do it again which I did. After the second interview obviously Bing trusted me because he gave me his home telephone number at the Hillsborough mansion near San Francisco which I call to this very day when I call the widow Crosby to determine how she is.

At times the telephone at the Crosby house was answered by the butler, Allan Fisher. Fisher's job before he went to work for the Crosbys was at Buckingham Palace. I might note that Bing was very fond of Britain and most of his last recordings including the very last one were recorded there.

Once when I called Fisher went to get Bing only to come back to say, "You know he's done something he doesn't normally do, he's driven Harry to school. Please call back in a few minutes." Another time I was told that Bing was walking the dogs. As a past President of the Regina Kennel and Obedience Club I was curious about the breed. They were Labs and Bing couldn't say enough good about them. There were about a half dozen with some as pets and others used for hunting which Bing called "meat dogs." Crosby hunted all over the world. He was a scratch golfer but he told me, "When hunting season comes I put away the sticks" and he hunted in such widely separated places as safaris in Africa and upland game birds south of Swift Current Saskatchewan.

Bing told me that on one hunting trip to Saskatchewan he and his party came upon a bitterly cold day. He said that it was so cold that they decided to knock on the door of the first farm house they found in order to warm up. I would have loved to see the look on the face of the one who answered the door when he or she saw that it was Bing Crosby asking if he could come in to warm up. Once they were over the shock Bing said the lady of the house prepared a splendid brunch.

On one of his trips Bing attended a hockey game in Swift Current and toured a high school which impressed him. He also sent a greeting via my show to Ernie Vogel who operated a motel in the southern Saskatchewan city. I asked Bing if he was recognized on the streets of Swift Current and he said, "No not much."

On May 16, 17 and 18 of 2003 I was honoured to have been asked to moderate two panel discussions at Gonzaga University in Spokane Washington which celebrated the 100th anniversary of Bing's birth. This was Bing's alma mater where he came close to earning a law degree. It is a small university of about 5 thousand students which is operated by the Jesuit Order. The early Crosby house is now within the campus and is used for university purposes. In front of the student building there is a statue of Bing with a pipe clenched in his teeth. The problem is that the university is forever replacing the pipe because the students keep removing and keeping them.

The panels included Kathryn Crosby, nephew Howard Crosby, niece Carolyn Schneider, Bing biographer Garry Giddens, his British record producer, Ken Barnes, Bing's longtime secretary and personal accountant, Mozelle Seger, band leader, Buddy Bregman and for comic relief, Rich Little.

Mozelle Seger had a funny story to tell as it related to Bing's funeral. Bing didn't want it to turn out to be a media circus so he only wanted family and friends in attendance and that the location not be announced. The funeral Mass was held before daybreak at St. Paul's Catholic Church in Westwood. When Mozelle arrived at the church media were already waiting in the parking lot. Mozelle was amused that she was mistaken for Maureen O'Hara! The burial took place at Holy Cross Cemetery in Culver City California. The tombstone reads "Beloved By All, Harry Lillis Crosby 1903 – 1977."

I want to address a matter of great controversy which surrounded the Crosbys after Bing's death. Oldest son from the first marriage, Gary, wrote a book in which he charged that his father was a cold, mean tyrant who was a disciplinarian who resorted to physical punishment.

Philip Crosby, a brother, told Neil Blincow of the Globe that Gary was "a vicious, no good liar" who wrote out of greed. He said, "To my dying day I'll hate Gary for dragging my Dad's name through the mud." Philip added, "My Dad was my hero. I loved him very much and he loved all of us including Gary." Philip was so angry that he didn't attend brother Gary's funeral. The boys of that first marriage were in constant trouble which has partly been attributed to their young mother's death and Bing said his absences didn't help either. The children of the second marriage have turned out fine in every case.

There was some discussion about Gary's book at the Gonzaga event in 2003 and Buddy Bregman the band leader I mentioned earlier said he and Gary were friends in their younger days. Bregman said that if things were as serious as Gary stated in his book he is certain that Gary would have said something. The point is that he didn't.

Yes my connection with Bing endures a long time after my competitor unwittingly gave me the idea.

What follows is a transcript of one of my interviews with Bing. It was a friendly chat that fitted in with the Christmas season. We left discussion about the nuclear test ban and the trade imbalance to others.

Harasen: Bing, has 1972 been good to you?

Crosby: Very good, indeed. I didn't have too much work, not enough work to interfere with other pursuits, such as golfing, fishing, shooting, and travel. That's a pretty good way to arrange it and I think I did well.

Harasen: I guess we want to begin the broadcast perhaps on a sombre note. You lost a very good Canadian friend during the past year, Max Bell.

Crosby: Mr. Bell. Yes, a dear friend, a man I admired very much, and we're sure going to miss him.

Harasen: Yes, he was well known in this part of the country for his good deeds in the interest of education and that kind of thing, and of course, a great horseman.

Crosby: I'd have to say he's one of the finest men I ever knew in all respects—a humanitarian, a great family man, a good sense of humor, a great sportsman, a kind, gentle man, sympathetic—all the qualities you admire most in a human being were to be found in Max Bell, in my opinion.

Harasen: Bing, during the past year, one of your albums had a very popular run at this radio station and I rather suspect at a number of others and that was that LP with the Count Basie band.

Crosby: He's great fun to work with, the Count. I enjoyed making that album because I've been a fan of the band for years and always went to see them when they toured through this way, and it's a great band, as you know. The organization has almost been the same for years, well-disciplined. These guys really know what they're doing. The arrangements were interesting and colourful. It was an exciting date I really enjoyed.

Harasen: There were a couple of selections in that album written by a Canadian fellow, Gene MacLellan.

Crosby: Which ones were they?

Harasen: "Put your Hand in the Hand." Gene has written a number of top tunes like that so we were certainly interested in the album. You know this has been the fiftieth anniversary year of CKCK, Bing, and we were able to go back into the archives and we resurrected a couple of old Bing Crosby shows back in those old Kraft and Philco radio programs. I remember one in particular when Jack Benny was your guest. How long were you on radio?

Crosby: I started really in the Cocoanut Grove on a steady basis when I was with the Rhythm Boys. We had a radio outlet up and down the Pacific Coast for an hour every night. Then, of course, I went back east and went on sustaining for CBS; that was in 1930. I guess I was on radio almost continuously then from 1930 up until the advent of television. What would that be, '51, '52, when television became regularly scheduled?

Harasen: The interesting thing about those early television shows, but particularly the radio shows, is that they were done live. That must have been a little nerve-wracking.

Crosby: Well, I didn't do much television live, I don't think. I still had the radio going. I always thought tape was a very good way to do a show, either radio or television. It gives the editor a chance to make changes, deletions, interpolations, shorten, lengthen, and program, do whatever he wants with it, a very convenient facility.

Harasen: A couple of television shows I'd like to discuss with you: one of them was that TV show from Ireland, which was a very enjoyable thing. Did you look up any of your kin?

Crosby: Well, they were down around Cork and we didn't get up to Cork, but I've been through there before and I've met some of my kin who go a way back.

Harasen: I was interested in the closing to that program. It took place in an Irish whisky distillery. Do you like that stuff?

Crosby: Well, no, it wasn't in a distillery. It was in a big brewery, in the Guinness Brewery, I think, if I'm not mistaken. It was a brewery where they make the ale and the stout and the beer, the mild and the bitter.

Harasen: You gestured at the very end of the program that seemed to indicate you were going to retire to the parlor.

Crosby: Aha! Well, maybe we had a little whiskey in there, quite likely, had a few neat ones!

Harasen: I want to comment on this year's Christmas special as well. I though that ballet sequence was a tremendous part of that program. I really enjoyed it.

Crosby: [Edward Villella]'s a beautiful dancer, probably the best American male dancer that we've ever had.

Harasen: You shouldn't tease us with this business of whether or not you're going to sing "White Christmas."

Crosby: Oh, they've got to have some sort of device to wind the show up with, you know.

Harasen: After you finished, my wife said, "Now Christmas has begun."

Crosby: You know, I had an amazing thing happen the other day. My son, Nathaniel, is a great follower of the Minnesota Vikings and has been for years, since Joe Capp was there, and he corresponds with all the teams and they're out here now to play the 49ers tomorrow.

They're training down at Stanford University, so, of course, I had to take him down there to the training grounds so he could meet all his friends and see them work out and they were running plays, the offence against the defense. We were standing on the sidelines. There were just a few people around, the trainers and assistant coaches and one or two newsmen. They were running plays and when they went into the defensive huddle, in full-throated choral arrangement, "White Christmas" came floating out of the huddle. Very unexpected, very surprising. Then everybody laughed and they snapped the ball and away they went again.

Harasen: Well, we had Joe as a guest on one of my radio programs just a few months ago. He was a guest in this city and, of course, Bud Grant, the coach of the Vikings, played up in Canada, coached in Canada, in Winnipeg, for a good many years.

Crosby: We had quite a visit with him too. They got beat out of any chance for a division title last Saturday so they're just out here for a take-it-easy trip. They came out early on a Tuesday, and then they're going to stay the week and then play Saturday. I suppose they'll try to win, though. They have a certain pride, these professional teams, to salvage something out of the season and if they can knock off a contender, that'll really make the season for them.

Harasen: Have you ever watched Canadian football, Bing?

Crosby: Well, yes! I've seen a couple of games in person and then it was televised here last year, several games. Of course, I know a lot of people up there connected with Canadian football, like Frank McMahon and different guys and Wilder Ripley and, of course, Max Bell. I think it's a fast, interesting, exciting game.

Harasen: We think it's all right. Those three downs and the wider field make for a wide-open contest.

Crosby: There's no downfield blocking on kick-offs or punts, is there?

Harasen: That's right, that's one kind of technicality. Another, for example, you kick off in American football after a field goal; we do not. We put it in play. You were talking about your hunting. I read somewhere where you have Miss Mary Frances Crosby now hunting with her father.

Crosby: I took her to Africa this year on a safari. The year before I took her older brother, Harry. I'll take Nathaniel next, probably, in a year or two. I think it's an exciting experience for them, particularly the opportunity to see another culture, another sort of civilization, another environment, and they have a big time.

Harasen: That entire gang all look like their mother.

Crosby: You think so? That's good. I think they got a break if that's true. I wouldn't want them to look like me.

Harasen: The other day we were talking about, maybe it's a legend, maybe it's a fairy tale, I don't know. What it was that we were talking about was mistaken identities. Somebody said at one time, during a hunting trip somewhere in Canada, Bing Crosby walked into a hotel with a few days growth of beard, in his hunting togs, and the guy at the desk was reluctant to rent a room to him. Now is that a fairy tale or did that, in fact, happen?

Crosby: It's quite true. We'd been in Canada, somewhere up around Prince Rupert, hunting and fishing. I had a full beard, really quite a full beard. I guess we'd been out about a month. I came into Vancouver in the old hunting trousers and the hob-nailed boots and the big heavy jacket, an old hat, smoking a pipe. I was with a friend of mine, a writer named Bill Morrow. It was at the Vancouver Hotel; I always stayed there when I was in the area. We drove up to the Vancouver Hotel and got out of the car and went into the desk and asked if they had a couple of single rooms. The fellow looked at me and there was a hurried consultation with somebody in another alcove there and he came back and said; "No, I'm sorry, we just don't have a thing right now." So I started out with my friend and we walked about halfway down the block to the car and the manager came running out. He discovered my identity and gave us a room and that was it.

Harasen: Well, you shouldn't feel too badly because that happened during the recent Canadian election campaign to the wife of the Prime Minister.

Crosby: Oh Lord!

Harasen: The Prime Minister had a room booked in Vancouver and, of course, the Prime Minister's wife's family lives in Vancouver. She had arrived in Vancouver ahead of him and, of course, came into the hotel, asked the desk clerk to be directed to that part of the hotel, and they refused to do it. They didn't recognize her and she had a bit of a problem for a while before she was able to convince them that she was, in fact, Mrs. Trudeau. Now, last year, you were talking about Bob Hope and Agnew playing golf. Have you had that golf game with the vice-president yet?

Crosby: No, I haven't. I've been travelling a great deal, Lorne. I've been gone all summer and into the late fall. I was in Europe and back east and then I just came back from the middle west where I did a couple of films for the American Sportsman and I just haven't had any time for any golf.

Harasen: What are you doing in 1973 in the way of albums, television, or whatever?

Crosby: I've got a special to do in the early spring, a comedy special with Gleason and Carol Burnett, and then I've got another golf show to do and I've got a guest shot with Flip Wilson to do. Not too much.

Harasen: I gather that Flip is a very fine guy to work with?

Crosby: Yes, he is. He's a perfectionist. He gets everything well-organized, well-rehearsed, well-staged. He knows the material. He's a good editor. He can eliminate things that are going to be deadweight or going to be heavy or not going to play and he has very good taste. He's a very excellent professional, I would say.

Harasen: That's really theatre in the round. You really work on a small stage in the middle of the audience.

Crosby: It's theatre in the round exactly.

Harasen: And an interesting departure. Well, old friend, it's been good talking to you again.

Crosby: Thank you very much, Lorne.

Harasen: You look hale and hearty when we catch you on the tube the odd time and it's always a great pleasure to have you here during the Christmas period. Are you coming to Canada in the next little while for anything—hunting?

Crosby: I'll be up there next fall probably, for the sharp-tail grouse and the Hungarian pheasant.

Harasen: Going to get to Saskatchewan?

Crosby: I always go to a place called Swift Current.

Harasen: Yes, well, that's not far away.

Crosby: Yes, we flew over Regina several times, I remember.

Harasen: Yes, it's the capital city. Well, maybe we can look for you at that time. In the meantime, let's hope that the Crosbys have a pleasant Christmas.

Crosby: Same to you, Lorne, and to everybody at the station and all my friends in Saskatchewan.

Harasen: Good.

Crosby: Who won the Grey Cup?

Harasen: The Grey Cup was won by the Hamilton Tiger-Cats. They defeated the Saskatchewan Roughriders in the last play of the game. It was tied 10-10 for about four quarters of the game until finally the last play and the Cats put it through the uprights for a field goal and all of us in Saskatchewan went into deep depression for about a week.

Crosby: That's a great finish. Who did Joe Theismann play for up there?

Harasen: Toronto. He's with the Toronto Argonauts. He broke his leg at the beginning of the season and was out until the very end of it so Toronto wound up out of the play-offs and the coach, Leo Cahill, of course was fired.

Crosby: Oh, I thought Theismann would go great up there with his style of play. You know he can scramble and run and throw.

Harasen: Well, I think the fact that they finished out of the playoffs and were in the final last year indicates just how important he is to that team.

Crosby: Well, I love Canadian football. I think it's a very exciting game.

Harasen: Well, we're glad that you do and I think that you will be getting a little more television coverage of it as it goes along.

Crosby: Yes, I hope so. Say hello to everybody up there.

Harasen: I will, Bing.

Crosby: Okay, Lorne.

Harasen: The very best.

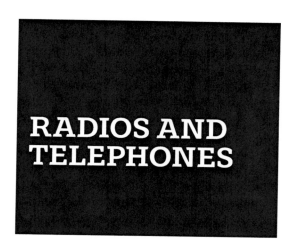

RADIOS AND TELEPHONES

I READ A MAGAZINE ARTICLE ONCE THAT STATED THAT A new community is formed when you combine radios and telephones. The article was written during the 1960s when the open line format was spreading throughout North America. I'm not sure when the first open line show was born but suffice it to say that the '60s were the years that saw the largest growth of the format in Canada.

I often had discussions with the late Johnny Sandison, my broadcast colleague and friend, about trends in broadcasting and he often wondered about the shelf life of open line radio or "hot lines" as they were called (even though all open lines were not "hot").

During my years as a staff announcer, I was once host of a program that invited people with household problems to call the program and state the problem in the hope that someone might call in with a solution based on past experience. For many years, George McCloy of CJOB Winnipeg had a feature called "Problem Corner" during his mid-morning show. Callers would ask how to remove a stain from their carpets or shirts or couches. Without exception, there was always someone who had experienced the same problem and called the program with a solution that worked for them.

Broadcasters soon realized that the common device known as the telephone could be a very useful item in the fastest medium in the media world. While some of the early programs were about two-way communication, the CBC's *As It Happens,* originally hosted by Barbara Frum, was and is a very successful format, calling out to people of interest almost anywhere in Canada and the world. I guess you could call it open line in reverse.

At one time, radio telephones had a bell-like tone that sounded at certain intervals to alert people at the other end that their voices were being heard live on the air or recorded for broadcast either in whole or in part. It was generally understood that recording a voice or being placed directly on the air without informing the person was unethical. It has been a long time since I have heard that tone, so maybe the rules have changed and those being interviewed are just more relaxed when they speak to a reporter. Needless to say, unethical broadcast types would try to sneak their way through an interview. I guess it can be said that some people being interviewed may be more forthcoming if they think they are only speaking to the reporter and not thousands of people. Mind you, there are unscrupulous politicians and others who deserve to be exposed, but everyone is innocent until proven otherwise.

I note that entrapment is more prevalent these days, with deliberately hidden tape recorders and cameras. The method was used in apprehending and convicting Colin Thatcher. I'm reminded of a true story about one RCMP officer, when communists were pursued by our police. This young officer was in plain clothes and carrying a briefcase with a tape recorder inside. He was given a tape recorder that started to squeak and squawk so loudly that there was no doubt what he was up to. It was something like you would see on television's *Get Smart!*

I must take my hat off to salute the late Howard Dean, who was Chief Engineer at CKCK radio during my time there. I wanted a delay device that was a protection against profanity and comment that was actionable. The telephone company didn't have anything like that nor did they understand what we wanted. Howard Dean developed one; even though it wasn't a perfectly operating device, Howie kept working on it until he had it refined and working smoothly. I also wanted a device that would enable me to put someone on the line who I could interview and callers could speak to. Again, the telephone company thought such a thing was from Mars and they didn't show any interest in trying to develop something. Again, Howie Dean went to work on the idea and before long built such an item.

A point has to be made that in my long years in broadcasting I found that engineers simply didn't speak the language that program people spoke. They were from different planets. Howard Dean was different. He put himself in the shoes of the guy working behind the microphone and acted accordingly. Howie knew that he was working for a broadcasting station and that it was his job to keep the place on the air and functioning smoothly while serving the ultimate master, the listening public.

Not only did Engineer Dean look after the technical side of what I did, he had a studio desk designed for me that would accommodate several guests, with a microphone for each. The physical requirements for me were all taken care of. All I had to be concerned with was the program itself and that is a very good arrangement.

By the time I moved my program to CKRM Regina, the telephone company was coming around to the realization that they needed to consider the various needs of their customers. I should say that a better studio situation was developed there, and near the end of my time the telephone company provided a very good telephone device that was versatile and simple to operate. CKRM now operates out of new quarters with the latest equipment. The drafty old former Hebrew school building that housed CKRM for decades still stands in an area where hookers ply their trade and the surroundings are less than inviting.

The telephone has been useful in reporting from the scene of a story, with the cell phone giving reporters portability, versatility, and flexibility. I remember the reporter who covered the trial of Colin Thatcher for CKRM when the verdict had been handed down. The telephone that he used was located far enough from the scene of the trial that the reporter had to run to it and was almost out of breath when he gave his report, in a bulletin that interrupted programming live on the air. If he had had a cell phone, he could have calmly provided his report completely without gasping for air—although the verdict itself took the breath away for many who followed the drama of that arrest and trial with great anticipation.

The telephone provided me with great flexibility. I took the program on the road with a show from the scene of a First Ministers' conference in Calgary and once from Saskatoon, which was the scene of the Canada Winter Games. I also participated in a program from a beach in Normandy, France, celebrating the anniversary of D-day. The program also included two D-day veterans back in my studio in Regina. I could hear and speak with them and vice versa. It was the first time that I was away for our wedding anniversary but I told my wife, on air, that I loved her and regretted being away. She didn't hear that broadcast but all kinds of people who heard me faithfully reported my sentiments to Velma. She kind of liked my public declaration.

I once asked my listeners if they would like to be a hotline host for a day. I invited letters that would include the reasons why the person would like to host and, of course, the topic that the guest host would like to pursue. I also indicated that, rather than coming to the radio station, which might be intimidating for the guest hotliner, that they could do the program from the comfort of their own home, on the telephone. We would look after taking the telephone calls and the commercial breaks. It was great fun and it gave at least one person, the guest host, a new perspective on what my job was all about.

I have always thought that the existence of CBC's radio network was a great asset for the public broadcaster's open line show *Cross Country Checkup*. While time zones might pose some small problems, the ability to get in touch with Canadian thought in every region of this far-flung country was and is a wonderful thing. The logistics are very basic and in many ways bind this country together in a superior way, more effective in many ways than the ways in which our politicians try to reach Canadians.

The privately owned radio stations in Canada have, at times, joined together in open line networks and have done so very effectively. Program hosts in this country's private sector have included such exceptional performers as Jack Webster in Vancouver, John Gilbert in Toronto, Peter Warren in Winnipeg, and Lowell Green in Ottawa. I'm not certain about the category in which Pat Burns belongs but suffice it to say that you couldn't ignore him. He took on issues that were volatile, to say the least. Language issues in Canada, particularly when he worked in Montreal (the city in which he was born) and a series of programs from Selma, Alabama, where things were changing for African-Americans, are examples.

Burns and Webster did battle for listeners in Vancouver, where Webster would usually win the day. Even though Burns had a background as a reporter, Jack Webster was generally credited with being a better investigative reporter. My personal experience with Webster was that he brought integrity to his work. I never met Pat Burns.

Open lines present opportunities for people in authority to defend or clarify matters that relate to them. It was not unusual for some members of provincial cabinet and local politicians like Harry Walker, when he was Mayor of Regina, to telephone the program and speak their pieces. The same would apply to people of various backgrounds who would call the program to challenge or clarify.

If my switchboard was jammed with callers, some people in authority knew enough to call my assistant and indicate that they wanted "on!" My assistant would inform me and then would call the person on the first free line and away we went. Some, of course, were skittish about going on the air, which is understandable. When my program ended for the day they would call my office.

The great versatility of radio and telephones is demonstrated in the following two examples. First, at the time when a Canadian diplomat helped to successfully spirit six American foreign workers out of Iran, I decided that I would give American people an opportunity to say thank you to Canadians. I had my assistant call the largest radio stations in Los Angeles, Denver, and Chicago and asked them if they would read our invitation on air and provide their listeners with our telephone number. Our program switchboard exploded as Americans telephoned our number to express gratitude and regard for our country.

Unfortunately, many years later Hollywood produced a movie that downplayed Canada's diplomatic heroics and made this look like an American operation. Dear old Hollywood screwed up or just couldn't accept that little old Canada rescued them. Former President Jimmy Carter apologized for that travesty and went public with a statement that decried the insult to Canadian diplomat Ken Taylor and this country.

Second, during the Gulf War, in 1991, there were three Canadian naval ships serving in the Persian Gulf. We were able to determine that one of them, *HMCS Terra Nova*, had a significant number of crew members from Saskatchewan. I went on the air and advised my listeners that the next day I would open the lines for friends and relatives in particular but also members of the general public to call the program and extend greetings to specific crew members plus add any family or community news. For those members of my audience who were not directly involved, it was still interesting to listen to the human side of things and for some of our older listeners it brought back memories of war in past times, when the wait for letters often took a long time.

We recorded the program and immediately sent the tape to the ship. Some days later we received a reply from Commander Stuart D. Andrews, Commanding Officer, who reported that the tape was made available to all on board.

Interestingly, he thanked us for our "support" and commented that "it has made a difference."

None of that effort would have been possible without that unique collaboration of radio and telephones.

The telephone has been useful to broadcasters for many reasons and it has been helpful to the listener. The expression of opinion by listeners has been a fundamental part of open line radio but so has information in various forms and from various sources. It isn't every day that you have an opportunity to question or admonish your member of Parliament or mayor or the Prime Minister or Premier. This also applies to those who want to compliment these same people or favorite musicians or singers or community activists. The radio and telephone make that possible.

Your telephone enables you to direct questions to tax or medical experts or ask questions of various types of legal and investment experts. People who love gardening or other hobbies can compare notes with some of the most knowledgeable in those fields. Sports on open line radio can also be informative and entertaining, and in a province like Saskatchewan, the Roughriders and other sports provide all sorts of grist for the mill.

I always tried to give agriculture enough time, dealing with market conditions, scientific breakthroughs, or just polling around the province to get crop conditions and opinions in various areas of agricultural production. Farmers, while working on their tractors and combines equipped with radios and telephones (and some with air conditioning), expressed themselves on general public issues but also those agricultural issues which can make politics and farming so political at times. Livestock production and dairy farming would also generate opinions and information. There were times when I would provide time, particularly in small towns and villages, to call and publicize sports days or fairs and, particularly, reunions.

There were times when I would get a call from a student in a school somewhere in Saskatchewan who would inform me that he or she and their class was listening to the program and either taking a vote on the question I was asking or wished to ask my guest or me a question. There were teachers who would write to me and ask if it was possible to announce my topics in advance and indicate who my guests would be. I was always sorry that I couldn't do that, for a variety of reasons. For the most part, I tried to remain topical. We were largely driven by the news of the day. A development overnight would often bump a previously chosen topic or guest. If the guest was a big name in politics or public affairs, however, we would stick to that plan even though the overnight development might have generated more spirited and greater response.

I must emphasize again that the number of calls received was not always an accurate measure of the size of the audience on that day. I did have one listener who asked in a letter if I would announce the content of my programs in advance. She said it was spring and that she was working in the garden. Her point was that if I was featuring something that didn't interest her, she would leave her radio turned off and work in the garden. I didn't answer her; my job was to get people to turn their radios on and I wasn't interested in informing my competitors what I was up to in advance all the time. Obviously, if we had a major guest coming, we would promote that, but not always.

IT'S ALL PART OF THE JOB

REGULARS

Virtually every open line show has its three or four regular callers. I was no exception. D. A. McLeod and Jim and Max Rutherford were almost fanatical about supporting the CCF and the NDP. Mrs. Inez Hosie was somewhere to the right of Attila the Hun. She once said that she was opposed to marriage between blacks and whites because that results in "a mottled race."

I once caught McLeod in a bit of mischief during a city mayoralty election campaign. He was supporting Henry Baker and called in to say that his property taxes had escalated to some fantastic level while Henry was out of office. Good old Hank was thunderstruck and wondered if they had paved McLeod's street with gold. It all didn't sound quite right to me. I asked my assistant to call City Hall and check the facts. You can get the tax situation of any property owner in the city. I also asked her to get me a recording of McLeod's statement on my program and to get it ready for his next call.

McLeod soon called and I invited him to listen to his actual statement. I didn't want to tell him myself because he would accuse me of twisting his comment. I then told him that City Hall had indicated that his taxes had increased by only a fraction of what he had claimed and that they were paid in full. I think I can still hear him shouting as I went to the next caller.

DO YOU KNOW WHERE YOU ARE?

My wife had someone from one of the department stores in the city to hang some drapes in our home. The man arrived and unfolded his step-ladder just as the introduction to my show came on the radio in the kitchen. The drape-hanger looked down from his perch and asked if she listened to "that program." She replied that she did so on occasion. Obviously, the man had been given an address only and not the name of the people who lived there. He stated that he would like to "punch that guy on the nose!"

It didn't end there because I could drive a quick way home on the bypass and have lunch and return for my afternoon broadcast. I came into the house, hung up my coat, walked into the living room, and greeted the man on his ladder. As I recall, he quickly folded his ladder and was gone. My wife, meanwhile, was convulsed with laughter in another room. I would have liked to have been a fly on the wall when the drape man told his wife about his morning.

Something similar happened to my father-in-law in a small-town barbershop in Saskatchewan. He was waiting for his turn when my show came on the air on the barbershop radio. This time it was the fellow who was already in the chair who ranted and raved about me. The barber, as it was related to me, was highly uncomfortable, but he didn't blow my father-in-law's cover and my wife's father just sat there and smiled. I used to tell my relatives and friends not to defend me but there were times, no doubt, when it was awkward.

POLICE AND THREATS

My wife and I were visiting at the home of friends one evening when the telephone rang; the call was for me. At the other end was a city policeman. He had called our home and, without divulging his purpose, was referred by our oldest son to our friends' number.

The policeman suggested that my wife and I go home, because some wacko threatened that he was going to shoot up our house that night. The officer said they would keep a patrol car in the area. Nothing came of it but you never know, particularly with young people at home alone.

SCHOOL

My children took abuse on the school ground because of me. They were spat upon and unkind things were said about me. My program was on the air at the same time that they were in class, so other kids must have picked up things that their parents were saying about me. Generally my kids handled things in a mature way even though there were tough times.

A teacher in one of our high schools didn't like me and would take out his frustrations on one of my sons. I approached him at a parent-teacher night and he couldn't say anything good about the boy. I was more than a little irked, since our instructions to our kids were that they would be disciplined at home if for some reason they stepped out of line in school. Before I sought an explanation from my son, I thought I would discuss the matter with the school principal and chaplain. I was flabbergasted when the principal said there was nothing wrong with the boy and that the real problem was the teacher. The chaplain agreed.

I got my son's side of the story and reminded him that his mother and I expected all three of our kids to be attentive and respectful in school. I then wrote to the teacher to advise him on admonishing our son and suggested that they both work out any differences they may have had. The teacher sent me a blistering, highly personal reply. At that point I had had enough. I wrote to him and thanked him for convincing me that reincarnation was real and that I wondered who the front half of the horse was in his previous existence. That seemed to be the end of it. Some time later, I learned of the teacher's death. I say categorically that my letter was not the cause; otherwise, I would have written sooner.

I might add that my son received an award for his marks in all four years of high school and that he went on to a professional career in which the profession's provincial and national associations have honoured him. Were my kids perfect? Of course not, but they had a right to respect and fairness.

SMALLNESS

In sorting out my personal finances one day, I reached the conclusion that I was carrying too much life insurance. I called the company's local office and informed them of my desire to cancel my policy. The man I was talking to said he would need signatures from my wife and from me. I asked him to send me the form and told him that we would look after it. Oh no, he said, he would drive to my home immediately to get my wife to sign and then he would come to my office for my signature. This was real service, when I expected a sales talk aimed at getting me to change my mind.

Once the insurance man got my signature and I thanked him, he asked me to direct him to our sales office, which I did. Not long after, the sales manager came to me to tell me that the smiling, wonderfully cooperative insurance guy wanted to know if he could cancel an ad campaign that his company was running on the station. "No," he had been told; the campaign had been placed nationally by the station's eastern representatives, which is a separate source from local ads.

DILL PICKLE JAR

I had a woman who would call from time to time. She had a shrill, high-pitched voice. I would ask her not to shout because I wasn't her husband but she shouted all the more. One day she called the program when my guest was a local doctor. As she was speaking, er, shouting, I looked at the doctor and there was a look of recognition on his face. When we took a break, I asked the doctor if he knew the woman. "Oh yes," he replied, "when I first went to that community she came to see me and, apparently in the interest of being prepared, she brought along a sealer jar of her own urine." He went on, "A few days later she brought me the same kind of jar of cream." I still laugh when I think of it.

CRANK CALLS

There were many but one in particular was over the top. I would get this call while I was on the air. The caller would make some nonsensical statement and hang up. I finally asked the security people at SaskTel for help after I locked the caller's line open. They soon came back with the answer. The crank caller was a resident in a home for the blind. Did I want to press charges? All of a sudden, my vindictive thoughts crumbled to the ground. "No," I said, "just tell the people in charge to make sure it doesn't happen again." Actually, the blind residents invited me to spend some time with them when I was leaving CKCK, which I was pleased to do. The lady who called said that my program was a regular part of their mornings and that they were sorry I was leaving. The staff took a photo of me, which I have kept, sitting between some of the residents.

LAWSUITS

I was threatened with law suits and some even went so far as to drawing up legal papers but nothing ever came of any. The threats were largely aimed at keeping us silent or have me tone down my commentary. That didn't stop us from bringing before the public issues and questions in their interest. Lawsuits are not unknown to open line broadcasters. But I was never sued.

IT WASN'T ALL BAD

For every bad or strange experience, there had to be ten that were good or interesting or rewarding. I was invited to address many groups and organizations in our listening area. I was treated wonderfully on many occasions. The Montana State Bankers Association sent out a plane for me and flew me back to Regina after a talk. It had to be that way because travel by car would not have returned me in time for my broadcast. I still have and wear the cowboy boots they gave me as a gift.

The Junior Ranks Mess at Canadian Forces Base Moose Jaw invited me to address a special dinner at the base. They sent a car out for me and returned me after the event was over. When the car pulled up in front of our house, our eleven-year-old daughter, Lori, looked out from an upstairs window. She knew nothing about what was happening. She saw two uniformed men come to the front door and escort me to the car. Our young daughter called out to her mother, "Mmmom...they are taking Dad away!"

I should say that it was a very pleasant evening. The young airmen had many questions for me. My driver shadowed me at a discreet distance and my glass was refilled promptly when I drained it. Being relieved of driving meant it was a relaxed evening. They gave me a very nice souvenir and once I gave the driver the high sign I was transported back to Regina.

My wife and I were invited to many functions that included royalty, political figures, writers, sports personalities, and movers and shakers in business. I was courted by political parties to run provincially and federally. They didn't want to attract me because they thought I would be brilliant in office. What was useful to them was that I was a public figure with an instantly recognizable name.

I was also a school trustee and a library trustee because I was interested in those activities.

WHITHER RADIO IN SASKATCHEWAN?

To suggest that radio has changed over the years is to state what should be obvious. Someone once said that in the old days people would gather around the radio. Today, with telephones, remote broadcasts, satellites, and portability, radio gathers around the people.

I remember my grandfather, George Harasen, would sit next to his floor model radio with battery power and those tubes that always needed to be replaced and he would without exception dial in Foster Hewitt and *Hockey Night in Canada* on Saturdays for the entire hockey season. The sad fact was that he died a couple of years before television service came to his farm. He would have loved to have actually seen his beloved Maple Leafs.

While I mention television, it was believed by some that television would sound the death knell of radio. All that it did was prompt radio to reinvent itself. I should say that, on the other hand, there were some in radio who argued that in the small and middle markets television wouldn't last because as a medium it was much too expensive and advertisers couldn't afford to buy advertising on it.

The predicted demise of radio and television that was deemed to be too expensive was nonsense. Today the radio broadcaster and television service in Yorkton are separate companies. CKCK Regina was the first television station to hit the airwaves in western Canada. Saskatoon and Prince Albert were examples of joint radio and TV operations. Eventually, a second television service came to some areas or a single television station offered more than one channel in those areas that couldn't support a competing alternate station.

With the number of channels available today to the home viewer, the question, increasingly, is "What is the role of the local television station? What does it have to offer that isn't available elsewhere on your remote control?" Virtually everything is offered and in many cases it is better quality than what the local station offers. When services in the near future will allow viewers to see what they want to see when they want to see it, those features will present a headache for the local television station. The writing is already on the wall.

Radio soon realized that it had to change. When I entered the broadcast industry I was a staff announcer. Initially, I read commercials, spun 78 rpm recordings, read the news and sometimes sports, operated large disc transcriptions of such shows as *Liberace* or tapes of *Boston Blackie*, and hit the network on time and gave station breaks. CJGX was on the Dominion Network of the CBC while other stations, such as CKCK, were on the TransCanada Network of the CBC (which, in my opinion, had better network programs, such as Edgar Bergen and Charlie McCarthy and popular "soaps," such as *Ma Perkins*). There were exceptions on the Dominion Network, such as the World Series, Gillette Cavalcade of Sports, and *The Woolworth Hour*, to name just a few.

In the time period between 9:00 a.m. and noon on CJGX Yorkton, when the station adopted a new program philosophy that we called "Family Radio," there were eight different programs, each with its own introduction, musical theme, and format. One program featured the choral music of

Fred Waring, another the music of Lawrence Welk, and yet another, keyboard music. There were at least two different quiz programs, a farm market show, an interview and show business program, plus news and weather reports; that kind of diversity continued throughout the day.

The weekday music was picked by the program director. It was all 78 rpm records and believe it or not each bundle of recordings was repeated every two weeks. A couple of my fellow announcers had a way of dealing with recordings they hated and a means of injecting some fresher material into the bundles. They would make like they tripped when they entered the control room and always four or five records would "fall" on the floor and break, like all 78 rpm recordings would do so easily. They were flat and about the size of an Aunt Jemima pancake and they were fragile and became scratchy very quickly. The broken ones had to be replaced and four or five different 78s were placed in the rotation. I didn't arrange to break some of the musical monotony because, as a younger staff member, I feared risking my job if I were caught in the act of breakage. Slowly but surely, 45 rpm recordings were coming on the scene along with an occasional vinyl long play album. The 45s were smaller, like CDs, and more durable, although they also wore down.

Saturday had programs that departed from the piecemeal approach and hinted at what listeners wanted to hear but our program department didn't get the hint. Starting at 9:00 a.m., the country top forty plus new recordings that had not yet reached the country hit parade were played right up until noon. The afternoon featured the top fifty pop hits; most were rock hits with some new recordings. The point is that every measurement and opinion indicated that listeners wanted to hear what we were doing on Saturday. Everywhere you went, radios in stores, lunch counters, homes, and cars were tuned to us on Saturday. The rest of the week it was like we didn't exist. We had some listeners because we were the only show in town but we didn't scare the so-called competition in larger markets.

I well recall, in the late 1950s, when CKCK Radio Regina abandoned its regular programs in one moment and came back as CK62, with fast-moving hit music, on-air personalities, news and sports, contests, and public or community service. The reaction of many people was shock. Among the brain trust where I worked, they were convinced that the program department at CKCK had lost its collective mind. The fact is that the change made CKCK radio the leader in the province for a very long time. Bob Macdonald was a thinking man's programmer who, I found, was always thinking. Bob started out as a teacher who started broadcasting at CJGX Yorkton and CFAR Flin Flon before joining CKCK radio as an announcer in 1952. He concluded his work life as an executive in the Sifton media empire.

Eventually, the rest of the radio community in Saskatchewan changed their programming to something a little more modern and directed it to a particular audience. About a year after I began my broadcast career, I started to drift into the newsroom.

My short CFQC stint had a profound effect on me, even though I still did some announcer work. We didn't have a large news staff but there was recognition that keeping our audience informed was a major duty. We needed to do more than rip and read from the Broadcast News teletype. In my view, we needed to do more at the local level than chase sirens. Some of the national stories needed to be probed to indicate what they meant to us in Saskatchewan. We also had to take the initiative to create stories at the local and provincial levels. Would the cost of living go up? What about the working man? Would he have a job next year? Would farmers see increases in the prices for their products or was payday going to be delayed again?

CJGX was one of the first private radio stations to hire a farm director. The late Doug Sherwin, a boy straight from the farm, did a commendable job of keeping in touch with all aspects of agriculture. CBC was already doing a first-rate job of agro coverage. Eventually private broadcasters in Saskatchewan realized that some coverage of agriculture, our number-one industry for many years, was an absolute necessity. I guess mining is number one today. When I was leaving CKCK, they asked me if I had any suggestions of ways they might do a better job in serving their large audience. Without a moment's hesitation, I said, "Hire a farm reporter." They did, almost immediately.

They hired Jim Smalley, who was broadcasting in Weyburn. After a time, Jim found his way to CKRM Regina. He knows about agriculture and he generally covers it in a very objective way. Jim can always use a hundred words when twenty-five would do! I also like the work of Bob Simpson, who works at CTV Saskatoon. He has a very professional television show and he produces good stories for newscasts. Simpson isn't entirely relaxed on his show but he makes up for that with very good content.

I guess the first sports broadcaster who made an impression on me was Lloyd Saunders of CKCK. His direct competition was provided very strongly by Johnny Esaw at CKRM. Ed Whelan was at CFQC for a time before moving to Calgary, where he toiled for decades. The first sports broadcaster that I worked with was Linus Westberg, at CJGX Yorkton. Linus was thorough and as a result would go long on some of his broadcasts, up to ten or fifteen minutes. This would drive the sales and traffic departments—not to mention the news department—up the wall. Linus still has the first and second dollars he earned and indeed if you can't take "it" with you then Linus will not be going! He was broad in his coverage. He was one of my attendants when I got married.

Lloyd Saunders apparently had a troubled marriage and a drinking problem. I don't know which came first, but a wonderful promising national career didn't happen. When he was still at CKCK, the station would send the overnight teletype copy to Lloyd's home, where he would do his morning sportscast. During the early part of his career he did much to keep the province aware of and interested in the Roughriders. Very much later, he went to work for CBC locally.

John Badham, who, at one time was at CKCK (and was an Anglican priest's son), has golden tonsils and calls football games with the best of them.

Johnny Esaw was from North Battleford and moved to Winnipeg's CKRC after his stint in Regina at CKRM. His next stop was in Toronto for CFTO Television when it first went on the air; it eventually became CTV's flagship. Johnny did some great work for skating in Canada and for many years he was highly supportive of the Canadian Football League.

One thing is certain; in Saskatchewan, the radio station that holds the broadcast rights for the Roughriders has a prized possession. The cost of those rights is not a giveaway but the promotional value to the station is priceless. CKRM is the originating station of the play-by-play, with a network of Saskatchewan stations picking up the broadcasts. Rod Pedersen took over from the competent Geoff Currier, who took his broadcast career to Winnipeg. Pedersen should have a good career if he isn't derailed somewhere along the way.

We have had our share of characters in Saskatchewan's broadcast community.

DAN WORDEN, the great storyteller on Saskatoon's CKOM.

MOLLY GEORGE, of CJGX Yorkton, was an oddity as an announcer in the 1940s, when many thought announcing was exclusively a man's job.

JACK CENNON, of CKBI Prince Albert, was a top-rated morning man and community person.

EUGENE (PORKY) CHARBONNEAU was a country music disc jockey on CKCK Regina and CKY Winnipeg, complete with a Tennessee accent (which he must have acquired when he attended Campion High School in south Regina).

RED ALIX was at CKOM Saskatoon before going to Winnipeg's CJOB, where he was a popular early morning man.

PETER SCOTT, who at times was known as **SCOTT PETERS** (and whose real name was **PETER SIKORSKI**), was a highly entertaining disc jockey on CKOM Saskatoon and CKRM Regina. He also made some forgettable low-budget movies.

BILL WALKER, of Rouleau, started announcing at CKRM at the tender age of sixteen. He flew bombers in World War II and earned the Distinguished Flying Cross for thirty-five trips over Germany. Bill returned to CKRM and then CKRC Winnipeg before heading to Toronto television. He could memorize a commercial script virtually instantly and edit and change as he went along, all within the time limit. Bill was an actor and at a Saskatchewan drama festival he won best actor five years in a row.

CY KNIGHT, of CHAB Moose Jaw, was for many years the uncomplicated, down-to-earth personality that seemed to fit with the city's slogan of being "friendly."

GODFREY HUDSON was the hard-driving, award-winning news director at CFQC Saskatoon, where he was a taskmaster in an unrelenting way.

JIM MACLEOD, the sterling newscaster at CKCK, was considered for the national newscaster's job when the CTV network went on the air but he was dogged by ill health and didn't accept the offer. He died well before his time.

JACK WELLS, who did sports on Winnipeg radio for decades, started his broadcasting career at CFQC Saskatoon.

JIM KEILBACK came to CJGX Yorkton from CKY Winnipeg, where he was a kind of backup to Jack Wells. He was one of the finest hockey play-by-play broadcasters. His son **Curt,**

who grew up in a house across the street from our house, eventually became play-by-play voice for the Winnipeg Jets (and continued when they became the Phoenix Coyotes). The press box was named after Curt and then, with no warning, after twenty-seven years with the team, Keilback the younger was fired. Jim retired in Phoenix after an association with the Phoenix Road Runners of the Central and Western Leagues.

FRED SEAR was a long-time announcer at CKCK, who at one time hosted an afternoon program from his home with wife **BETTY**. At various times he did the early morning show and mid-morning show. Fred was referred to as "Friendly Fred." I couldn't understand that because I found him rather gruff and unfriendly. Alcohol brought his long-time career at CKCK to an end. Alcohol brought many broadcast careers to an abrupt end. **GREN MARSH** was a popular announcer at CKCK who moved to CBC Winnipeg when CKCK's musical format changed to rock. I made contact with Gren after he retired and was doing some work for Winnipeg's community FM station. His wife, **LORRAINE**, was a jazz singer who sang on a program heard on CKCK on Saturday evenings. Gren died in 2014 at age eighty-nine.

HARVEY DAWES was another first-rate newscaster at CKCK who eventually had a long career at CBC Vancouver. I always thought his delivery was flawless. I met him during a reunion weekend of former CKCK people who gathered because the venerable old station was no longer with us. Dawes passed away not long after that.

CKRM at one point had three **HILL BROTHERS** on staff. I knew **BOB**, who was a highly competent on-air person with a distinctive sound. One by one, they each left for work elsewhere.

BARRIE DUNSMORE is a name with Regina beginnings; he broadcasted at CKRM. For more than thirty years,

Dunsmore was a foreign correspondent for ABC in the United States. Henry Kissinger, no less, said that Dunsmore was a significant journalist of his era. After retiring, he has done some lecturing on media and public policy at Harvard, where his work has also been applauded. Barrie Dunsmore guested on my program many years ago. He lives in Charlotte, Vermont.

ROY CURRIE was an announcer, a program director, and station manager at CFQC Saskatoon. Currie was a real stickler for proper pronunciation and good English. The part that amused me to no end was that, in a friendly way of correcting you, he would use the saltiest profanity to make his point. Roy Currie was really the founder of CJWW Saskatoon. Between his time at CFQC and the launch of CJWW, he hosted an all-night show on a Toronto radio station.

FRANK CALLAGHAN was the country DJ at CFQC in the mid-1950s. He had his own dance band and in 1957 he had country performer Billy Barnes play some dates with him. Callaghan moved to Vancouver, where he was program director at one of the Moffat stations, which played hit music.

I first met **BOB WASHINGTON** when he was at CKOM Saskatoon but had accepted a job offer from CJOB Winnipeg. From there, he went to CKRC Winnipeg, where he completed his career as program director. Bob was a Wadena boy whose dad was the local dentist. "Wash" used to do those annoying commercials for K-Tel!

Moose Jaw contributed two announcers to the CBC. One was newscaster **EARL CAMERON** and the other was **ELWOOD GLOVER**. Both guested on my show; when Glover came on I had **KEN JEFFERSON** and his group play music, which Glover and listeners identified. It was great fun.

In its early stages, radio was not the greatest source of news. What little was broadcast came from any handy source. Newspapers, daily and weekly, probably were the biggest source of news for radio. In fact, in the 1940s and early '50s, CKCK Regina had a station break which went something like this: "This is CKCK Regina, the *Leader Post* broadcasting station." Major decisions relating to the radio station were made by the newspaper. That wasn't the case for all privately owned stations but in the case of CKCK and the *Leader Post* it was, because both station and newspaper were owned by the same people.

Radio people began to understand that they had an important role to play in keeping listeners informed. It had a very great advantage over other news sources and that was speed. A daily newspaper could report only once in twenty-four hours, while weeklies needed a week. Radio could follow a story to conclusion before the newspaper could report. The main advantage for print media was the ability to report a story in depth. Time was a discipline for radio while space was an important consideration for newspapers, it didn't make the same demands as radio time.

British United Press provided newswire service initially, even though it was written in newspaper style and had to be edited for style and length. Broadcast News, an arm of Canadian Press, came on the scene in the 1940s and was really appreciated by broadcasters because it was written for broadcast and included a large variety of news categories, including world, national, regional, sports, weather, markets, and entertainment.

It took a long time for broadcasters to be regarded as worthy journalists. I use as an example the Saskatchewan Legislative Press Gallery Association. In my first year covering the legislature, a number of us tried to get the late Ron Chester of the CBC elected President of the Gallery Association. He didn't make it. It was always, in the past, a newspaperman elected to serve as our president. The President of the Gallery keeps Mr. Speaker informed about who is going to work in the gallery. You can't walk into the gallery and begin work with no one knowing who you are or who you represent. The legislative chamber and Mr. Speaker must know that there are no "strangers" in the gallery.

My boss at the time, Grant Kennedy, was most determined that a broadcaster should be elected Gallery President. When the next election came up, he saw to it that I was duly nominated for the post. Success! I was elected president in 1970, bringing to an end the long rule of many good newspapermen. I was the Jackie Robinson of the broadcast news business!

Charlie Edwards was the long-time boss of Broadcast News, a division of Canadian Press, he would preside over spring meetings with subscribers in the various regions of Canada. News directors and news editors from stations would make requests for new or added services and changes in existing services. Charlie could talk the hind leg off an elephant and he could sit up and socially imbibe till the wee hours of the morning but he was always bright and chipper come meeting time. He also had the memory of an elephant for names. He had two associates who I often think of, Don Covey and Dave Rogers.

There was one thing about Charlie Edwards and that was his regard for newsmen and his desire that newsrooms have the resources to provide good, competent service. Charlie made certain that station owners and managers knew that, because it always seemed that in tougher economic times the first reductions in station personnel and budgets were in the newsroom.

The Radio Television News Directors Association (RTNDA) was first born in the United States. The organization is committed to improving the quality of broadcast news, maintaining a code of ethics, and providing awards or recognition for excellence in broadcast journalism. CFQC Saskatoon had a membership in the American association as far back as the 1950s and the station received awards from RTNDA at that time. It was many years later that an all-Canadian organization came into being. I attended the first all-Canadian convention of RTNDA in Ottawa in 1975.

It should be noted that Charlie Edwards was supportive of RTNDA and that it would be part of the Broadcast News meeting either the day before or after.

There have really been some very able news directors in Saskatchewan. I recall Godfrey Hudson, Bill Cameron, Les Edwards of CFQC Saskatoon, Jim Struthers, Grant Kennedy of CKCK Regina, Frank Flegel of CKRM and CKCK Regina, Del Delmage of CKOM Saskatoon and CBC, and Bill Armstrong of CJVR Melfort.

I also think of newspeople from out of province that I was pleased to know when I was going to Broadcast News and RTNDA meetings: Bill Trebilcoe of CKY and CJOB Winnipeg, Steve Halinda of CJOB Winnipeg, Bruce Hogle of CFRN Edmonton, Ed Whelan of CFAC Calgary, and Bill Skelton of CJOC Lethbridge. They were all fine people who were ethical, professional, and innovative.

It goes without saying that one of my proudest possessions is a Lifetime Achievement Award from RTNDA Canada, which was presented in 2003, the year that the award was established. There were seven of us from across Canada, including Frank Flegel of Regina, who received the award that inaugural year (including two posthumous presentations). I should note that I have been privileged to act as judge for RTNDA awards for newspeople and stations from outside of Saskatchewan.

The grand vision as far as radio is concerned was that there would be a move to FM radio for music; AM would be left with the talk, news, and sports formats. FM was appropriate for music because of the fidelity and AM for talk, because of the reach. What has happened is that AM has either moved to FM or has gone out of business. There has been a steady decline in AM stations, totaling about 150 stations in Canada since the year 2000. New FM licenses were about double the number of AM stations. Most stations went to the FM band or simply died.

It hasn't been a bed of roses for AM stations that moved to the talk format. A number simply didn't make it and went out of business. CKO, the radio news network that was born with high hopes, died piece by piece until there was nothing left.

There is no doubt that one of the biggest problems for those wanting to adopt a news, sports, and talk format is getting staff who know what they are doing. They should not, as Allan Fotheringham once said, be "jockeys with tape machines who would be rendered sterile if someone had taken away their Duracell batteries." Meaning, of course, that they were either sensationalists who chase sirens or simply don't understand the issues. They would likely lead a newscast with a small chicken coop fire rather than an economic forecast that predicted loss of jobs and higher prices. A former news director who shall go nameless told me once that radio listeners want to hear newscasts that reported blood and gore. Fires, highway fatalities, shootouts with police, and sexual assaults were good for ratings and building audience numbers. None of the news directors I referred to earlier would subscribe to such a philosophy.

The profitability of Canadian radio means the profit before interest and taxes. Ontario and Alberta radio stations have been the most profitable in the country, while those in Saskatchewan have been the least profitable. The profitability of Atlantic radio has been declining for several years. There are exceptions in certain markets, but in general FM has been generating most of the profit. All sorts of factors play a part in profitability, but I think, in general, Canadian radio doesn't come by its success easily.

Radio broadcasters are always concerned about getting radios turned on and keeping them on for as long as possible. Something that concerns the industry has been a decline in listenership, which has been more pronounced among teens.

A swallow doesn't make a spring, but I have been interested in the number of young people of post-high-school years who have discovered CBC radio. One told me she particularly likes to listen when she is at the wheel on a longer trip on the highway. Perhaps the public broadcaster has more to offer?

As I write this, the first radio station to go on the air in Saskatchewan, CKCK Regina, has been off the air for several years and the second station to go on the air, CFQC Saskatoon, has suffered the same fate. Their call letters are now being used at FM stations in each city. Since FM stations usually identify themselves as wolves or dogs or something, you don't get to hear the call letters very often.

Once CKCK stopped functioning, CKRM radio moved quickly to adopt 620 on the AM dial. That was a coup, because 620, with transmitter towers located just south of the city of Regina, provides a signal that is the envy of other broadcasters. It has a reach around the province and spills into Alberta, Manitoba, Montana, and North Dakota. I once had a caller from Lemmon, South Dakota. CJWW, in Saskatoon, claimed CFQC's place on the AM dial, 600, which was an improvement for them.

Has the demise of these two stations had something to do with the decline of AM stations in other parts of Canada? I can't be certain about CFQC, but CKCK may have forgotten what got them to number one. Basically, a station needs to appreciate the fact that information is most important and that a station that doesn't provide public service doesn't deserve to do business in its community. I remember that after a snowstorm in Regina almost fifty years ago, when we didn't know which roads in the city were open, News Manager Grant Kennedy (who lived quite close to me, in Whitmore Park) picked me up on a snowmobile and we took a long and cold ride to the radio station, where we proceeded to dig up information about streets and everything else.

Something that I saw in the later years of my time was the increasing use of program consultants. My experience with them is that most were based in the United States. They would come from places such as Los Angeles or Seattle for a fat fee. Usually, they would come to town and spend a day or two listening to the station in a hotel room. Then they would meet with senior station staff and disclose their findings. In most cases, they felt that changes had to be made. I was always cynical about a radioman coming from Los Angeles, who didn't know our listeners but would prescribe a remedy. Most didn't like too much talk. News and sportscasts usually had to be trimmed and an open line show was just too much spoken word on the station, even though it might have stronger audience numbers than most programs.

The music changes they suggested would have to be fine-tuned. In other words, the station would become nothing more than a jukebox. Categories included pop, in all its forms, the various kinds of rock, hip hop, various kinds of country, jazz, classical, etc. In fairness, these consultants were no doubt helpful to some stations, but I would not advise stations in San Francisco without knowing the people who listen. There are differences in the people in Saskatoon and those in Regina. I guess the search for a station's share of the audience is often a difficult task. You have to decide on a particular program style to attract specific listeners and then you have to be consistent if you want to hang on to that group of listeners. To deviate can spell disaster.

I heard someone say that the genius of radio is that it's portable. Indeed it is. You can find most of them in rooms in your house, the garage or workshop, the car, in stores, service stations, offices, in your pocket, and you can go on and on. Radio has reinvented itself several times and will probably go on reinventing itself.

I never cease to be amazed by the technical advances in radio. Tape machines provide a great example. When I was ending my time as a broadcaster, the reporters in the station newsroom were carrying tape machines that were light and compact and they recorded voices with studio quality. On my first interview assignment many years ago, I was given a machine that looked like a metal toolbox and was just as heavy. You didn't have batteries nor could you plug it into electric power. It was spring-wound. When you took the tape from the "portable" machine and placed it on the tape machine in the station, which was powered by electricity, the play-back dipped and wowed because the spring-wound machine just couldn't record at an even speed. I used to say that the playback was in three-quarter time!

As for most mediums, the computer has been a wonderful thing for radio. You can record music, news clips, commercials, and salt away all kinds of files. I never cease to be grateful for the word processor, which is helpful in so many ways. The computer is also a very effective means of communication. I think of the times when, as a staff announcer, you would ride levels in the main control room and you would have to get up and place commercials on reel-to-reel tape machines, cue them up, and then return to your chair in front of the control board, play them, and then take them off and replace them with others. Added to that was cueing up music, transcribed programs, and staying on schedule.

I'm pleased that the University of Regina has a school of journalism. I have seen the work of some of their graduates and on the whole it is quite good. Something I would like to see developed at the school is a Saskatchewan Media Hall of Fame and Museum. There have been many newspaper people and radio and television broadcasters in the province who merit that kind of recognition.

The sky is the limit as far as a museum is concerned. Equipment would be one part of the display but it would also have to include special editions of newspapers, radio and television scripts, film, videotape, photos, taped radio items, and a host of other items. The one concern I have is that some equipment has gone to the Canadian Association of Broadcasters' display in Ottawa and to private collections. The same concern applies to the disappearance of newspaper equipment.

As far as people who should be recognized, the list is long. Harold Crittenden and Tom Melville, who served the Sifton media empire, Irwin McIntosh of North Battleford, Vern Dallin in Saskatoon, Ken Mayhew in Yorkton, Stirling King in Estevan, and the list goes on. All played pivotal roles in print or before cameras and microphones, sometimes under difficult circumstances. Many were characters in their own right.

Do I think that more radio licenses will be approved for Saskatchewan? Probably. Do I think we need more radio stations in Saskatchewan? I would say no, because we have almost too many stations now. Much will depend on what happens to existing AM stations in a province that seems to want to hang on to AM. These include CKRM, CJME, and CBC Regina, CJWW and CKOM Saskatoon, CKBI Prince Albert, CJVR Melfort, CKSW Swift Current, CFSL Weyburn, CHAB Moose Jaw, and CJGX Yorkton.

Anyone who thinks that a broadcast license is a license to print money should think again. The dollar numbers for all of Canada are not that large. The Canadian Radio-Television and Telecommunications Commission (CRTC) looks at areas of the country that are not served by a particular broadcast specialty and more often than not they will issue a license to cover that area. If existing stations intervene and oppose the additional license, they are usually deemed selfish or greedy. We generally have enough radio signals in Saskatchewan, but the regulating body seems to enjoy handing out new licenses.

There might be room for an ethnic radio station when you consider how diverse Saskatchewan's ethnic population is. They have been successful in large markets like Toronto. Our national philosophy, that Canada's population is a mosaic rather than a melting pot like the United States, may make ethnic radio viable here.

The other possibility is broadcast instruction for radio and television located at the School of Journalism at the University of Regina. However, there is no doubt that both universities in Saskatchewan are feeling the pains of not enough revenue to maintain the basics, much less the embellishment of programs.

Whither radio for Lorne Harasen? I haven't been employed by a radio station for twenty years and I have been fully retired for about fifteen years. That doesn't mean that I haven't been broadcasting during that time. I am offered broadcast assignments from time to time. If I'm interested, I take them; if not, I decline the offers. I'm also developing broadcast projects of my own. An example is the program I did with Bing Crosby's widow, Kathryn, at Christmas time, on CJTR, Regina's community station, which has certainly been very generous and kind to me.

Broadcasting has been good to me and if I had it to do again I certainly would, with very few changes. I'm not a rich man but I'm not poor either. I have a loving wife and children who are very good to us. Grandchildren have been a wonderful dimension for us and Velma and I have been blessed to have the kind of friends that we have gained over the years. To my listeners, I say "thank you. You helped me raise three kids with that stuff!"

Ron Lancaster celebrates the 1972 Western Conference Championship

THE ROUGHRIDER CONNECTION

I WAS INTERESTED IN FOOTBALL AS A YOUNG BOY BUT my interest really blossomed when six-man football came to the Kamsack Collegiate. We had a coach who once played for a Winnipeg junior team and he made things interesting. I liked everything about football: spring training, practices, play-making, and the excitement of game day. The opposing team always looked bigger. I played on the line or at least I tried to play on the line but was much too small and moved to running back, where my participation made sense. I was also the placement kicker for converts and field goals. We didn't record many kicks, because you have to score touchdowns or get close often enough to try field goals. Suffice it to say I was smitten.

I should note that a very important influence as I grew up was my father. I don't think he saw his first game at Taylor Field until he was in his fifties. Dad was a railway labourer with too few pennies to spread around. He always caught the football radio play-by-play and related shows and he would pump an uncle who lived in Regina when he came to visit to find answers he couldn't get from the media. The coming of television made things much better.

Our move to Regina in 1965 began an involvement with the Roughriders that has continued for 45 years. I should note that this involvement includes my wife and my children. As the interest has grown, our family's growth, with marital partners and grandchildren, has also grown.

That first year in Regina was very exciting, with the first Grey Cup championship coming in 1966. We decided that buying tickets on a per-game basis didn't make sense, so we purchased season tickets. That was almost a half century ago. Needless to say, our recreational lives have centered on football. I've lost track of the number of Rider dinners I have attended and the various promotions we have supported.

I was covering City Hall in 1966, so I watched everyone there scurrying around trying to find ways to create Saskatchewan visibility at the Grey Cup Festival. When the Roughriders repeated as western champions in 1967, the scurrying about repeated itself. The problem was a poorly founded approach dictating that Regina and the province should only participate in Grey Cup festivities if the Riders were playing in the championship game. It was soon clear that such an approach would continue the panic and last-minute pressure. It took a bit of time but a new, more sensible approach prevailed; since the Roughriders were a part of the Canadian Football League and since the Grey Cup is the league's premier event, Saskatchewan should always be doing something at the Cup (as they do now).

During that 1966 championship year, I was assigned to Union Station to broadcast little reports about Saskatchewan fans boarding the Grey Cup train during Johnny Sandison's early morning show on CKCK Radio. To suggest that there was a festive air about the place would be an understatement. I watched as two or three trucks backed up to railway cars to unload what appeared to be liquid embellishments. It caused one to wonder how far down the track the train would proceed before it would have to reload. I once worked with a fellow who usually took the Grey Cup train to the big game and he was certain that at least two or three of his kids were conceived on that train.

As I was doing my brief colour pieces from the rail station, John Robertson, the very talented sports columnist for the *Leader Post,* walked into the place with a suitcase and a comely lass on his arm. As the intrepid reporter, I asked John to predict a winner in the Grey Cup game. He replied in the only way that such a question should be answered. He said, "I predict that two of the rum bottles in my suitcase will be broken before I get to the train!" After the Grey Cup was over, the late Ken Wade, who was managing the Rider ticket office, came to my office to ask if I would take responsibility, as a Roughrider director, to see to it that the Green and White be more visible in the Grey Cup city. I accepted and told him that participation in the Cup parade might be the place to start, particularly when there was national coverage of the parade on television.

The Roughriders didn't have any money for that kind of expenditure so we went to the provincial government for some assistance. I thought school bands would probably be the answer. The province had a youth department, so they were able to contribute a few thousand dollars and the rest of the cost for the bands came from support groups and parents. Some came up with original ideas about billeting, feeding, and busing the kids.

There was a kind of prestige to not only representing their communities and schools but also the football club and the province. Some bands made stops to play brief concerts in towns along the way. I thought the band directors really did an outstanding job and the young musicians played their hearts out in rain or shine on national television. I made my approach to the bands as early as possible, so that all had the time necessary to get ready. I thought they did an outstanding job of representing us. I held that chairmanship for five years and we were in the parade in all of those years.

I knew that the amateur football chairmanship was going to be open so I indicated to the football club that I was interested. They used to call that chairmanship "minor football." I thought the word "minor" had a negative tone to it, so it was changed to "amateur." My job was to establish good relations and provide encouragement for those in the various areas of amateur football, including everyone from the small tykes through to high school, junior, and university categories.

I don't think I have to tell any football fan in Saskatchewan how important the development of Canadians is to the CFL, particularly in Saskatchewan over many years. Let's just mention a few players: Roger Aldag from Gull Lake, Lorne Richardson from Moose Jaw, Dale West, born in Cabri, Bob Poley from Hudson Bay, Bill Baker, born in Kindersley, Henry Dorsch from Weyburn, Gordon Barwell of Saskatoon, Ted Urness of Regina, and the list goes on.

When I walked in to my first meeting of the Saskatchewan association that oversees the interests of amateur football in the province, if looks could kill I would have succumbed on the spot. This situation was the result of years of neglect by the Roughrider organization and usually negative responses when anyone in the amateur community came looking for assistance.

There was one example where one of the provincial teams had a player in camp who had a foot larger than most. There was no appropriate shoe size in stock and the team wondered if the Riders could help with a larger size. I'm not certain if the Riders didn't have the size in stock or the request was just dismissed as unimportant, but the Saskatchewan team got help from the Edmonton Eskimos. That is simply unacceptable. I like to think that such a situation would not occur in this day and age.

I got the Riders to provide a little financial help for junior football and we started a program of public recognition for coaches at the high school level. People such as George Lamb, of Wynyard, and Gerald Elmslie, of Gull Lake, were recognized. We would invite our honorees to join us for lunch in the Green and White Lounge and at halftime introduced them to the crowd, provided a rundown of their activities, and presented a plaque to each.

A popular program was our travelling clinic. A group of retired players would take a Saturday afternoon and provide instruction for local high school players in various communities around the province. Al Ford was perhaps the most faithful participant and would generally find other former players to travel with him. Needless to say, the local media often provided generous publicity and it was good for all concerned.

Some of these programs didn't cost very much money because the football club didn't have it to spend but it improved the feeling between those who ran the amateur game in the province and the Riders.

I represented the Roughriders at a luncheon in Saskatoon celebrating the thirty-fifth anniversary of the Hilltops in 1981. My wife and I were chatting with someone who noted that Bob Arn had entered the room. I had not heard that name for decades. Dr. Bob Arn was a high school teacher in Saskatoon who coached seven city and four provincial high school championships in a row and who participated in reorganizing the junior Hilltops after World War II. He was the head coach when the junior team won their first national championship in 1953. He was a coach who believed in strategy and he brought the split-T to his coaching. Early on, he would go to American colleges at his own expense during the summer months to broaden his knowledge of the game.

Having heard that respected name for the first time in a long time, I commented that Arn must have been named to the Saskatchewan Sports Hall of Fame long ago. Not so, said a friend; "We tried a couple of times but he didn't make it!" Right there and then I said that I would see to it that Bob Arn was inducted into our Sports Hall of Fame. Not because I felt that I had some extra-special capabilities or influence, but I felt strongly that Arn's achievements and his story were strong enough to get him into the Hall.

While I prepared my nomination, I arranged to have Bob Arn be a Rider guest at lunch, made a presentation to him at the fifty-five yard line, and, of course, had him watch the game from a box seat. When we got down to field level, the players were just coming off at halftime. I noted that Dr. Arn was impressed by the size of some of those Montreal players. It was also noted that included among the group were those expensive NFL players who just never got it done here.

In my nomination of Bob Arn, I included his entire football record and I underlined the fact that he was getting on in years. The Hall's selectors must have agreed that time was moving on because he was one of their inductees in 1982. I nominated him in 1981. He died in 1987, just days before his eighty-sixth birthday. A real football soldier if there ever was one.

I should note that Velma, my wife, whom I taught the game, picked it up readily and was soon picking up defensive formations more quickly and more often than me. She was called in to help in the ticket office and that soon became a full-time job, which led to being named Executive Secretary for General Manager Jim Spavital and President Dick Rendek. Rendek had some very nice things to say about her at one of the annual meetings. Velma soon had many friends among her workmates and the players as she does in all of her involvements. In all, she was a Rider employee for some fifteen years before she accepted an administrative position in the healthcare field.

I return now to my dad, who continued his keen interest in the Roughriders. He came down with chronic leukemia at the age of sixty. The chronic form usually gives you a few years, if you are lucky, while acute leukemia is over in a matter of months or even weeks.

Canadian National Railways, recognizing that Dad had at least some time left, retired him early. He had been living and working in Manitoba for a number of years but his football heart was still beating for the Jolly Green Giants.

There was one thing that Dad could do better than almost any fan, and that was formulating alibis or excuses for the shortcomings of the team. They were works of art! It was either injuries or poor officiating or a tough schedule or the weather or Lord knows what! Never once would he call them bums or call for firing the coach.

The last year of my dad's life, 1978-79, was lived in Regina; it was a good year. He had good housing and he joined Blessed Sacrament church. He quickly joined the local Legion branch and volunteered to be a pallbearer for Legion funerals. He was close to his grandchildren, made some great friends, and lived in the home of the Saskatchewan Roughriders. The football club was upgrading and expanding seating by some eight thousand seats at Taylor Field. Dad wanted one of those seats and he bought a season ticket.

Velma was still working for the Riders and took Dad to one of the noon Quarterback Luncheons. As it worked out, she was able to introduce my father to Ron Lancaster, who Dad greatly admired. Velma said the look on Dad's face as he clasped the Little General's hand was something she will never forget. She said he looked like he had just been introduced to the Almighty.

I was a member of the Roughrider expansion committee. My duty was public relations, which included advertising, news releases, and special promotions. It was a nine-million-dollar project, with the city and province picking up most of that and the Roughrider organization committed to raising one million dollars. Construction was aimed at a completion date in time for the 1978 season but a strike/lockout killed that hope. We all watched the building cranes sit motionless all summer. Frustration supreme.

My father became ill in June, 1979, and immediately went into hospital. The chronic form of leukemia had run its course with him. He died October 10, 1979, at age sixty-six. He would never sit in the seat he paid for at Taylor Field.

Actually, it was touch-and-go if the newly expanded and refurbished Taylor Field would be ready for the opening exhibition game in 1979. The artificial turf was acting up but President Gordon Staseson swung into action, as he usually did in extenuating circumstances, and the opening game kickoff was right on time.

My activities as the public relations man really started well before construction. In those days municipal councils had to seek approval in a vote by taxpayers before they could finance capital projects. That meant that we had to develop a campaign urging voters to vote "yes." It included posters, pamphlets, newspaper, radio and TV ads, interviews, speeches at service clubs, and we had a perfect model of what the stadium would look like which we carted to shopping malls, where we would answer questions and hand out information.

We felt that the best way to campaign was "run hard and run scared." The waters had been muddied, so to speak, by a professor at the University of Regina who decided to oppose the project; he provided a rallying point for the naysayers. When the votes were counted, the ratepayers approved the borrowing, in a very light turnout, by 3854 votes. We had reason to run scared. We never heard from the professor again.

With approval to borrow, it was time to get on with the Rider share of the cost. I thought a kickoff luncheon might just be a good starting point. You need a full house and some heavy hitters at the head table. We had a full house at noon on a crisp Saturday on January 28, 1978. The heavy hitters at the head table included CFL Commissioner Jake Gaudaur, that sterling sportswriter of the Southam newspapers, the late Jim Coleman, and the star of the show, Charlie Farquharson (better known as actor Don Harron), who received a spontaneous and prolonged standing ovation. All came on their own nickel. Charlie was presented with a Rider jersey and the number .08!

Jim Coleman, in his national column, pointed to people in Saskatchewan as "almost" unique and asked, "Where else would you expect five hundred relatively sane human beings to give up the leisure of a Saturday holiday to go out into the bitterest cold of a Canadian winter to pay their own good money to attend a public luncheon, the object of which is to persuade them to fork over another one million dollars of their own good money to build an eight-thousand-seat addition to an open-air football stadium?"

Four Saskatchewan firms reached over to Committee Chair Dick Rendek at the head table and gave him cheques totaling $80,000. The actions of an older lady living in a town just down the highway brought a lump to one's throat. She sent in a cheque for one hundred dollars. Committee Chair Dick Rendek tried to get the lady to come to the luncheon as our first donor. She said she couldn't do so, particularly in winter. Dick then offered to send a car to bring her to Regina and take her back but again she said no and pointed out that she was an invalid. That said it all. The lady would never sit in the new stands or any stands but she wanted to contribute.

I think the rest of the committee would agree that we soon learned how difficult it was to raise one million dollars when many individual contributors made donations of fifty or one hundred dollars. There were many firms and some individuals who insisted that they wished to be anonymous and did not want any publicity. As the campaign went into its closing stages, Dick Rendek entered into some fruitful negotiations with Sask Sport and Lotto Canada.

The point that seemed to be recognized by donors and people such as Jim Coleman was that the Canadian Football League couldn't afford to lose the franchise in the smallest market and so we wore two green and white badges, one reading, "I kicked in" and the other asking, "Have you kicked in?"

We eventually completed the campaign and enjoyed a much superior stadium. Joe Theismann, as a parting shot when he was leaving the CFL for the NFL, referred to the old Taylor Field as "a converted dog track." For one thing, the player's dressing room was at the refurbished stadium rather than under the Exhibition grandstand, where players had to be bused to the football field. The general manager had an office at Taylor Field rather than next to a livestock ring at the exhibition grounds or above a hardware store miles away. These were just some of the good things that the new facility offered.

When 1987 rolled around, our team was less than exciting. The lack of attendance and poor season ticket sales plus rising costs put the organization in serious financial shape. In fact, Tom Shepherd, who kept the books for a period of years and raised millions for the football club, says the situation had bankruptcy written all over it. Our credit had run down to the end of the rope. Knowing that the Roughriders had experienced near-doom in past years, the club's leaders decided to tie a knot at the end of that rope and hang on. What to do? They decided to go to the people of Saskatchewan in what they called a "Tickethon" in a weekend marathon broadcast carried on radio and television throughout the province.

I was given the task of rounding up as many former players, coaches, and executive members in Canada and the United States as I could, to see if they could come to the broadcast or at least videotape an appeal and send it to us for use on the broadcast. Some of these people were able to come. Others sent videotaped public appeals. When I called long-retired General Manager Ken Preston, he said, "Lorne, I can come to the telecast and be seen on it but I can't answer interview questions or make statements because I'm in the early stages of Alzheimer's." It gave one reason to pause and reflect.

John Robertson was a former *Leader Post* sportswriter who coined the term "Rider Pride" when helping to fill Taylor Field at another time. He worked for some of the biggest newspapers in Canada and was a gifted writer quite apart from being a prankster. He loved the Roughriders but baseball was one of his greatest loves. While in high school, he had a tryout with the Washington Senators as a pitcher. "Robbie," as he was known, was living in Winnipeg. In fact, we knew that he was dealing with some serious health problems. What do we do? We knew that he was bound to hear about the Tickethon and that if we failed to invite him there would be great hurt. I thought I better call his wife and explain the predicament. We concluded that we would bring him to Regina and really demand that he take rest breaks and not work marathon hours on the broadcast. Intent is one thing and reality another.

The day before the broadcast, Ted Urness and Ron Lancaster would fly in a private light plane with Ted as the pilot to Swift Current, North Battleford, Saskatoon, Prince Albert, and Yorkton to promote the Tickethon. We alerted the media in these communities and asked them if they would meet the plane and do their interviews. It all went very, very well.

Robertson, now in Regina, heard about this mercy flight and insisted that he was going along. I will spare the details but John Robertson went along! In fact, when talking about it, John's patented sense of humour was still there. When he talked about the flight, Robbie said Ted Urness, the best centre to ever play the game, actually piloted the craft by being bent over in the cockpit and looking through his legs in the centre snap position.

Once the broadcast was launched, I asked others in charge to keep an eye on Robertson.

When I returned in the morning I asked if Robertson got some rest and was told that he was up at all hours overnight. We checked on him and found a leg swollen by phlebitis, a dangerous condition which is not to be taken lightly. Robbie was taken to emergency and promptly admitted to hospital, where the clot was dissolved. His wife was advised that he would be released the next day provided that treatment relieved the problem (which it did). I picked him up at the hospital and took him to the airline lounge at the airport, where I thanked him for his dedication, urged him to take better care of himself, and turned him over to the air crew. The Tickethon was a smashing success, with some 77,000 tickets sold, assuring that the Riders would continue to play.

John Robertson died at Betel Home in Gimli, Manitoba, on January 25, 2014, at the age of seventy-nine.

I have had some very pleasant assignments for the Saskatchewan Roughriders, including writing a series of articles about the immortals in the game program magazine for the seventy-fifth anniversary of the team in 1985. These articles included such names as Glenn Dobbs and Ron Atchison. Later, for the one hundredth anniversary, I anchored twelve one-hour television shows, which dealt with the long and storied history of the Green and White.

A special honour was to act as master of ceremonies for the fortieth anniversary reunion, in 2006, of the 1966 Grey Cup championship team that won that first Grey Cup championship for Saskatchewan. It was great seeing such past players as Clyde Brock,

Jack Abendschan, and, of course, Ron Lancaster and George Reed. I also made a few away trips with the team as a guest of Ken Preston, Henry Dorsch, and Dick Rendek.

It was also an honour to have acted as MC for two Rider dinners, the Taylor Field

Expansion kick-off luncheon, and several Meet the Players evenings. In addition to volunteer jobs, I have done a fair number of game broadcasts, such as post-game call-in shows from a room at Taylor Field, then the weight room next to the team locker room, and then the radio station. One afternoon I waited in my car outside the radio station to listen to the closing minutes of the game play-by-play. The station was near an area where ladies of the night would ply their trade. Suddenly I felt eyes looking at me. I looked up and it was one of the "ladies" wondering if I needed her services. I said "Thank you, but I'm going to work in a minute."

For a number of years, I did a pre-game radio show from a hotel and a couple of

restaurants and the casino. In some cases we had a live audience. Prior to my coming to Regina, I was part of a CJGX broadcast from the Holiday Inn in Yorkton, which was hosted by Jim Keilback and featured former Rider Art McEwen and Dr. Steve Yaholnitsky, a Yorkton dentist who cheered for the Bombers. There were many good tussles between Art and Steve. We even had a football-shaped table made for the show. My last show was a half-time feature called *Rider Notebook*, which ranged from features about past legends to interviews, such as one with Weston Dressler's parents.

My most recent activity has been as a selector on the Plaza of Honour Committee. This has brought many satisfactions on the basis of recognizing deserving players and builders. The greatest satisfaction has been the gratitude of the recipients, some of them players or coaches who may have left the team with hurts or issues. These hurts or issues have not been the basis of selections, but with some recipients they were something that seemed to heal.

The Plaza selection has seemed to be one of the more misunderstood selections. It is made on the basis of merit as a player or coaching success. In addition, it has much to do with the recipient's loyalty and contribution to the team and even the community. Obviously, all-star rating and other CFL awards or recognitions are noted, but all-stars and CFL award winners don't need another award category. We all know about players over the years who were good journeyman players who produced for the team and just missed the award categories.

One of my pleasures over many years has been to act as master of ceremonies of the Plaza luncheon, which has been held at the Wascana Golf and Country Club on Plaza day. Besides including Plaza recipients of the past, it is an informal gathering primarily for the honorees and their families. There are always "good vibes" at this gathering.

I must make reference to a friend with whom I was associated with the Plaza and other Roughrider enterprises as well. I write of the late Dan Marce, who was taken from us in a traffic fatality way before his time. He had a generous and loyal heart. Dan loved his family just a bit more than he loved the Riders. His kindness to me will not be forgotten. I miss him throughout the year but particularly at football time. It's hard to understand why these things happen.

If I have left the impression that the Harasens are a football family, that is right. You already know about my dad and my wife, but it doesn't stop there. My oldest son, Greg, played high school football and has coached high school and minor league ball. Paul, our youngest, has coached minor league ball, had an undefeated record for two years, and was named Coach of the Year. Two of my grandsons, Luke and Mark, have played minor league ball and Luke has played with the South Saskatchewan Selects in several football tournaments in San Antonio, Texas. He is also part of the Leboldus Golden Suns high school football team.

Our only daughter, Lori, has lived and worked in Alberta for more than thirty years but is green and white to the core. She has also made certain that her Welsh husband, Nigel Lane, and our grandson, Owen, know what the priorities are in football. Lori likes to sit in the middle of Eskimo fans in Edmonton and bait them. You can find Rider fans in all CFL stadiums. Often there is more green in the stands than home colors. My wife was once attending a meeting in Lisbon Portugal only to notice a young man walking toward her on a street near her hotel. He was wearing a Rider Tshirt. She stopped him and asked him where he was from. He couldn't speak English! On another occasion my wife and I were in Milwaukee to watch some major league baseball. While there we realized that the National Football League spring training was underway. We had flown to Milwaukee so we climbed aboard a Greyhound bus and headed to Green Bay Wisconsin where the Packers were working out. After a good day of tours and visiting we hailed a cab for a ride back to the bus depot. The driver was a young man who was about 25 years old. Immediately he asked us where we were from. "Saskatchewan," was our reply. "Oh the Roughriders," he exclaimed. They are known everywhere. The Riders are often compared with the Green Bay Packers but Green Bay is significantly smaller than Regina.

No, football is not our religion. We have that in order, but we are grateful for the game, the fun we have enjoyed, and the good people we have met and been associated with over the years. Go Riders!

SASKATCHEWAN THEN AND NOW

I'M OFTEN ASKED ABOUT THE CHANGES I HAVE SEEN IN the province in the almost sixty years, full time and part time, that I have made my living behind a microphone. I take that to mean changes in attitude and values rather than technology or machines. There is no question that we have changed somewhat in values, but change has been very gradual. We are descendants of people who took a big chance in pulling up stakes in their countries of origin, where they may have been persecuted or had no future, and came here to start a new life.

I use as a reference something in Gerald Friesen's *The Canadian Prairies: A History,* which includes a telling letter. Mrs. Johanne Frederiksen, of Denmark, arrived with her six children in New York on May 13, 1911. Six days later, they got off the train in a driving snowstorm at Nokomis, Saskatchewan. They were met there by her husband, who had come ahead of them by about a year. Mrs. Frederiksen later wrote of exhaustion, cold, fear, and tears. Her letter went on, "Here it's still so desolate and frightening on the wild prairie. It is like the ocean. We are a tiny midpoint in a circle." Mrs. Frederiksen's experience was shared by many who built this province.

AGRICULTURE

The average farmer and working person are those who work hard, still cling to some values, and can see through the proverbial "snake oil salesman" very quickly. Things are changing but very slowly and deliberately. Some things for the better and some in the other direction.

I'm often irked by city dwellers who complain about what they consider to be many government handouts to farmers and a farm population that never stops begging for more. To begin with, farmers' produce earns foreign exchange for Canada, not to mention creates jobs in the processing sector. For the most part, farmers have virtually no power over the prices that they receive for their produce. That is because society generally believes in a cheap food policy. Raise the price on a loaf of bread or a dozen eggs and the cries of anguish are long and loud, but raise the price of a bottle of rye or some recreational item and all is silent.

It should be noted by those who think producers always have their hands out for government aid that farmers have done much to solve problems for themselves through the creation of co-operatives, credit unions, associations that concern themselves with the various commodities that farmers produce, and their support of communities. It is a fact that when farmers have money they spend it! They have little choice if they wish to stay in business.

There have been many changes on the farm. Not all of them good. Initially, with horses as the means of conveyance, average hauling distance from farm to wooden elevators was about eight miles. With the coming of the farm truck and more modern elevators, the distance was extended to sixteen or seventeen miles. Near the end of its time in business, Saskatchewan Wheat Pool was planning on what they called "high throughput elevators" that were faster and dust-free and about twenty-five miles hauling distance from the farms. I remember an executive for one of the privately owned elevator companies speaking in support of that concept, saying that he visualized a situation where an elevator agent sold a few chemical supplies and maintained direct contact with his farmer patrons.

The wooden elevator is all but gone. Those remaining are owned by farmers for their own storage. The first elevator built in Saskatchewan was located at Fleming but unfortunately burned to the ground in recent years. Grain is now largely trucked to inland terminals by custom truckers. The relationship between farmer and elevator manager is not the same with a middleman transporting grain. Just who profits from the new arrangement? Grain companies and the railways are the winners, with fewer stops and bigger loads. No advantage for the farmer.

The biggest bill of goods sold to farmers was the demise of the Crow Freight Rate for grain. Those who supported killing the Crow told farmers that if freight rates were compensatory the railways would have an incentive to transport grain and all would be happy. Well, what do we have? Railways are the same old railways. The federal government is fining and threatening actions against rail leadership and grain waits on the prairies.

The case for retaining the Crow Rate or something like it is that Prairie grain has to travel a long distance before it's in export position. Competing grain-producing countries like France and Australia produce their grain close to saltwater. In the United States, they are able to use their internal river system to move grain to export position. Water is the least costly form of transportation, followed by rail transport. That makes highway transport the most costly. Yet we see miles and miles of rail steel being taken out of service.

The prairie elevator system has never been responsible for the failure of Canadian grain to meet its export commitments. Strikes in the handling and transportation sectors have often been the problem.

Something that needs to be clarified is that, counter to popular belief, Canada is not the "bread basket" of the world. Countries like France and the United States are much bigger producers of wheat. Traditionally, about eighty percent of wheat produced in the world is consumed in the country that grew it. That means that about twenty percent of what is left over is available for export. Canada gets a fair chunk of that business, thanks to the great quality produced by prairie farmers and an effective selling job by the Canadian Wheat Board (which is no more). We were told that farmers wanted the CWB put to death but the politicians refused to hold a vote of producers to make certain that this was what producers wanted.

This little dance started when Otto Lang was responsible for the Wheat Board. Without anyone asking for it, farmers were called on to elect a Wheat Board Advisory Committee. Farmers see through such actions and went along with it. When the votes were counted, those who supported Wheat Board marketing held the majority of the seats on the Advisory Committee. Eventually the advisory role was replaced by elections for board directors. Again, the same result. Most directors were Wheat Board directors. Regardless of pro-Wheat Board directors, the executioners got their wish and the Board is gone. The Free Trade Agreement with the United States had a small hand in it. American politicians cried copious tears that the bad old Canadian Wheat Board was unfair competition. Some called it socialism, even though past U. S. governments contributed financial help to the private American grain trade by granting low-cost loans to countries buying American grain. This piece of "socialism," as the critics would have it, was created by a Progressive Conservative government headed up by that raging red, R. B. Bennett! I was always puzzled by the contradiction of American politicians who wanted our governments to scuttle the Wheat Board. Do you suppose they would have complained if the Board had not been effective?

The mixed, half-section farm is long gone. Thousands of acres is the norm, with farm machinery selling for hundreds of thousands of dollars. A friend of mine who had more than a little to do in agriculture once told me that in previous times he would drive down a country road and note that barns and machine sheds were always painted and kept in good condition. Now, he notes, all buildings are kept up, including the house, garden and lawn, one more example of the increased role that women are taking in managing the farm. Many are active in operating machinery in the fields or hauling grain to market and some are active in farm organizations. My one and only daughter is a city girl who is a graduate of the College of Agriculture at the University of Saskatchewan; she was an agrologist for Farm Credit Canada for over thirty years and is now retired. If you see a shabby farmstead, it might be that the place is occupied by a bachelor or that the family has moved to town and the farmer commutes to his land each working day. The children are bused to school, with the little country school virtually gone. Some schoolhouses have been converted to museums of sorts or district halls for country social events or meetings.

Agriculture continues to be an important part of Saskatchewan's economy but we no longer live and die by what happens on the farm. Mining and oil and gas moved up the ladder to lead. Even though oil and gas are temporarily having problems, that is bound to change for the better. A diversified economy was the goal of many Saskatchewan governments for many years. We seem to have turned that corner, perhaps for good.

ALCOHOL

Saskatchewan has always been straight-laced in some of the ways we approach things. Saskatoon was founded as a temperance colony and some of that thinking persists in some ways today. By and large, most Saskatchewan people have a more balanced approach to the subject.

Do you remember our liquor stores just fifty years ago? You would enter these places and look up a list of what you wanted to buy, write your choices down on a slip, and hand it to a clerk, who would take it to the back of the store and bring the bottle back to the counter and put it in a bag and take your money. Usually he didn't say hello or smile or show courtesy in any way. It was probably the only place of business where you couldn't handle or look at the goods before you bought them.

Who can forget the "men only" beer parlours? These were smoky, smelly places that can only be described as awful. It was yet another example of the idiotic way women were treated. Remember, also, that they were not allowed to vote at one time.

The provincial government allowed for local option votes in the late 1950s. Voters were given a choice of liquor outlets, such as mixed beverage rooms, bars, and nightclubs. The politicians wouldn't take the bull by the horns; they left that to voters. It was not an act of true democracy. I blame politicians for some of the problem. If one side of the House could pin some questionable thing involving liquor on the other side, they would do so with cheap shots in debate.

If voters didn't approve of one or all options, they would not be allowed to vote again until five years later. That was the dilemma in the city of Yorkton. They voted out all but one type of outlet and approved something that was immediately impractical: nightclubs. I rather suspect that large numbers of voters didn't understand what they were voting for. Willowbrook, a hamlet just down the road, approved mixed beverage rooms and night after night saw long lineups of men and their ladies waiting to get into the new facilities. That scene was repeated over and over in small places in the Yorkton area.

Five years later the Yorkton Jaycees called on the Chamber of Commerce to urge voters to vote yes for all options. The young men argued that the city couldn't afford another delay. In fact, the Jaycees brought an executive member of the Hotels Association to address a dinner meeting of the chamber, but the chamber didn't let him speak and took no public position on the question.

Well, the Jaycees did take a public position and urged voters to vote yes. Some employers sponsored their young employees' Jaycee membership fees and the cry went up that these sponsorships would be cancelled because of that endorsement. The votes were counted; all options were approved and no Jaycee memberships were cancelled either. It was yet another sign of the silliness that surrounded alcohol.

We had eased liquor laws but that didn't totally reduce the controversial nature of alcohol amongst some in Saskatchewan. Politicians were still scared of it. I recall an exchange between Premier Ross Thatcher and a hotel owner at a hotelmen's convention. The hotel owner wanted restrictions lifted so that beverage rooms could serve hard liquor in addition to beer and wine. Thatcher responded by saying that as long as he was Premier he would not approve such a measure. As it was reported to me, Allan Blakeney was driving his car on Albert Street in Regina with the radio on when a newscast came on the air including a voice clip of Premier Thatcher's bombastic statement. The story, either fact or fiction, is that Blakeney went directly to the hotel where the hotelmen's convention was being held and met the delegates as they were coming out of the session with the Premier.

I had a personal experience when a by-election had been called in one of our rural ridings. I wanted to get some tape and sound on film that reflected the views of those people who would have a vote in the by-election. You can set up on the street in a small town or attend a meeting. This time, I sent my technical crew to set up in the local beverage room. You can bet that politics were vigorously discussed in that beverage room at the time.

We had a very good discussion and packed up and headed for home quite satisfied that we had something of a good handle on the state of politics in that riding. About a week later, I received a letter from the beverage room owner, who wondered if our taping was legal. He indicated that he had received strong criticism about facilitating such a session. One can only guess that the complaints came from people who felt that their favourite party didn't come off well in the discussion. I wrote back to the owner and suggested that he relax because election time in Saskatchewan was often "ding-a-ling time!" The government side of that by-election lost the seat.

I remember a time some years back when an out-of-province brewery was forced to change the shape of their distinctive bottles to the shape that all other brands used if they wanted to sell beer in Saskatchewan. I guess the genius behind the Liquor Commission requirement for uniformity is that a distinctive bottle might give a brewery a marketing advantage. One wonders if that distinctiveness might have an opposite effect. What then?

As a broadcaster, I watched a situation develop over a long period of time in which representatives of my industry tried to get approval that would enable Saskatchewan broadcast stations to carry beer advertising. It seemed unfair that *Maclean's* magazine and the *Toronto Globe and Mail* could sell their advertising to breweries using me and all the rest of their subscribers in Saskatchewan to get advertising dollars but the stations I worked for could not.

Initially, when beer advertising finally came to us, there were conservative regulations. You couldn't depict people drinking and enjoying. It should not be too flashy and the scripts should be straightforward and not hard-sell the stuff. I thought the purpose of advertising is intended to increase awareness and urge people to try a particular product.

As the years have gone by, our attitudes have moderated. We have an experiment with private liquor store ownership and a privately owned wine store. In Regina, a government-owned liquor store carries every imaginable brand of wine, beer, and spirits. It holds tastings and it is equipped to include food. One store stays open till 3:00 a.m. and another is open on Sunday afternoon. Liquor store employees have become friendly and helpful and liquor is being sold in a limited way in grocery stores. Wine-tasting functions are popular and there has been an experiment with selling wine in bulk by bringing your own bottles and filling and corking by yourself. Brew pubs (where the pub brews its own beer) now exist here. Sports bars cater to a specific patron.

Beer is no longer the only advertised item on the air or in print. Spirits, wine, and specialty products are advertised. The government hasn't made a great noise about it or called another plebiscite and despite that the sun has risen every day.

Contrast today's approach with that of another time, when one hotel in a small town had a room made up for women with children who would wait for their husbands, who were drinking in the beer parlour on a Saturday night. That is such a sad story from every angle. I guess the male-only drinkers at the time had the same attitudes about women as most of the rest of society. The inequality at so many levels is scarcely believable in such recent times. Aboriginals were also discriminated against, for racist reasons that could not be proven in scientific trials. Things have improved but I wonder about attitudes.

There is no minimizing the fact that alcoholism is a social problem for some people. Provisions must be made to deal with the problem in a variety of ways. Prohibition didn't work, except for gangsters and bootleggers. Government profits from alcohol. A sensible portion of those profits should be earmarked for dealing with problem drinking. Some people also eat to excess and become obese. I'm certain that restrictive laws were passed with the best of intentions, but, looking back, there were restrictions that simply didn't make sense. We have grown up in so many ways, despite the fact that some people thought they knew what was good for us. As we know, "the road to hell is paved with good intentions."

GAMBLING

Gambling in our province has gone through some interesting changes. The bingo in church halls and basements with prizes of household goods has given way to cash prizes with large numbers of players. Charities have become the recipients of bingo revenues but the major concern has become players who spend major sums that they can ill-afford. It's another one of those mixed bags, where the charity gets some of the money while the person putting up the money maybe needs it almost as much or more than the charity it supports.

For many years, people in Saskatchewan purchased sweepstakes tickets from foreign countries. There were local low-profile people who were agents for these tickets; each generally had his list of local purchasers who bought the tickets regularly. It usually was hush-hush. During those years, people in the province would think about the millions of dollars that were going to a foreign country and wondered if that situation could be reversed. Well, that day came and we now have lotteries of all kinds, with agents operating in various handy locations. The Saskatchewan Roughriders and hospitals, among other organizations and causes, are involved in fundraising that is legal and highly successful. Every so often we see new millionaires or winners of expensive prizes like homes and cars announced in newspapers and television. TV bingo is also very popular.

I rather suspect that there are some fairly hefty poker games going on in many places in the province. There used to be a time many years ago in Kamsack where a neon sign indicated the location of something called the Tuxedo Club. I'm not certain what it offered or who could use it but it was better known among many people in town as "the gambling joint." How it managed to operate, while gambling in general was illegal at the time, I don't know. Something else I don't know is how poker can qualify as a sport that is carried by sports television.

The rise of casinos across the country and here in Saskatchewan has come about due to the demands of the gambling public. For a long time, plane-loads of people out of Saskatchewan went to places like Las Vegas and Reno to play the slots, craps, poker, and roulette. Big spenders were always watched very closely and if it looked like they were addicted or enthusiastic, Vegas casinos offered them free transportation or accommodations to come back and spend more. I was sometimes amused by the little old ladies carrying paper cups, hands black from handling silver coins. Some were bleary-eyed and walking about as if lost. Some would spend a long time feeding coins unsuccessfully into one slot machine only to walk away and see someone go to the same machine and hit the jackpot. The look on the bleary-eyed lady's face is pure dejection! Life is unfair, she thinks.

Well, Las Vegas has come to Canada. We now have palatial casinos right across the country. Tour groups can find places that offer special rates and full buses carry patrons to just about anywhere that offers food, drink, entertainment, and gambling.

Again, as is the case with big bingo, profits go to a good cause or disadvantaged people. Does that excuse the exercise? I doubt it. I think governments want to do the right thing on the basis of lesser evil. I buy lottery tickets but that is about it. I just think that when my ship comes in, I will probably be at the airport! There are people who want to gamble and if gambling isn't available here they will find it somewhere. How in a free society do you protect people from themselves—or should you?

SEX & CENSORSHIP

Saskatchewan people have generally believed that sex is not a topic for public discussion. That has modified somewhat, particularly among young people. You can now find books on a variety of sexual topics. Movies now leave little to the imagination. I think that will continue and content will become even be more explicit. Censorship has supporters here but prostitutes were in Regina before the roof was on the rail station and a house of ill repute was here before the first church was built.

I remember some movies in the distant past, such as one with Johnny Belinda starring a very young Jane Wyman playing a deaf-mute. The movie includes a rape scene that people in this province talked about for weeks. The scene is in a loft, if I remember it, featured a cowering Jane Wyman with a look of terror on her face and a shadow coming over her and that was it. If I remember it, you didn't get a look at the rapist. *The Outlaw*, a western starring a very young Jane Russell, with ample cleavage and long legs on display, was filmed in a haystack. You were left to draw your own conclusion. Initially, it was regarded as a notorious western. Completed in 1941, it was given a limited release in 1946 and it was not generally available until 1950.

The work of censors has always intrigued me. I gather that their purpose is to protect the rest of us. At least that was generally their purpose in the past. I often wondered who looked after the censors' interests.

Film censorship has had an interesting evolution in Saskatchewan. When the CCF came to power in 1944, film censorship became the responsibility of the Department of Labour. How that connection came about I surely don't know. Mr. C. C. Williams, a dear man who I knew, was Minister. It was said at the time that the Department brought in some of the most progressive labour regulations in North America but had the most conservative film censor anywhere. It was said of Charlie Williams that when his department took over a movie and censored it, it turned into a travelogue!

I appreciate one service that film classifiers provide today and that is information about what the movie does in terms of content. Is there excessive violence, gratuitous sex, constant profanity, or attempts to shock or nauseate with stomach-turning hideous depictions? A little of that can be tolerated but a constant diet turns people off. I use as an example Spielberg's *Saving Private Ryan*. The opening scene of storming the beach at Normandy is not *Sesame Street*. It is tough business, which veterans of that invasion say is closer to what they experienced on D-day than any other movie ever made on that event. On the other hand, some movies that depict partly decayed bodies coming from the grave to terrorize is sickening nonsense. I use as another example a movie about a crooked labour boss, Jimmy Hoffa. Danny Devito appears in the movie and every time he opens his mouth excessive profanity comes forth. People are not being holier than thou when they say they are offended. Hour after hour of that stuff becomes tiresome.

An admirable film that I like to use as example is the movie about the great racehorse Seabiscuit. It had the excitement of a small horse who didn't know he was small. It portrayed a man who demonstrated that a wealthy man could be a good man and a jockey and trainer who had special gifts and yet came from underprivileged backgrounds. I don't recall any serious profanity, if any.

I have a personal experience on the topic of profanity that may demonstrate how things have changed. In my grade nine year, I performed in a play in a regional drama festival. It was entitled *John Doe*. We were the first high school to do it. Previous performances were staged by university players. John Doe represented humanity and we were all in Limbo waiting for judgment just outside of heaven. The script included two words that were considered profanity at that time. These were "hell" and "damn." As I remember it, they were uttered only once each. The first time, there was an audible gasp from the Yorkton audience. When the adjudicator gave us his judgment, he advised, "Don't use profanity if your audience can't take it!" Needless to say, we didn't win.

Today, movies, books, magazines, radio, television and many plays include profanity much stronger than "damn" and "hell." Some of the larger networks in the United States bleep out offending words but others don't touch them. I am sometimes amused by print media, particularly newspapers, when the first and last letters in a word are provided and blank spaces are left between them for you to fill in. What is the difference between spelling out the entire word and uttering it completely in speech? Or do we think that there are vast numbers of people out there who don't know these words? I guess the answer is to make no reference to the words at all. I'm reminded of two little eight-year-old girls; one says, "Look at the condom on the verandah" and the other asks "What's a verandah?"

I generally found, in my open line programs, that listeners became a bit more comfortable talking about human sexuality but not very much. I would gather that it was okay for me to carry on asking questions in their place. When I started broadcasting, you wouldn't dare approach the subject but gradually things warmed up a bit. There are some couples who can't discuss the topic between themselves, so we shouldn't be surprised if they can't call a radio program with a large audience and professionals they don't know.

Yet a question asked is a question that a host of other people would also ask but are afraid to ask. I had one woman who called once about oral sex and a man who wanted to know how to deal with a wife who was not interested in sex. I concluded that both were desperate and wanted help.

We had a long list of "experts" on the topic, including Dr. Alex Comfort, of *The Joy of Sex* fame and Dr. David Reuben, of the bestseller *Everything You Always Wanted To Know About Sex*. These were all good resource people, but as far as I'm concerned, the best was a couple from Saskatchewan: Dr. William and Nurse Carolyn Chernenkoff, co-therapists in marital and sexual counselling in Saskatoon, who brought knowledge, sensitivity, approachability, and empathy to their work. They could act out various scenarios and communicate brilliantly. I recorded a series of five-minute programs for radio with the Chernenkoffs which many people found helpful.

POLITICS

People in Saskatchewan have taken their politics very seriously over the years. The Liberals were early favorites. Six Liberal Premiers governed the province, including the first Premier, Walter Scott. The others were William Martin, Charles Dunning, James Gardiner, William Patterson and Ross Thatcher. There were only two Conservative Premiers, J.T.M. Anderson and Grant Devine. The CCF and NDP had five Premiers, including Tommy Douglas, Woodrow Lloyd, Allan Blakeney, Roy Romanow, and Lorne Calvert. The present Premier is Brad Wall, who leads a party calling itself the Saskatchewan Party. It includes Conservatives of various kinds and some Liberals. In terms of personal popularity, Tommy Douglas would have been tough to beat and Brad Wall has been personally popular for a period of time.

A political science study some years ago tried to determine which party was most popular. Ross Thatcher used to say that in Saskatchewan there were socialists and free enterprisers. Not so, said the study. It identified Liberal voters and those who would vote for anyone BUT a Liberal. That has probably changed somewhat over the years.

In earlier years we had candidates run under such banners as the Provincial Rights Party, the Non-Partisan League, Progressives, Labour, Labour Liberal, the Farmer Labour group, the United Front, the CCF, and Social Credit (in 1938), among others. Later, there was an Aboriginal People's Party but they had little success and apparently vanished.

In 1938, the Labour Progressive Party (or, put another way, the Communist Party) ran in the election. They ran in a few elections and then later as "Communists." Noteworthy was that they continued to lose those few votes as they went along. They ran in such constituencies as Pelly, Meadow Lake, Saskatoon, and Regina. Their candidacy was probably a test of their support. Which party they hurt is anybody's guess. The CCF and NDP won election after election with such large majorities that it didn't matter.

We like our politics in Saskatchewan and elections in the past were fought hard and in many cases bitterly. Neighbour against neighbour, brother against brother, and friend against friend. One prairie legend that I doubt is true is about a mythical farmer who tuned in to his local channel only to find that a political leader he detested was holding forth on the screen. As the legend goes, the farmer fetched his shotgun and aimed it at his television set and shot while the politician was doing his thing. I think that story is a bit of a stretch but that kind of political hate has been alive among many party supporters of various types in Saskatchewan.

I'm reminded of a personal experience just a short time after the Medicare crisis was settled here. Two men came to a cottage I happened to be visiting at one of our provincial parks. One of the men had a fishhook deeply embedded in his hand and he wanted to know if I might know if there was a doctor at the lake. Neither he nor his friend would have been able to remove it. As it turned out, I did know of a doctor who happened to be at the lake and offered to drive them there. As we drove along, the man with the problem said to his friend that he wondered if the doctor might know that he (the wounded one) supported the government side in the Medicare dispute. I suggested that he keep his politics to himself and remember to thank the doctor if he removed the hook. It was another example of the paranoid atmosphere that enveloped the province at the time.

People changing their politics, particularly if they were high-profile, made for delicate times. To begin with, I would think that some Liberals and Conservatives must have chosen to throw in their lot with the CCF, while uncommitted voters, a significant number, would do likewise. Ross Thatcher and Hazen Argue were first elected to Parliament as CCF candidates. Part of that was due to the Liberals and Conservatives not naming candidates who were not at least gray at their temples. Thatcher switched horses to the Liberal one and he became Premier. Argue, a fidgeting, restless sort, became a Liberal Senator and I don't think Liberals ever embraced him. Walter Erb left the CCF in the middle of the Medicare crisis. The avuncular former cabinet minister tried to get elected as a Liberal but was unsuccessful.

RELIGION

Although we now have Muslims, Hindus, and Sikhs in our province, such was not the case as I was growing up and when I began my broadcast career. Cities and towns had their churches but churches were also built in rural areas of the province. In fact, rural churches not only served religious purposes, they also played a key role as places for meetings and cultural activities. This was so not only in Saskatchewan but right across Canada.

Reginald Bibby is a sociologist at the University of Lethbridge who has studied and written extensively about religion in Canada. Bibby says that, with rural depopulation, attendance at rural churches dropped from sixty to thirty percent. Those denominations hardest hit were Lutheran, Presbyterian, Anglican, and the United Church.

The Roman Catholic Church has seen lower attendance but is relatively stable by comparison. One of the greatest challenges facing the Catholic Church is a shortage of priests.

Bibby notes that evangelical churches such as Baptist, Pentecostal, Mennonite, Nazarene, and Alliance increased from eight percent to eleven percent during a fifteen-year period. Minority groups such as Muslims, Sikhs, and Hindus jumped from three percent to eight percent. The biggest change in Canada was the number of Canadians who said that they did not have or practice a religion. That increased from one percent to twenty-five percent.

Most interesting is Bibby's contention that religion is not dead in Canada but, in fact, is making a strong comeback. For those who left the church, he says one in three are re-affiliating and he expects that to grow to two of three. Dr. Bibby says that, led by Catholicism and Pentecostalism Christianity, the world is on the "biggest roll" in two thousand years. Ministers and priests who are having trouble paying the bills would be anxious to know just when we will be feeling that "roll."

A few years ago I was working on a project which involved taking photographs of rural churches in southern Saskatchewan. These had to be churches standing alone in the country and not in a hamlet or village. I didn't want cars parked around them or people standing around them.

I found that almost all were not locked. Once inside, you were invited to sign a guest book. Some provided a brief history. Some had an honour roll of those from the congregation who served in the Second World War and some indicated which of their own didn't return from war. Some had Sunday school lists of children and there was usually an adjoining cemetery with tombstones that often told an interesting story.

Most of the churches that I photographed were either Anglican or Lutheran or United Church. There were some Roman Catholic or Ukrainian Orthodox or Ukrainian Catholic. I particularly remember one church, sitting all alone on a country road. It always had a car or cars parked around it. I came back a few times but a car was always there. I finally did some checking around and found that the building was not used as a church but had been turned into a house, with one person living there.

I remember St. Mary's Roman Catholic, south of Moosomin, where there were concrete sidewalks down each row of tombstones in the cemetery. Even more than that, I found Scottish names on the tombstones. You will not find a plentiful supply of Scots who are members of the Roman Catholic Church anywhere but here was a colony of them in Saskatchewan.

Some experts claim that before 1950, people attended church out of obligation. Now, they will attend if they think they will get value for time spent. Homilies that are slapped together at the last minute and liturgies that are delivered poorly just don't cut it anymore.

It has been suggested that rural churches are more resilient than some of their urban cousins. I do recall attending a rural church once, in the middle of winter, with an uncle of mine. It was very cold and I watched while a fire was built in a heater near the front of the church. I thought I was going to freeze to death. Eventually things warmed up and we proceeded with the service.

Dr. Cam Harder is an ordained Lutheran minister and Professor of Theology at the University of Saskatchewan. Dr. Harder has had a hand in developing a program that is intended to prepare ministers and priests for rural ministry at the Centre for Rural Community Leadership and Ministry at the University.

The program is intended to help clergy to assist in times of crisis, provide ritual to process life events, and develop skills in care-giving and reconciliation. Reverend Harder said that, with cars and technology, people aren't as tied to a community as they once were. He said rural churches still offer buildings, volunteers, leaders, fundraising structures, and a focus on building hope and human capacity.

A psychiatric study at the University of Saskatchewan medical school carried out over a fourteen-year period with some 12,600 people has demonstrated that at least monthly attendance at church acts as a buffer against major depression. Dr. Marilyn Baetz, of the medical school, says the study indicated that regular religious activity fosters feelings of well-being and gives a sense of meaning and purpose and a sense that people have something to live for. She noted that church attenders tend to live healthier lives and display unselfishness.

HEALTH CARE

In the cradle of hospitalization and Medicare, the topic of health care is discussed constantly. For the most part, the discussion is negative. It's either a question of surgical waiting lists, a shortage of doctors, not enough nurses, lack of medical equipment, and mostly not enough money to pay for the things that are needed.

I like to think that we are constantly talking about health care because we welcome and value the program and we want to make it better. I also think that maybe some of us take Medicare for granted. You walk into a doctor's office, show them your health card, and then get the service without reaching into your pocket for the usually considerable dollars that your service costs. People here who are unfortunate enough to contract cancer or some other terminal illness are not bankrupted.

If there are genuine opponents to Medicare, I'm not aware of them. Right-wing think tanks come up with statistics or their own studies that demonstrate that medical care as we know it is not financially sustainable deep into the future. According to them, our government and/or people must pay more in some form. That couldn't be utilization or "deterrent fees," as the NDP cleverly named them, because they helped to defeat a Liberal government here in the 1960s. Annual premiums or fees, as we used to pay for hospitalization before Medicare, would not raise enough money to make it worthwhile, according to some people. Yet we have a situation where lotteries are used to help finance hospitals and a helicopter ambulance service. It should be remembered that there used to be hospital auxilliaries around the province that would raise modest amounts of money for hospitals.

It's interesting to see reconciliation at work when you consider that in 1998 the Canadian Medical Association inducted Tommy Douglas into the CMA Hall of Fame. I was a young adult when the Medicare crisis struck this province. There were heart attacks from stress, communities that were divided; it was often brother against brother, neighbour against neighbour. Saskatchewan was front-page news all over the world. You could cut the tension with a knife. It took the mediation of a British peer and physician to come up with a solution that may not have been completely satisfactory to both sides but that brought to an end a battle that threatened the stability of the province.

There have been some who have referred to Emmett Hall, the eminent jurist and public policy advocate, as the "Father of Medicare." While Hall did some work in that area, I think he would admit that the title belonged to Tommy Douglas and even a little to Woodrow Lloyd, who piloted the tense times in Saskatchewan when it came to a showdown. Tommy raised the concept and campaigned on it. Mr. Lloyd had to endure the agony of that birth. I wonder about the time and money spent on fixing Medicare. Studies like Roy Romanow's Commission, given to him by Prime Minister Jean Chretien, sits gathering dust. If not Romanow's Commission, whose?

THEN AND NOW, BRIEFLY

The very existence of Saskatchewan as we know it might never have come to pass had it not been for a pioneer doctor from Yorkton. Dr. T. A. Patrick was a member of the Legislature of the Northwest Territories from 1897 to 1904. The original plan was that everything from Moose Jaw east would become part of Manitoba. Patrick didn't agree. In the legislative session of 1898, Patrick proposed the present-day boundaries of Saskatchewan and Alberta. He faced for-midable opposition from people like Frederick W. Haultain and A. L. Sifton, but the Patrick plan prevailed. In reversals that only politics can explain, Haultain became Chief Justice of Saskatchewan and Sifton became Premier of Alberta.

I once covered a conference in Lethbridge that examined the possibility of uniting Manitoba, Saskatchewan, and Alberta into one prairie province. The conference drew politicians, senior civil servants, and thinkers of various shapes and forms. Allan Blakeney and Peter Lougheed participated before either was elected Premier of their province. Conference papers noted that such a union was possible and even advantageous but not likely to happen. I guess it was a case of "we've come too far in the way we are."

HUTTERIAN BRETHREN

Hutterites came to Canada around 1918 but didn't settle in Saskatchewan until the 1940s, when they established eight colonies. There are over forty colonies in the province today (the biggest concentration of Hutterites in Canada can be found in Alberta). They can be traced back to 1528. They are Christian but were persecuted in Europe by both Catholics and Protestants. Their founder, Jacob Hutter, was burned at the stake. They are pacifists, own everything in common, share the work that must be done, and dress and live in a manner that sets them apart.

They are noteworthy farmers who often take a poor bit of land and turn it into a top grain producer. They have machine shops in which they claim they can even repair "a broken heart." Some try to leave their colony to live in the outside world but apparently most return. Their farm equipment is mostly up-to-date and fully paid for.

CHINESE

Immigrants coming here from China experienced shameful discrimination. They were denied the vote until 1947. In 1912, there was a law in Saskatchewan preventing Chinese from hiring white restaurant waitresses. Canada also had a restrictive immigration policy that applied to Chinese. They were here before Saskatchewan became a province, with Chinese cemeteries appearing between 1880 and 1911 in Moose Jaw, Saskatoon, and Regina. Moose Jaw had the largest settlement, with over 160 residents as well as some twenty Chinese-owned businesses. Initially, Chinese immigrants also settled in Swift Current, Battleford, and Saskatoon.

I'm glad to see that classic racism here is somewhat gone. Apologies seem to be a growth industry in Canada. Notice that the Chinese have not been overly demanding on that score.

WOMEN VOTE

On March 14, 1916, a bill was passed that gave Saskatchewan women the right to vote. Men and women here voted together later that year and by a margin of four to one brought in prohibition. The debate surrounding the issue of giving women the right to vote was treated by some politicians as a joke. Our first Prime Minister, Sir John A. Macdonald, once said only single women and widows should be given the vote, because "It does not follow that because we go to a certain length, we have to go the whole length."

Strangely, Sir John didn't subscribe to that kind of restraint when his nose was in the gin. I think Macdonald's reasoning was the same adopted by men and some women for all aspects of feminine equality. Women still fail to be paid equally with men for the same work and I doubt that they have the same opportunities for advancement. They have come a long way but there are still more hills to climb.

UNITED CHURCH

Saskatchewan congregations were early and eager supporters of what became the United Church of Canada on June 10, 1925. It was a union of Presbyterian, Methodist, Congregational, and the General Council of local Union Churches, mainly in Saskatchewan, who united in anticipation of the larger union. The Evangelical United Brethren joined in 1968. The United Church is Canada's largest Protestant denomination, with about three million members. As is the case with other Christian denominations, church attendance is dwindling and there is a clergy shortage. Candidates for ministry study at St. Andrew's College in Saskatoon. Moderators have included women, men, lay-people, black, Korean, First Nations Canadians, and some Saskatchewan people.

The Christian Gospel which speaks of modest living and service to others doesn't appeal to some people, who are told repeatedly by advertising that they should first take care of themselves and be comfortable and accumulate more material goods.

JEWISH POPULATION

Jewish people have contributed mightily to the growth and development of Saskatchewan. Jewish farm colonies were established here before we became a province. The first, with twenty-six families, was founded near Moosomin in 1882. Others were located near Wappella, Hirsch, and Lipton. After 1905, Jewish farm colonies were started near Sonnenfeld, Edenbridge, and Alsask. Like other early settlers, Jewish farmers suffered dreadful hardship. Some were escaping persecution. They had little agricultural experience, there were no schools, winter was bitter and lonely, and crop failure was common.

It may come as a surprise to some, but you can still find people in Saskatchewan who hold anti-Jewish views that would make Adolf Hitler blush. Still, our Jewish people are to be found in commerce, the professions, the arts, and they are generous givers to good causes.

CAPITAL PUNISHMENT

At one time, capital punishment was meted out in all Canadian provinces, including Saskatchewan. Our final hanging took place on February 20, 1946. The condemned man was twenty-year-old Jack Loran of Burstall, who, on

June 29, 1945, left a dance where he was drinking heavily and without motive killed a neighbour, Gustav Angerman. That same night, eighteen-year-old Vincent Manastryski killed his abusive father on a farm near Yorkton. Both killers were sentenced to die but there were efforts to commute their sentences. Manastryski was spared but Loran was hanged.

The hanging prompted one brewery to provide free beer for selected guests picked to watch the hanging. The guests included some Saskatchewan members of the legislature, who watched Loran take his final breath. There is still a considerable amount of support for capital punishment in Canada. Some support it for reasons of revenge while others believe that it acts as a deterrent. Many American states still have capital punishment in their justice systems and some countries of the world have methods of capital punishment that go back to the dark ages.

ACTOR

The late Gordon Tootoosis, of Saskatchewan's Poundmaker Reserve, was one of the busiest and best actors this province produced. He was always in demand as an award-winning actor, narrator, and spokesperson; he made dozens of appearances in movies and on television. Tootoosis, who had a noble air about him, listed Marlon Brando and the late Chief Dan George as role models. His favorite role was in the movie *Legends of the Fall* and he was noted for his part in the TV series *North of 60*. Tootoosis once said his toughest role was that of Chief Big Bear, largely because of his admiration for the man.

It's always rewarding to see people who didn't have opportunities in early life make something of themselves in the arts or business or other professions. You wonder how far they would have gone with more opportunities in their formative years. It's a very slow process but First Nations people are making progress in so many ways. There are more and more teachers, social workers, lawyers, and other professionals graduating

from post-secondary education institutions. Not only are they doing something for themselves and their people, but they are contributing to this country. First Nations leaders in this country are proving to be most capable in their work. They are able to deal with the leaders of the rest of Canadian society in a thorough and eloquent manner.

OFFICIAL THINGS

As Saskatchewan has evolved, we have adopted a number of items as "official" in the province. The western red lily was named our official flower in 1941. It is a threatened species so don't get caught picking or digging it up, because you could be fined up to $500. The sharp-tailed grouse was chosen as Saskatchewan's official bird in 1945 and curling became our official game or sport in 2001. This is interesting because curling popularity has declined and we have fewer curling rinks in Regina. The white birch became our official tree in 1988 and sylvite or potash is our official mineral. We also have an official animal, the white-tailed deer, officially adopted in 2001. Our motto is "From Many Peoples Strength" and our license plates proclaim to all that Saskatchewan is "The Land of Living Skies" or contain a couple of Roughrider slogans or they may point out that the car belongs to a veteran. We got an official, distinctive flag in 1969.

IN CONCLUSION

Between Saskatchewan then and now, much has been achieved in building a province that is modern, forward-thinking, and humane. We have more miles of roads and highways per capita than anywhere in Canada, yet by having an ombudsman and Child Advocate and an arts board (which was the first of its kind in Canada so many years ago), the province has indicated that building people is just as important as building strong buildings and highways.

We are a more tolerant people than before but we still have some distance to go. A children's hospital will soon be built and the building of new and better schools and hospitals is an ongoing need. Post-secondary education faces demands for relevance and the money to pay for that relevance.

We need political leadership and choices that are clear and far-thinking. If we expect that our politicians will be self-serving and lacking integrity, they won't disappoint us. If we don't demand excellence or if we fail to pay attention to the democratic process or even fail to vote, we break faith with those who settled here and built this province. Not only do we break faith with pioneers who suffered unspeakable hardship, but we also forget the more than ten thousand of our own who gave their lives in war.

I always felt that the Moose Jaw Band Festival fancy drill competition provided a great example of what this country is all about. The big arena doors would go up and in would march a Scottish pipe band and in the middle would be a boy of Chinese descent wearing a kilt and blowing vigorously into his Bagpipes!

Our motto, "From Many Peoples, Strength," includes First Nations people and all who have come here. In the final analysis, people is what all of this is about.

CPSIA information can be obtained
at www.ICGtesting.com
Printed in the USA
LVOW12*1724190816

500813LV00005B/7/P